SAVING
Sterling Forest

photograph by Richard Botshon

SAVING
Sterling Forest

The Epic Struggle to Preserve
New York's Highlands

Ann Botshon

STATE UNIVERSITY OF NEW YORK PRESS

Cover art: "Sterling Lake from Fire Tower (spring)" by George M. Aronson
Used by permission of the artist.

Published by
STATE UNIVERSITY OF NEW YORK PRESS
ALBANY

© 2007 State University of New York

For information, address
State University of New York Press
194 Washington Avenue, Suite 305, Albany, NY 12210-2384

Production and book design, Laurie Searl
Marketing, Susan Petrie

Library of Congress Cataloging-in-Publication Data
Botshon, Ann, 1942–
    Saving Sterling Forest : the epic struggle to preserve New York's highlands /
Ann Botshon.
        p. cm.
    Includes bibliographical references and index.
    ISBN-13: 978-0-7914-6939-2 (hardcover : alk. paper)
    ISBN-10: 0-7914-6939-5 (hardcover : alk. paper)
    ISBN-13: 978-0-7914-6940-8 (pbk. : alk. paper)
    ISBN-10: 0-7914-6940-9 (pbk. : alk. paper)   1. Forest conservation—New
York (State)—Sterling Forest.   2. Forest management—New York (State)—
Sterling Forest.   3. Sterling Forest (N.Y.)   I. Title.

SD428.A2N727 2007
333.75'160974737--dc22

2006003066

10   9   8   7   6   5   4   3   2   1

Contents

List of Illustrations

Foreword

ON SEPTEMBER 3, 2004, AT THE AGE OF SIXTY-TWO, a few months after finishing this book, Ann Botshon lost her battle with cancer. As this book goes to press, many of the same people who were in the trenches with Ann for decades to save Sterling Forest from development are still on the forefront to preserve the remaining 570 acres, continuing the story that she depicts here.

In 2004, the Sterling Forest Partnership was able to temporarily halt the development of a golf course in Sterling Forest by making the DEC aware of the presence of the threatened timber rattlesnake. That same year, President Bush signed the Highlands Conservation Act, authorizing over $100 million to preserve open space in the Hudson Highlands from Pennsylvania to Connecticut, including Sterling Forest; Sterling advocates were jubilant. But, in the summer of 2005, a proposal to build 107 homes in the center of the park diminished their elation; those who came to testify against the project at the public hearings included the ever-stalwart individuals and organizations of the Sterling Forest Partnership.

Like these lifelong activists, Ann wore many hats. Soon after moving with her family to an old farm in Orange County, New York, in 1979, Ann immersed herself in local environmental issues and was instrumental in the nascence of several important organizations, including the Ramapo/Catskill group of the New York State Sierra Club and the Orange County Land Trust. She lent her time, energy, and insights to others as well, such as Orange Environment, the Stewart Park and Reserve Coalition, the Bashakill Area Association, and local political organizations. She served on the Orange County Vegetable Growers Task Force and the Orange County Planning Board. Her most recent work was as coordinator of the Wallkill River Task Force.

Those involved in environmental activism know how frustrating conservation efforts can be; rewards are few and the burnout rate is high. However, the multifaceted effort to save Sterling Forest, an effort that was decades long in the making, and that involved the creative cooperation and collaboration of many (sometimes unlikely) allies across state lines, ultimately resulted in an incredible success, one that Ann was quite inspired by. Ann's unwavering belief in the creation of the Sterling Forest State Park, and her conviction that the intertwining paths that led to its creation were stranger than fiction, motivated her to write this book. *Saving Sterling Forest* was also conceived with the hope that it would encourage others who believe that we should value the land as much more than a mere commodity.

We know that Ann would want to thank everyone who has worked throughout the years to preserve Sterling Forest for future generations, and especially those who helped her with this project; this book is dedicated to you.

RICHARD BOTSHON
LISA BOTSHON

CHAPTER ONE

A Forest Is at Stake

AT THE NORTHERN AND WESTERN FRONTIER of the vast urbanized New York City metropolitan area is a long swath of rugged upland, called the Highlands, that runs more than 170 miles, southwest to northeast, from Reading, Pennsylvania, to Litchfield, Connecticut.[1] Near the geographical center of this corridor and only 40 miles northwest of New York City is Sterling Forest, a large tract of land, more than 20,000 acres, with landscapes that are among the most beautiful in the East: masses of forested hills that recede into the far distance, narrow valleys over which loom rugged, steep-sided ridges up to about 1,400 feet, near-vertical drops along sheer rock outcrops, fantastically beautiful rock formations where the bedrock has broken through the thin soils, and dramatic views of lakes and wetlands from the hilltops.

This is a place of great natural drama: A young bear strips ripe berries from slender shadbush and leaves a tempest of broken branches and a trail of berry-rich scat; the force of winter meltwater punches holes in the ice covering a creek; a spring walk yields an unexpected encounter with a rare salamander or hard-to-identify warbler. Here you can still find mysterious stone walls as wide across as a rural highway, old rock constructions whose remains are still recognizable as iron furnaces, and 200-year-old pieces of slag littering the forest floor.

Although most of Sterling Forest is in New York State, its streams and creeks provide clean water to a number of New Jersey's major reservoirs. The forest also contains thousands of acres of varied wetland, forest, and rocky upland wildlife habitat, including sanctuary for dozens of imperiled plant and animal species. It preserves scenic, historic, and cultural riches that have been eroded or erased by the feverish pace of creative destruction that has gone on in more densely populated places. It provides an undeveloped land link to the vast Palisades Interstate

1

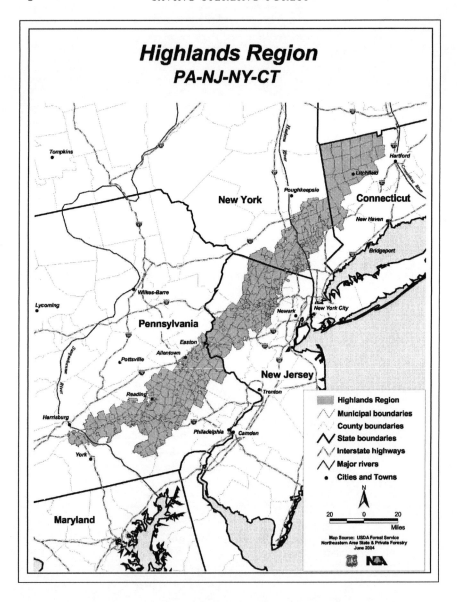

FIGURE I. *USDA Forest Service map of the Highlands region (2004). This map depicts the span of 3.5 million acres stretching from Harrisburg, Pennsylvania, to Hartford, Connecticut, that make up the Hudson Highlands, of which Sterling Forest is a key piece. In the fall of 2004, President George W. Bush signed the Highlands Conservation Act into law, committing $100 million of federal funds to help conserve this region. Courtesy of the USDA Forest Service.*

Park to its east and to several large protected New Jersey tracts to its west and south. And with its lakes, creeks, and trails it offers abundant opportunity for hiking, fishing, hunting—even the experience of solitude and quiet—all of which are hard to find in this busy region.

The battle to save this forest jewel from development embodied every painful and controversial facet of land-use conflict and the most basic economic and environmental aspects of land-use policy. Since few large tracts of private undeveloped land close to the metropolitan area remain, suburban development of Sterling Forest became a highly attractive goal for its long-time corporate owner, the Sterling Forest Corporation. The development also was important to the real estate community at large, as the forest's subdivision could trigger spillover development activity elsewhere. But the fact of its being a single large tract also made Sterling Forest an especially important place to environmentalists and area residents. While elsewhere in the outer metropolitan region open space was being lost night after night at municipal planning boards, with one piece after another falling to subdivision, environmentalists saw that focusing a single concerted effort on Sterling Forest might attain protection of this one large, critically located piece.

But the environmental community failed to anticipate just how difficult and how long the Sterling Forest fight would be—a quarter-century struggle, if you count an early but extremely bitter skirmish in the Town of Tuxedo, where the corporation first advanced plans to build on a large scale. Ultimately the battle for the forest was all about money—it came down to the question of how to negotiate a deal on 20,000 acres with a tough corporate adversary determined to squeeze the most profit possible out of its only asset—a corporation whose own fortunes came to be held hostage by larger global entities. The environmental community had the specially vexing problem of how to negotiate a deal on behalf of the public with no public or private money firmly in hand (for many years, not even in remote sight). New Jersey might have been willing to pay because its precious drinking water originated in the forest's New York uplands, but for a full decade New York was unwilling, and in some years unable, to open its purse strings; and the federal government, richly endowed with potential funding possibilities, was held in check by powerful regional and ideological conflicts. Luckily, the Sterling Forest struggle attracted a core group of the most impassioned and determined of the region's environmental advocates, and it was these hard workers and sophisticated strategizers, unflaggingly persistent, who made the deal happen.

The Sterling Forest struggle ended with a victory for the public and the forest, but the Highlands as a whole are now intensely vulnerable to the kind of pressure that once threatened the Sterling lands. Of the more than two million

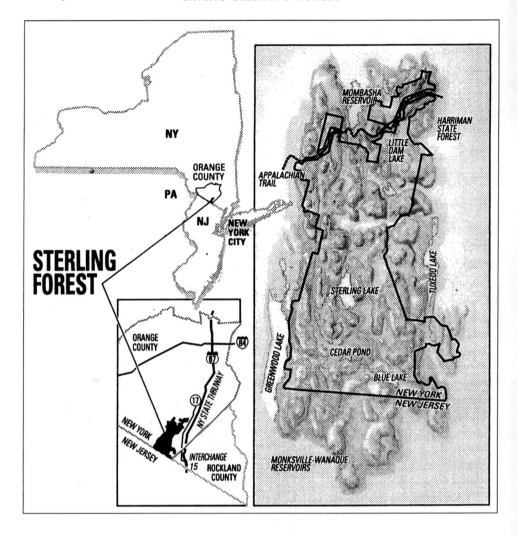

FIGURE 2. *Tri-part map indicating location of Sterling Forest. Courtesy of Steve Butfilowski.*

acres in the Highlands, several hundred thousand acres have been protected, but four-fifths remain in private hands. And, responding to market forces, the privately owned tracts are quickly being developed. Interstate highways have enabled commercial and industrial development to leapfrog out from traditional downtowns and inner suburbs to campus-style settings in bucolic exurbs, opening up big new markets for suburban housing tracts that are, literally, gouged out of the rocky upland forest.

Sprawl has begun to overtake the once sparsely populated Highlands much as it overran more accessible locales only decades before. Year by year, farms are lost and the traditional community fades, the watersheds and aquifers become degraded, and the rich biological diversity vanishes.[2] In town after town, people are fighting development projects; environmentalist Jeff Tittel summed up the despair: "For every parcel of land that gets saved, we lose another three or four. It's like the Janis Joplin song: 'Every new development tears a little piece of my heart out.'"[3]

This book is the story of the twenty-five-year struggle to save Sterling Forest from the fate that has befallen thousands of acres of land across the vast New York City megalopolis—conversion to lawn or median strip or simply, irreversibly, asphalt. The successful outcome of the Sterling Forest struggle—a large state park within easy access of millions of people living along our crowded seaboard—holds out hope for new solutions to what are long-festering problems of land use and for new land-use policies to replace those that are long out-moded. If the Highlands and other vulnerable areas can be saved, it will be in part because the struggle for Sterling Forest has provided a model and an inspiration for preserving essential but rapidly vanishing resources.

CHAPTER TWO

Money from the Colonial Rocks

THE NEW YORK–NEW JERSEY HIGHLANDS, that dense cluster of hills within the wide curving swath of ancient, worn mountains of the northeastern United States, are uncommonly rich in iron. Rock outcrops at the surface of these hills often sport thick veins of the Precambrian gray-black stuff, long since solidified and contained.[1]

These Highlands are iron-rich because over a billion years ago miles-thick layers of coastal sediments plunged 20 to 30 miles below the surface and the resulting pressure and heat shot liquefied rivers of molten iron into the surrounding rocks. The iron-rich rocks, among many others, were displaced 300 million years ago or more as colliding and submerging tectonic plates pushed vast masses of material upward, creating mountain ranges, and as wind and water acting inexorably over millions of years ground down the resulting peaks. Then, three times over the last 200 million years, forces from within the Earth slowly pushed the ranges upward to great heights once again; these, too, were worn down by the erosive power of wind and water.

It is the geologically recent Ice Age that brought the Highlands landscape near to its present shape—and its iron to the surface. At least four times over the last two million years, until about 10,000 to 15,000 years ago, vast ice sheets spread south over North America and through New York and northern New Jersey, leaving valleys and depressions where the ice gouged the earth down to its underlying bedrock.[2] After the glaciers retreated, the bedrock outcrops were left uncovered, creating the ancient veins of iron close to the surface.

The land's rich iron deposits were pretty much ignored by the indigenous Lenape Indians, who for a few thousand years combed these hilly woodlands for the game, herbs, and toolmaking rocks that they needed for their subsistence way of life. But in the late seventeenth century, the Lenape were largely displaced by

Dutch, German, and Scottish settlers who moved into the Highlands around the Hudson River. These European colonists hated the hills whose thin soils, rocky outcrops, and rock-strewn flanks made farming a near impossibility, but it didn't take long for them to discover the great value of the iron ore in the rocks.[3] It was this iron that, even before the Revolutionary War, fed the Ringwood and Sterling blasting furnaces on Ringwood Creek, the Charlotteburg and Pompton ironworks on the Pequannock River, the Long Pond ironworks on the Wanaque River, and many others. Iron ore soon became the source of wealth and commerce in the Highlands.

Until the eighteenth century, most of the iron needed in the New World came from England and elsewhere in Europe. But it cost the colonists dearly— and this cost was increasing. The mines of the Old World were old ones, and, as they became played out, the expenditures for working them edged up. And of course the long transatlantic voyage itself also kept the price of iron punishingly high.

These Highlands offered the colonies a welcome homegrown solution to the high cost of European iron. Ramapo iron was largely magnetite, an iron oxide ore with unusually high iron content. Dense forests promised an unlimited source of wood for charcoal to fuel the iron furnaces. Highlands rivers, which over eons had eroded away overlying rock, had left ancient rocks exposed above the streams, their veins of ore often visible and workable right at the surface. And the abundant and muscular waterways tumbling out of the hills provided ample waterpower for both industrial use and transportation to East Coast deep-water ports.

Almost overnight a new industry flourished in the American settlements. Proprietors brought over miners from England and Wales to open veins of ore and charcoal burners from Germany to turn trees into charcoal. As James Ransom notes,

> Furnaces and forges were in operation up and down the Atlantic coast in every Colony except Georgia, and the industry was spreading inland and westward with the frontier. Export of American iron began as early as 1718. By the time the Revolution broke out these Colonial furnaces were producing about 14 percent of the world's supply of iron. . . . The eve of the Revolution found the Colonies well able to furnish their own most basic sinew of war, iron for tools, for guns, for cannon and for shot.[4]

The Hudson Highlands were not the only place where iron was being produced, but they were in a key area—the Revolutionary War played out right in the neighborhood—and they have been called the "cradle of the Industrial Revolution. And because they were an unusually rich source of ore for the East, in the years after the Revolution, the mountains were invaded by a swarm of ironworks employing thousands of workers.[5] The hills saw bustling communities of small villages growing up around the ironworks, with homes, churches, schools, and small businesses. By the mid-eighteenth century, dozens of iron mines pocked the beautiful hills and bore deep into subterranean veins; dozens of stone furnaces and forges nestled along the region's waterways. Iron-smelting furnaces, astride the fast-flowing streams, were sending clouds of steam and smoke into the once-clear mountain air, while slag heaps and cinder piles littered the ground and smoldering charcoal-producing mounds smudged the hills and sent clouds of gritty charcoal dust to settle everywhere. And on thousands of acres around every furnace, the land was brutally denuded of its trees, its wood commandeered for the much-needed charcoal to melt the iron.

STERLING FOREST—A GEM OF HIGHLANDS REAL ESTATE

No piece of land was more caught up in the land-use and political changes that transformed the colonial-era regional landscape than Sterling Forest, some 25,000 acres of hills to the west of the Ramapo River, which wends its way south for about 14 miles before freeing itself at a wide cleft in the mountains at the Ramapo Pass and turning southwest into the New Jersey lowlands. Sterling was part of a vast tract—called Cheesecock—that seven English colonists bought from Iroquois Indians in 1702. Five years later, Queen Anne of England granted the colonists Royal Title to this land and, in 1735, the heirs hired surveyor Charles Clinton to plot out the queen's Cheesecock patent. After Clinton surveyed the tract, he divided it into shares for each of the patent holders.

Cornelius Board, a Scotsman who had come to colonial America to search for precious metals, discovered iron ore at the southwest end of what is now known as Sterling Lake and is likely the founder of the first iron mines and ironworks in that area. He first purchased 100 Cheesecock acres from John Burnet in 1736. He then added another 50 from Burnet and built a "bloomery"—a small, forge-like hearth furnace—in 1738. Board and his two partners Timothy Ward and Nicholas Colden (or Colton) operated the modest Sterling facilities until 1740, when Board sold his share and moved a few miles south to Ringwood, New Jersey, where he found still more workable veins of iron ore.[6]

In 1750, the Sterling works were sold to William and Abel Noble, who enlarged the business by building a furnace. Peter Townsend married the daughter of Abel Noble and in 1777 joined the family's firm. By early 1776, Noble,

Townsend & Company completed a large forge at the Sterling Iron Works, just south of Sterling Lake on Ringwood Creek, and soon Sterling was supplying the Continental Army with anchors, steel, and other items.

Sterling Iron Works gained a modicum of fame through its connection with the well-known Hudson River iron chain. In February 1778, the Continental Army asked Sterling to produce, as quickly as it could, a 750-link iron chain, to be set in place across the Hudson River, some 25 miles to the northeast. An earlier chain, forged in 1777, and other river obstructions had failed to stop the British fleet from moving upriver. To assure rapid completion of the new chain, the colonial army guaranteed Sterling owner William Townsend a large workforce and he in turn agreed to keep his forging and welding fires operating round the clock.

According to Lincoln Diamant in his book *Chaining the Hudson*,

> Throughout February and March of 1778, the Sterling ironworks op-
> erated 24 hours a day, reddening the dark winter skies with periodic
> showers of sparks each time the great stone stack was recharged. An
> attendant necklace of charcoal-making tumuli smoldered all over the
> surrounding Ramapo hills; for charcoal-making each day's furnace op-
> eration consumed an acre of forest converted into charcoal.[7]

Through February and March of that winter, hundreds of sledge loads drawn by pairs of oxen laboriously hauled the heavy sections of chain from Sterling Pond northeastward through Central Valley and to New Windsor to a small foundry on the south shore of Murderer's (now Moodna) Creek, a mile inland of the Hudson. There the outsize chain and boom sections were linked.

On April 30, 1778, the finished chain was made fast to a huge rock crib on the west bank, and soldiers painstakingly drew the fortification across the deep Hudson and fixed the end to a crib on the east bank. The chain forged at the Sterling Iron Works in a mere two months' time dissuaded the British navy from attempting the upper Hudson for the duration of the Revolution.

Soon after the Revolution, William Townsend began purchasing large tracts of land from the owners of the Cheesecock Patent. The partnership Noble, Townsend and Company lasted until 1798, when the Nobles sold their interest in Sterling Forest to the Townsend family, which continued to oper-ate the property. Eventually fourteen Sterling mines and two charcoal blast furnaces were located at the Sterling works. The large tracts of land around the ironworks, including the mines and wood lots, referred to as the Sterling Estate as early as colonial times, grew from 16,500 acres in 1827 to 18,489 acres in 1836.

IRON MINES FLOURISH, THEN FADE

Continued need for iron for rapid growth and industrial expansion in the new nation led to a boom in the industry in the last years of the eighteenth century, the early decades of the nineteenth century, and, with ever-intensifying demand, through the War of 1812 and the Civil War. Soon the entire area was dotted with iron mines.

And the ironworks in the Highlands flourished. The Sterling Iron Works produced a wide range of implements as well as anchors, cannonballs, and war equipment. Completed in the late 1780s, the Augusta Furnace, on the west bank of the Ramapo River near the present-day village of Tuxedo, produced bar iron, crowbars, anchors, and other ware. The Ramapo Works, in Ramapo, New York, started operations in 1797. The Southfield ironworks, established in 1804, eventually made the first blistered steel in New York. The Greenwood Furnace, on the east side of the Ramapo Valley, founded in 1810 and run by the Parrott family, drew from a half dozen iron mines in the vicinity and became famous for its design and production of the Parrott gun, considered the most effective artillery weapon of the Union army. The Wawayanda Furnace, further west and

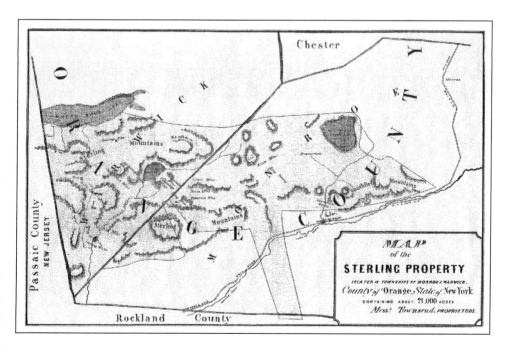

FIGURE 3. *Nineteenth-century map. This map accompanied the prospectus offering Sterling Ironworks for sale in 1856. Courtesy of the Orange County Historical Society.*

completed in 1846, specialized in making wheels for railroad cars. A prosperous local economy spawned forges and furnaces and villages around the mines. An entire local culture grew up around the iron industry.

Meanwhile, railroad fever grabbed the country in the early 1830s, and it took shape in New York as an ambitious aim of connecting the key locations and major markets of the East Coast with the frontier economy that began at the Great Lakes. The railroad routes touched the Highlands gingerly, warily approaching the morass of steep grades and dangerous mountain curves. In 1841, the New York and Erie Railroad completed a rail line that connected Ramapo, in the valley at the entrance to the Ramapo Pass on the New York–New Jersey border, with the Hudson River hamlet of Piermont, almost 20 miles to the east. A mile-long pier built into the Hudson shallows allowed passengers and freight to New York City to continue by boat down the Hudson. The same year, this Erie line was extended north through the valley along the eastern edge of Sterling Forest and parallel to the Ramapo River, then west through farm country into central Orange County; in 1848, the line reached another 30-plus miles to Port Jervis on the Delaware River.[8] That same year, 1848, the Paterson & Ramapo Railroad completed a line that would eventually connect with the Erie at the Ramapo Pass; this line went south into Jersey City, New Jersey.

In 1865, the Sterling Iron and Railway Company, then owner of the Sterling Iron Works, constructed a 7.6-mile rail spur to take its iron products from the foot of Sterling Lake down to the Erie Railroad line running parallel to the Ramapo River. Sterling Junction, also known as Sterlington Junction, was about a mile north of the hamlet of Ramapo. (Another ironworks spur, coming from the Southfield ironworks, met the Erie in the village of Southfield.)

Another rail company, the Montclair Railway, completed its Greenwood Lake line from Jersey City north to the New York–New Jersey state line in 1874. In the Highlands, it ran parallel to the Erie line and about 7 miles west, and was eventually acquired by the Erie.[9] In the early 1900s, the name of the line's terminus on the east shore of the bustling resort destination of Greenwood Lake was changed from State Line to Sterling Forest.[10]

The presence of the recently arrived rail transportation was not enough to save the eastern iron industry, even though rail was bringing coal to the Highlands furnaces—indeed, ironically, the railroads had made readily available the iron sources from further west—and by 1880 the mines and furnaces of the New York-New Jersey Highlands were all closed or on the way out. The Panic of 1873 and other misfortunes of the economy were national events that also adversely affected the entire iron industry; at the same time, the Highlands iron industry was being forced to compete with the rich Mesabi Range ores of Minnesota, which were considerably cheaper to produce, stripped as they were from open

FIGURE 4. *Nineteenth-century photograph of ironworks and employees. Sterling furnace #3 was one of the buildings used to manufacture raw iron products in the nineteenth century. Courtesy of the Orange County Historical Society.*

pits right at the surface. Through the middle and late years of the nineteenth century, virtually all the Highlands furnaces, and most of the mines, shut down.

The Ramapo Works closed down in 1855, when its owner Jeremiah Pierson died at age ninety. The Wawayanda Furnace shut down forever in 1856, only a decade after its startup. The Greenwood Furnace, having switched from charcoal to Pennsylvania anthracite in its last years, was fired for the last time in 1885. The Southfield Furnace ceased operation in 1887. The Ringwood works stopped furnace activity in 1880, although its Peters mine was worked sporadically until 1931. The Augusta Furnace closed down early in the nineteenth century. The boomtowns, fed by mining and railroads, mostly faded into small isolated mountain hamlets. An exception was the 7,000-acre Augusta tract[11] that was sold to Peter Lorillard, the tobacco baron: Lorillard's descendants eventually developed about 2,000 acres of the area into Tuxedo Park, the spectacular private enclave of the social elite.

KEY TRACTS CHANGE HANDS

In the nineteenth century, the mines around the Greenwood Furnace complex, predominantly on the east side of the Ramapo River Valley and into the Hudson Highlands, were still owned by the Parrott family; the family's total holdings were approximately 10,000 acres, acquired over time in dozens of separate transactions. In the early 1880s, with all the eastern iron facilities suffering, the Parrotts' Greenwood ironworks property went into receivership, and in 1885 the Parrotts were forced to put 9,300 acres of their Orange County estate up for auction—keeping only their immediate homestead. Edward H. Harriman, the powerful railroad magnate, bought his friends' property for $52,500. Harriman, for his part, argued that the tract was "two to three times as much land as he really needed" and claimed he had entered the bidding merely to prevent the forested hills from being plundered by timber speculators and lumbermen.[12]

Harriman named the estate Arden for Mrs. Parrott's family; nevertheless, the Parrotts, offended that Harriman had simply taken the opportunity to benefit from their financial plight, severed their friendship with him. The Parrott estate became the first Harriman acquisition in what would eventually grow to a vast fiefdom of lakes, streams, and forested hillsides and about forty farms.

The major Harriman purchase was the Sterling works and surrounding lands, long owned by the Townsend family. By the nineteenth century, the descendants of William Townsend owned tens of thousands of ironmaking acres in the Orange County towns of Tuxedo, Monroe, and Warwick, as well as northern New Jersey. The tract included the Sterling Works, the Augusta Furnace, and the Southfield ironworks.

By 1856, with the iron industry in severe decline, the Townsend family decided to sell, in its entirety, its Ramapo Mountain estate, which included virtually all of Sterling Forest. No buyers appeared for a long while, but, in 1864, 18,489 acres were sold to the Sterling Iron and Railway Company.[13] In 1892, that company was reorganized, and, in 1893 Edward H. Harriman purchased a considerable amount of the company stock from two of the principal owners, the Clarks, of Clark, Dodge & Company of New York and Philadelphia. In 1895, Theodore Price purchased nearly all of the remaining stock, and a year later sold his entire interest to Harriman. Thus, the railroad titan acquired full ownership of the forest.

By the time Harriman acquired the Townsend properties, even the Sterling furnaces had ceased operation. Sterling's 1848 furnace, the only one still operating in the Ramapos, shut down in 1891. This ended the era of Ramapo blast furnaces—although ore was still being taken from a few of the mines to be shipped to more modern furnace facilities in Pennsylvania and elsewhere. Activity at

Sterling resumed briefly with the coming of World War I: The Ramapo Ore Company, Incorporated leased the property and planned to mine.

The armistice, though, signaled an end to the venture and the Sterling Works were finally closed in 1923. Ransom writes,

> For most of the period between 1923 and 1952, the only human contact was the watchmen who acted as caretakers for the abandoned ironworks . . . few had occasion to visit or see the decaying works. . . . Sterling had become a ghost works whose active days were over although its past was still evidence in the shadows surrounding the mines, millraces, and piles of slag. Perhaps the most obvious and attractive feature that Sterling still had for a prospective purchaser was its rich history.[14]

During World War II, as part of the nation's wartime inventory of its mineral reserves, the U.S. Bureau of Mines and the U.S. Geological Survey made field studies of the iron deposits at Sterling, but, despite this, the forest reclaimed the mine-scarred land. Today, walking the streamside trails near the old furnaces, one can easily find long-discarded iron slag.

EARLY CONSERVATION EFFORTS IN THE HIGHLANDS

E. H. Harriman's purchase of vast acreages seemed to be a facet of his compulsive need to trump his peers in business, and his habits of mind extended into exerting his financial power to trump his social peers in creating beauty in his holdings. In 1905, Harriman began building his magnificent house, Arden, on a mountaintop on his property. Historian Rudy Abramson asserts,

> When it was begun, the mansion was a technological marvel, lighted by electricity from its own power plant, served by its own railroad, and supplied by greenhouses that provided not only an unlimited supply of potted plants and flowers but nectarines and vegetables in every season. . . . Mary Harriman stuck faithfully to E.H.'s detailed plans for a house that would represent American art and craftsmanship from its limestone and granite walls to furniture carved, assembled, and finished in the estate's own woodworking shops.[15]

From 1905 until his death in 1909, E. H. Harriman continued to expand the estate. The *Newburgh Daily Journal*'s "Memorial to E. H. Harriman" noted that at the time of his death Harriman owned nearly 40,000 acres: "The estate was the envy of all the city rich who kept country places in the Hudson Valley."[16] The Harriman family continued the acquisition of lands even after E. H.'s death.

In 1909, New Yorkers discovered that the state had developed plans to build a penitentiary on Bear Mountain in the Highlands overlooking the Hudson River. This discovery launched an auspicious collaboration between Harriman and George W. Perkins, a banking partner of J. P. Morgan. Perkins, who had devoted years to saving from blasting by quarrymen the spectacular Palisades cliffs along the Hudson River—by purchase—was spectacularly successful in eliciting generous contributions from the wealthy and the powerful. His efforts enabled the purchase of about 13 miles of Palisades in northern New Jersey and adjacent New York State. As commissioner of the fledgling Palisades Interstate Park Commission, Perkins began working with Harriman on a plan to preserve the entire New York–New Jersey Highlands, from the Ramapo Mountains section to the Hudson. In a letter dated June 1, 1909, Harriman proposed to New York Governor Charles Evans Hughes that he and other property owners contribute toward creation of a vast wild park between the Ramapo Mountains and the west bank of the Hudson:

> I have thought that possibly some of the other property owners might join with me in this move, making it possible to secure practically the whole wild area between the Ramapo and the Hudson Rivers, extending from West Point down to below Stony Point, and again north of West Point, taking in the Crow's Nest. I feel if this should be accomplished the State's prison should be moved again to the other side of the river, so as not to destroy the natural beauty which can never again be replaced.[17]

Governor Hughes, who recognized the urgent need for additional parkland so close to the burgeoning New York City population center and the need to develop some control over a vital watershed, indicated his interest in the project. Edward Harriman died in September 1909 before his plan could be realized, but that December Harriman's widow Mary carried out his wishes by offering the state nearly 19 square miles of the family holdings as well as a gift of $1 million to enable the state to acquire additional property between Arden and the Hudson River. Mary Harriman required that by January 1, 1910, a further $1.5 million in private subscriptions be secured; that New Jersey contribute an amount determined by the Interstate Park Commission to be "its fair share"; and that New York State contribute an additional $2.5 million for land acquisition, road building, and park purposes. Mary Harriman further required that the state drop its plans for siting a prison in the Highlands.[18]

Spurred by the brilliant fundraiser George Perkins, John D. Rockefeller Sr. and J. Pierpont Morgan each donated half a million dollars. The remaining half million was given by fourteen other subscribers, including George Perkins himself. New Yorkers also passed a $2.5-million bond issue to allow the state to provide the required cash match. This successfully extended the Palisades Interstate Park into the Highlands and the Ramapos. In October 1910, the Harrimans' son Averell, who was then a freshman at Yale, returned home to spearhead the formal ceremonies that provided the state with the Harriman gift of $1 million and transferred the deed to 10,000 acres of Arden land.

Following Mary Harriman's mandate that the state use the fund to acquire other parcels of land adjacent to the Harriman lands, every year after 1910 the commissioners purchased additional tracts. The Harriman donation became the northern and western anchor of the Palisades Interstate Park. Successive maps of the park show it growing from scattered blocks to a solid area, as wide as 8 miles across and extending from Bear Mountain 15 miles south nearly to Tuxedo and Sloatsburgh. Averell Harriman donated more than 2,000 additional acres, much of it in the northwest portion of the park, and funded the purchase of still other lands. The Harriman family also donated about 1,000 acres around Arden House to Columbia University. Eventually, through the gradual and incremental acquisition of hundreds of parcels, some as small as a few tenths of an acre, some as large as 1,200 acres, some by donation, some by exchange or purchase, some to prevent quarrying, some for road rights of way, most quietly but some through dramatic and contentious litigation, the Bear Mountain-Harriman Park grew to over 51,000 acres and the entire Palisades Park system to more than 86,000 acres—some of it bordering on Sterling Forest.

The jurisdiction of the Palisades Interstate Park Commission was extended to Newburgh and into the Ramapo-area Highlands early on, and by 1930 the commission increased its activities, especially in Rockland and Orange counties.

The 1910 Harriman gift, together with other private donations, constituted an incredibly important legacy to the people of New York State. In 1940, the great New York park and road builder Robert Moses said, "the Harriman gift was a piece of statesmanship and philanthropy so far-sighted that few people understood its significance."[19]

THE NINETEENTH AND TWENTIETH CENTURY PRESERVATION MOVEMENT EMERGES

The Harriman contributions were part of a larger national environmental sensibility that began to take shape in the latter decades of the nineteenth century and grew into a full-blown movement by the end of that period. Through the early years of the nineteenth century, the development of powerful new machines, new mechanical devices for farming, and government land giveaways—all with the underlying assumption that subduing nature and exploiting its resources were civilizing and beneficent acts—encouraged pioneers to tame the land and speculators to appropriate it. Lumber became the foremost industry, as wood was needed for everything from paper to house beams to railroad ties. With the forests of New England and New York pretty much logged out by 1840, the timber industry moved further west, first to the forests of the upper Midwest and later to the productive temperate rainforests of the Northwest.[20] The deforestation over millions of acres changed climate, destroyed watershed, and obliterated wildlife habitat.

Mining permanently defaced the land; as Philip Shabecoff notes,

Mining both preceded and quickly followed settlement of the interior and left deep and permanent scars on the continent's land and waters. Gold in California, copper in Montana, coal and oil in Pennsylvania, iron ore in Minnesota and lead in Illinois attracted fortune hunters and job seekers. . . . Mines were operated without care for the surrounding countryside—the idea that such concern was important would simply not have occurred to most nineteenth-century Americans. The picks and shovels, the hoses and dredges, and the smelter fires of the miners created the nation's first widespread pollution and environmental health problems.[21]

New roads and the expansion of canals and railroad networks encouraged the population to Go West, away from the densely populated East Coast, even as new immigrants arrived to replace those who had moved on. The cities, however, merely increased in attractiveness to the young and ambitious after the Civil War because they were both the biggest markets and held the most wealth. But the mid-nineteenth century, cities had not yet instituted the large public water-supply and sanitation systems that could keep typhoid, cholera, and other infectious diseases under control, and they remained festering centers of filth and disease.

After the Civil War, the nation saw even greater industrial expansion and economic activity—and concomitant growing losses of fertile soil, cherished vistas, and wild places. It was the dawn of the age of the robber barons and their corporations; the aim was maximum profit, and environmental and social costs were easy to ignore. The need for public intervention was clear, but for most of this period the federal government was too weak to intervene and moreover lacked the regulatory structure to bring excesses under control. Moreover, acquisition of lands for the public good was a still-new notion in this county.

Nonetheless, through this period the population was slowly recognizing the tremendous destruction that was a by-product of the world's most rapid rate of industrialization and was even more slowly arriving at an awareness that something had to be done about it. There was, for example, a growing concern for nature that began to be felt and expressed several decades before the populace as a whole was ready to act on it. Americans had absorbed the ideas of nineteenth-century European romanticism, one of whose themes was a mystic feeling for the natural world, and transmuted it into a mid-century American version, transcendentalism, which emphasized the spirituality inherent in nature. Following the transcendentalists, artists embraced the immense and powerful, the unconstrained and uncorrupted American wilderness. Painters of the American landscape movement, with their scenes of serene pastoral vistas, fascinating wildlife, and majestic wilderness, reflected this vision and for the first time gave America a unifying artistic tradition of its own. Frederick Law Olmsted, Henry David Thoreau, Ralph Waldo Emerson, and others urged that part of the pristine wilderness still in government hands be protected for future generations.

The first environmental writers articulated more or less utilitarian arguments for better management of nature. George Perkins Marsh's 1864 book, *Man and Nature; or, Physical Geography as Modified by Human Action,* argued that human activities, magnified by technology, can devastate what he termed "the web of life" and what we call ecosystems. And he made the further point that wherever people destroy nature, the impacts, often severe—ranging from an explosion of insect pests to climate change and transformation of productive farmland into desert—can end up affecting people themselves.[22]

For a long while, the ideas of the transcendentalists failed to translate into public action, and it was not until the 1860s that popular concern had grown enough to inspire political activity. One of the earliest efforts was the movement to protect Yosemite Valley, which became a California park in 1864; that success was followed by creation of the 2-million-acre Yellowstone National Park in 1872. These actions marked the beginning of the first wave of resource protection in the United States.

Toward the end of the century, Progressive-era citizens initiated reforms of all kinds: they began to campaign aggressively for control of air pollution as well as better management of public lands, especially forests. Starting in 1879, government on both federal and state levels began to respond with new laws and new agencies to assure protection of public resources. These actions were reinforced by the establishment of the Sierra Club, the Audubon Society, and many other citizens' groups that advocated ongoing protection. At the dawn of the new century, with the presidency of Theodore Roosevelt, conservation entered a golden decade, with establishment of wildlife refuges and the addition of vast tracts to the national forest reserves.

In New York State, community leaders, seeing lands across the state become the object of an escalating tug of war between private profit-taking and the public good, began to take strong and courageous steps to protect tracts with great public value. Preservation of Niagara Falls in 1885 marked the first state purchase of land for its scenic value. Public outcry about voracious logging and watershed degradation of the Adirondack Mountains in upstate New York, coupled with a growing appreciation of the area's natural beauty and recreational potential, resulted in the creation of the enormous Adirondack Park in 1892. In 1894, the passage of Article 14 of New York's Constitution protected the lands of the Adirondacks as well as about 700,000 acres of the Catskill Mountains, west of the Hudson. Outrage over the rapacious quarrying of the Hudson Palisades in the 1890s led to growing public effort to preserve these spectacular cliffs and ended with establishment of the Palisades Interstate Park Commission in 1900.

The vigorous campaign of a single individual, William Thompson Howell, to publicize the beauty of the Highlands resulted in a widespread recognition of the value of this wilderness so close to the growing metropolis at the Hudson's mouth; it helped inspire the extraordinary Harriman family gift to New York State in 1910.[23]

Finally, there was the visionary effort of regional planner Benton MacKaye to create a footpath along the entire length of the Appalachian Mountains, from Georgia to Maine. He envisioned the trail as a bridge to the rural and wild lands of the Appalachian Mountains, providing industrial workers a nurturing connection with the land and its wilderness values; he also hoped the lands would deter urban encroachment. MacKaye's Appalachian Trail project began in 1921 and was not completed until 1937.[24]

But the Sterling lands—although adjacent to Harriman Park in the Palisades system, and despite decades of sporadic acquisition attempts by the hiking and outdoors community—failed to benefit from the vigorous and widespread protection efforts. For example, in 1930, Raymond Torrey, co-founder of the New York–New Jersey Trail Conference, wrote, "Sterling Lake is one of the most beautiful bodies of water within fifty miles of New York City. It may be hoped that some time it will come under public ownership, possibly by a western extension of the Harriman section of the Palisades Interstate Park."[25]

Reportedly, the Harriman family offered the Sterling tract to New York State as a gift. In a decision that would later come to haunt, the Palisades Interstate

Park Commission declined the offering, feeling that in the financially tight years of the Depression, it could not manage a major expansion.[26] The Harrimans put the tract up for sale sometime before 1950 for $975,000.

In January 1951, Louis Sigaud of the New York–New Jersey Trail Conference wrote to R. W. Hart, superintendent of the Harrimans' Arden Estate, expressing interest in incorporating the tract into the interstate park system, for recreation and for protection of the northern New Jersey water supply. In this, he noted, the Trail Conference had the support of the Palisades Interstate Park Commission, the Regional Plan Association, and the North Jersey District Water Supply Commission. Sigaud mentioned that Robert Moses, New York State's parks advocate, suggested that "some of the tract could be acquired by donation and the balance paid for." And he noted that the sale of the Sterling Park tract to private interests would be "a matter of very grave concern to the water supply system of a highly industrialized section of northern new Jersey and to production for national defense."[27]

But because Averell Harriman was in Washington on government business and his brother Roland, heading up the Red Cross, was also unavailable, the disposition of Sterling Forest property was left in the hands of a more strictly business-minded executor, Superintendent R. W. Hart. Hart, who apparently had the power to make decisions on such matters—or who assumed such power for himself—wrote back:

> It is not possible for me to at this time make a recommendation that might be helpful to you in approaching either of these gentlemen. The best that can be done at the moment is to give you the benefit of my knowledge of their feelings at the last time this subject was under discussion. As you know the Harrimans have been quite liberal in making contributions of land and substance to the Palisades Interstate Park over the years . . . however there is a limit on what they can do and on what should be expected of them.[28]

The tract could have sold easily, Hart continued, but he intimated that the family was looking for a buyer who would be sensitive to the use of the property. Moreover, in matters relating to the Sterling tract, the Harrimans were not free agents but answered to the stockholders of the Sterling Iron and Railway Company. In short, Hart said,

You and the others at interest may find it to the advantage of all involved to . . . look to the outright purchase of the property. I am sure every consideration would be given to a fair and reasonable offer. . . . [Y]our offer . . . would be a starting point with earnestly interested folks and for a purpose that the

Harriman Family has already evidenced their interest in and support of in a very substantial way.

> The subject of your letter will be discussed with whichever the Messrs. Harriman I come in contact with first. If there is a change in their attitude from what has been expressed in this letter you will hear from us further.[29]

Immediately, Risdale Ellis, of the New York–New Jersey Trail Conference suggested to John D. Rockefeller, Jr. that he purchase the forest from the Harrimans. Declining to do so, Rockefeller passed the letter on to the Palisades Interstate Park Commission. Observing the unfolding of this transaction, the Palisades Interstate Park Commission concluded, "in the light of this reply there is no chance that the Commission will get this property by donation in the foreseeable future."[30]

In 1952, after years of public tinkering with the idea of incorporating Sterling Forest into the Palisades park system, the City Investing Company, a venerable private real estate investment firm, acquired the Sterling tract from E. Roland and W. Averell Harriman, heirs to the Harriman estate. The historical central portion of the vast tract remained the heart of the transaction; seven additional parcels were acquired from various other owners in order to eliminate irregular property boundaries. The final transfer of 18,500 acres of Sterling land to City Investing, with a total purchase price close to a million dollars, was completed in 1954.[31]

The Sprawl Wars Begin

LOOKING AT LAND AS A HIGH-PROFIT INVESTMENT

IN THE YEARS AFTER IT BOUGHT THE HARRIMAN STERLING FOREST TRACT, City Investing also bought additional parcels in the area, eventually owning about 21,000 contiguous acres. The City Investing domain included 9,527 acres in the town of Warwick, 833 acres in Monroe, 8,349 acres in Tuxedo in Orange County, a few acres in Rockland County—all in New York—and, across the state line to the south, 2,074 acres in New Jersey. The forest on its westernmost boundary descended to the eastern shore of Greenwood Lake.

With its purchases, City Investing acquired a large portion of some of the most beautiful real estate remaining in the eastern United States. The tract contained enormously valuable wildlife habitat, due to its diverse natural features, its large size, contiguity with tens of thousands of acres of already-protected public land in the immediate area, and its central location within the broad swath of the Appalachian Mountain chain that runs from Alabama to Maine.

After the silencing of the ironworks and decades of benign neglect the woodlands had restored themselves to an approximation of eastern old-growth forest—the forested hills noisy only with birdsong and the sibilant chatter of streams descending their rock-strewn ravines. Once again the mountains provided excellent hardwood forest community, mostly oak, ash, and hickory, with a rich diversity of natural features. The hills, critical to the migration routes of nearly a hundred species of migratory songbirds, were resettled by many bird and mammal species that require extensive breeding, feeding, and territorial ranges, including turkeys, owls, hawks and other raptors, black bear, and bobcat. Sterling Forest again came to support numerous species of concern to biologists, including the timber rattler and copperhead, southern leopard frog, northern cricket frog, spotted salamander, spotted turtle, wood turtle, eastern worm snake, eastern woodrat and Indiana bat, red-shouldered hawk, barred owl, certain warblers, and a number of uncommon butterflies—many considered endangered, threatened, or rare.

Some of the forest provided unique habitat. The retreat of the ice sheets after the last Ice Age had left a natural rubble of sand, clay, and gravel that blocked the glacial meltwater and created myriad ponds, lakes, marshes, bogs, and other wetland types. Dozens of freshwater wetlands contributed to the forest's diverse wetlands communities, which included wooded swamps and shrubby swamps, acidic bogs, open fresh water, seasonally flooded basins, and fresh meadows. Some supported a few rare species or species that were rare locally; for example, an Atlantic white cedar swamp supported the rare bog turtle as well as two un-common insectivorous plants, the pitcher plant and the sundew. Of particular interest were several very large wetlands: the 600-acre Pine Meadow, really a red maple swamp, the highly acidic Cedar Pond and adjacent kettle bog, and Spruce Swamp and nearby McKeags Meadow, wetlands of some 700 acres containing white and black spruce and red maple. Other unique habitat included scrub oak/pitch pine and hemlock-hardwood forest.

In the valleys and hills flourished species from both southern and north-ern ranges of the Appalachians. The five-lined skink, a lizard common in the south but rare this far north, lived here, but so did the pale laurel, considerably more common in northern habitats. And of course there were also the common northeastern creatures: loon, woodcock, great horned owl, belted kingfisher, two dozen species of warblers, white-tailed deer, black bear, red fox, and several turtle species.

Long freed of the pollution of the iron industry, the forest's waters returned to an earlier time of sparkling purity. Yellow perch, chain pickerel, and large-mouth bass populated Sterling Lake, brook and brown trout Sterling Creek.

As important as the forest's high-quality waters were for the fish, they were even more important for people. Most of the Sterling Forest watershed drains westward into several creeks that flow south into Ringwood and Jennings creeks and thence into New Jersey's North Jersey Water District reservoir system. More than a fifth of the watershed of New Jersey's Wanaque-Monksville reservoir system is in Sterling Forest. The remaining Sterling drainage, about a third of the total, flows east into the Ramapo River via the Indian Kill. (The Wanaque system also receives, by pipeline, up to a quarter of its water from the Ramapo River.) Both of these sources ultimately serve the more than two million residents of northern New Jersey; in addition, more than 300,000 residents in northern New Jersey and in New York's suburban Rockland County depend on the Ramapo River aquifer for about half of their primary water supply.

Having been left largely untouched for much of the twentieth century, the Sterling Forest tract retained many clues to the early industrial activity, its dozens of remnants of the furnaces, forges, and mines, as well as Native American rock shelters and charcoal pits dating back more than 10,000 years, making it a rich archeological resource. The abandoned and poorly mapped old pits and deep shafts, although a hazard to unsuspecting hikers and an obstacle to development, also presented an opportunity for future generations to glimpse the once-bustling but now vanished way of life of the iron works. (Some of the old Highlands furnaces are now being restored.)

Perhaps most obviously, the forest tract was a great recreational and open space resource. When it was owned by the Harriman family, Sterling Forest had been open to the public for hunting, fishing, and hiking, although in later years the property had been posted against all trespassing because the Harrimans wanted to keep hikers out of the many unmarked mines, some deep and dangerous, and to keep out smokers. The new owner allowed access to about 16,000 acres, using a permit system, private security patrols, and the maintenance of hiking and hunting trails by community trail groups.

But City Investing (CI) had not paid $775,000 to the Harrimans and another quarter of a million to the individual landowners whose contiguous smaller parcels it acquired in order to quietly contemplate the magnificent vistas and the rich flora and fauna or to make life good for a handful of hikers. City Investing had only one mission—to make money. In the past its investment activities had been in urban settings, in the planning of major urban centers in New York City, Pittsburgh, and Philadelphia, in city office buildings and theaters, where it acted as a conduit for investment capital. Now, recognizing the increasing potential for profit at the urban fringe, CI was beginning to invest in large tracts of land strategically located, not in the urban cores but at the suburban frontier.

SPRAWL IMPOSES MAJOR CHANGES ON THE REGION

The New York City metropolitan region, the country's most populous, experienced the same kind of accelerating land-consuming expansion as other large American cities, reflecting nearly a century of development outward from the center cities. By the mid-1950s, the unrestrained growth and expansion that followed World War II was like a popped cork releasing an explosive froth of champagne: The war's end had sprung open the bottleneck of wartime shortages and restrictions and unleashed a powerful outpouring of demand. That, together with a postwar spurt in population, resulted in burgeoning consumption, soaring energy use, ever-greater industrial production—and the boom in house construction and auto production accommodated by the explosive expansion of the suburbs. Acre by acre, mile by mile, new low-density suburbs encroached on open space, steadily and inexorably taking over vast reaches of farmland, woodland, hillsides, river corridors, and coastline along the full length of the eastern seaboard. As open land vanished, people fled to open spaces still further from the cities—spaces that, in turn, soon became the next ring of suburbs.

The postwar sprawl development in New York and the country's other metropolitan centers was partly fueled by people's desire for a suburban dream house and for a quiet, green and clean landscape, and was made possible by a growing affluence. But it was also powerfully propelled by top-down government policies over many decades and implemented through enormous public subsidies—subsidies for highway construction, mortgages, flood insurance, and infrastructure like water supply and sewer systems. By the early 1950s, the entire economy had become critically dependent on house-building and auto production. Then, in 1956, Congress approved funding for interstate highways, with the federal government agreeing to pay 90 percent of the cost of a 41,000-mile system.[1]

Making commuting by auto easy, fast, and attractive, the interstates opened up thousands of nearby quiet communities to land speculation and to auto-dependent housing developments in former pastures and potato fields.

In the 1950s, the population in the suburbs rose by 49 percent over the decade, nearly three times faster than the U.S. population as a whole—a pattern that reversed five previous decades of expansion of the cities. Starting with urban centers whose population was high even before mid-century, vast corridors of high population and urban-type construction developed—making the loss of open space particularly severe in these areas. Coastal regions sustained especially heavy increases in population along with extensive sprawl development.

Nowhere in the East was the change more dramatic than in the New York City metropolitan region, the nation's largest center of population: it experienced the same shifts as other urban centers but in absolute numbers an even greater shift of population to outer rural regions. Between 1950 and 1970, the population in the "urban" counties (Manhattan, Bronx, Brooklyn, and Queens in New York City and Hudson County in New Jersey) remained about the same, before actually declining, according to the 1980 and 1990 census figures. In the next ring out, the so-called suburban counties of the metropolitan region, the population increased dramatically, from 5 million to 8 million—an increase of 60 percent—between 1950 and 1970, before declining slightly in the 1970s and 1980s. But it is the outer exurban and rural counties that showed the most explosive population growth. As the urban and inner suburban areas lost population, the population of the fifteen-county outer ring mushroomed: from 1.6 million in 1950 to 2.5 million in 1960, an increase of 73 percent in only ten years. In

1970, the population in these counties was 3.7 million; in 1980, 4.3 million, and in 1990, 4.6 million.

Put another way, in 1950, more than half of the region's population lived in the urban counties, while only a tenth lived in the rural areas; by 1970, only 41 percent of the region's population lived in cities, while nearly the same number (40 percent) lived in the suburban counties and the proportion living in rural areas had increased to more than 18 percent. [2]

Put still another way, by the early 1960s, 1.5 million acres of this 8-million-acre region had been converted from open space to urban use. And, by the late 1960s, it was obvious that the entire Lower Hudson Valley (Orange, Rockland, Putnam, Westchester) was especially vulnerable to being overtaken by low-density development. The population of this four-county region, which had increased 31 percent in the decade 1950–1960, continued to transform historic forests and farms into suburban enclaves.

The problems associated with sprawl in the New York metropolitan region had been identified fairly early by the Regional Plan Association (RPA), a private nonprofit group created in 1929 to provide long-range comprehensive planning for the region as a whole. As the one powerful and credible voice for regionwide planning for both economic development and quality of life, RPA commanded the attention and respect of government and business alike. As early as 1929, RPA had called attention to the opportunity to preserve much of the open space of Sterling Forest. Its interest in the forest, it said, was "motivated by the property's unique combination of critical watersheds, wildlife habitat, diverse natural features, recreational opportunities, aesthetic quality, large size and central location within the densely populated Tri-State Region." [3] The Sterling Forest property lay within one of the tri-state region's most critical greenways, the open lands that extended from the Delaware River to the Hudson River.[4]

In 1968, the RPA weighed in with its second regional plan that, reflecting the worry that sprawl would cause the New York City metro region to lose its global leadership in the competition with other world capitals, called for revitalization of the region's cities, preservation of important open spaces, and reinvestment in the area's transit system.[5]

The plan also recommended that some control be placed on the trend to decentralize development, to control the sprawl that had dominated since the 1940s. Partly as a result of RPA's assessment, state and regional transportation agencies were created and additional investment made in commuter and public transit systems.

The RPA warned that a demographic change in which a million people left those parts of the New York City metropolitan region having the highest population density and roughly the same number of people moved to the areas of low density would increase energy consumption by about 50 percent, weaken public transportation, and increase dependency on the auto. The RPA also predicted that a redistribution of population outward would weaken Manhattan's labor market, undermine economic opportunity in the city, and increase racial segregation. In a 1969 report, the RPA, predicting mushrooming growth of Orange County in the Hudson Valley, recommended preservation of the county's Appalachian Highlands, including Sterling Forest, and acquisition of fully one-quarter of the land in the mid-Hudson Valley for public use.[6]

Unfortunately, there was little government machinery—New York was a planning backwater—to impose order on chaotic consumption of the land. One student of sprawl notes, "New York state is quite progressive in many areas, but makes up for it by being retrograde when it comes to land use. In decades early in this century, Republicans were land stewardship advocates—they considered land use a good-government issue. So we've got the Adirondack and Catskill Parks, we've got zoning in all urbanized communities. But with autos, rural land became reasonable for scattered-site residential development—it was not possible before cars. In rural areas the thought was, anybody could make a nickel converting the land to something else, and had the right to do it. Unfortunately a whole new paradigm of land-use planning became necessary because of autos. We in New York didn't get that paradigm. And consequently changes in planning and zoning didn't happen."[7]

BIG PLANS AFOOT FOR THE FOREST

Situated at the northern edge of the developing front of new growth in the New York-New Jersey metropolitan area was Sterling Forest. The Highlands region, bordered by several major highways and interstates, was only an easy hour's drive by car from New York City. Having been largely spared development for most of the century because of its rugged terrain, the Highlands in and around Sterling Forest seemed ripe for development of the kind that had hit the New Jersey Highlands to the south and was encroaching on the Putnam County Highlands to the east of the Hudson River. The bedrock lying just under the shallow Highlands soils resisted conversion to house foundations and the steep slopes were a deterrent to construction, but powerful modern drilling rigs and houses erected on cement piers made possible construction feats not considered economical just decades earlier.

After its Sterling Forest purchase, City Investing entertained a wide and even unconventional range of options for exploiting the tract: harvesting and marketing peat for horticultural use and transforming the old mining holes into new lakes to form the picturesque backdrop to new factories. A plan for intensive resource extraction—harvesting timber and mining limestone, ball clay, iron ore, building stone, trap rock, and gravel—was intended to provide the market with a wide range of products to be sold under the trade name Sterling Forest.

But the main thrust of the Sterling Forest development, its ultimate product after its natural resources had been mined, was residential subdivision. In the halcyon days of 1954, the company envisioned an enormous community, 400,000 to 500,000 people, served by shopping centers, churches, and community centers. Little more than 40 miles from the George Washington Bridge, it would be highly desirable for its convenience alongside the New York State Thruway and near major parkways.[8]

The company was bullish on development, and with reason. City Investing saw Sterling Forest as the ideal location for the next suburban development boomlet. Major corporations in droves were moving their headquarters out of New York City, many heading for the suburbs where their CEOs lived. City Investing formed a subsidiary, the Sterling Forest Corporation, for management of its newly acquired land.

Within three years of the City Investing purchase of Sterling Forest, Robert Dowling, then head of City Investing, proposed turning the forest into a giant, totally planned, scientific, educational, and residential campus that also included a theater, gardens, and other cultural and recreational facilities "for the highest human satisfaction and to foster a climate for creative expression."[9] The corporation put its faith in careful planning, to avoid what it deplored as the "uglification" of America, to preserve the beauty of the land, and also to provide "the finest living and working environment" for the community. Resolutely high-minded, the corporation vowed to create an "industrial utopia" and to "inspire a more beautiful America and a better way of life."[10]

Jürgen Wekerle, a Hudson valley resident and long-time watcher of City Investing in Sterling Forest, says now, "CI was a development company, but it had the somewhat romantic notion of having this corporate park and university think tank, where scientists could stroll through the beautiful landscape and commune with each other and develop new insights and new discoveries."[11]

Union Carbide Corporation was the first tenant corporation; its residency was notable for the swimming pool-style 5-megawatt nuclear research reactor it built (three decades later, under other owners, it leaked radioactivity into surrounding soils and a drinking water reservoir and had to be dismantled). In 1960, a family recreation center opened: Sterling Forest Gardens, a 125-acre attraction with two million tulips, daffodils, and other bulbs, acres of flowers spring through fall, and fountains, waterfalls, and exotic birds. The Gardens, popular with local residents and visitors, were followed in 1963 by the Sterling Ski Center.

MAJOR CONSTRAINTS TO LARGE-SCALE SUBDIVISION

Although development fever was heating up in the Hudson Valley and City Investing was working hard to capitalize on the value of its large tract so close to New York City, three years of ownership had tempered the company's enthusiasm with a strong dose of reality: the potential for development in Sterling Forest was severely limited. The extensive steep slopes alone—there were fourteen peaks between 1,200 and 1,300 feet—created a significant problem since construction there would be an invitation to erosion and sedimentation of streams and expensive to build on. Additionally, the tract had mostly thin soils lying just above bedrock, making grading difficult and—from the point of view of developers—there was an unfortunate abundance of swamps and bogs. It was a beautiful but problematic tract.

Still, from City Investing's perspective, even if only 15 or 20 percent of Sterling Forest was developable, several thousand acres would still be available for intensive development—and few such tracts of that size were available within an hour's drive of Manhattan. The City Investing Company suggested a Thruway interchange halfway between Harriman and Suffern in the early 1960s.[12]

In the late 1960s, the corporation began working on a development plan for the forest. In 1967 the *Sterling Forest News*, a monthly corporate newsletter that went to households in the Sterling-area community, buried among its reports of bake sales, marriages, and the fire department annual election the following announcement about City Investing's development plans:

> City Investing believes that by 1971 the present population migration outward from New York [City] will have largely surrounded Sterling Forest and will be putting real pressure on the area for additional housing. It is expected that new residential areas will be opened up to meet this need, and that the growth of both industry and residential development will move at an accelerated pace in the '70s. By 1980–1985 it is expected that the Forest land will be almost wholly developed. The residential development would be carried out by builder/developers as the need develops and as such developers satisfactory to City become interested.[13]

Indeed, in addition to Union Carbide and the recreation facilities, a number of big corporations and institutions did build facilities at the forest in the 1960s and early 1970s—Reichold Chemicals plastics research and development laboratory, Incomation, and International Nickel (all in 1965), International Paper research center, the New York University Medical Center Laboratory for Experimental

Medicine and Surgery in Primates (LEMSIP) and apartments for staff, IBM research facility, and Xicom conference center (all in 1972). In addition, starting in the late 1950s, the corporation itself built about 200 houses on a total of about 200 acres in three residential communities in Sterling Forest: Laurel Ridge, Clinton Woods, and Maple Brook.

THE STERLING FOREST CORPORATION'S FIRST PLAN

In 1971, City Investing's Sterling Forest development arm, known as Sterling Forest Corporation, came forward with a plan for further developing its tract. Preparatory to the plan, William L. Pereira Associates carried out a study of the forest lands. The Pereira report made a number of points that struck a cautionary note: the steep slopes and shallow depth to bedrock or actual bedrock outcroppings through much of the forest indicated that only about 8 percent of the land was prime for development and another 40 percent had major constraints. Moreover, most of the prime developable land was in the southernmost portion of the tract, south of the state line in New Jersey.

This information forced the corporation to scale down its initial pie-in-the-sky forecast of half a million souls; now it projected a population of 80,000 in 22,000 residential units plus 5,500 vacation homes overlooking the eastern shore of Greenwood Lake—a development on 12,000 acres overall. The corporation was not prepared to underwrite this still-gargantuan venture itself—rather, it asked the Department of Housing and Urban Development to underwrite the plan to the tune of $37 million under the New Communities Development Act of 1971.[14]

This legislation was an outgrowth of the concern of President Richard Nixon over depopulation in rural areas, particularly in the Midwest. While in 1900 two-thirds of the population lived in rural communities, by 1950, reflecting the half-century-long move to cities and then suburbs, only 36 percent were rural residents. The act was another federal push to encourage growth into the countryside, and it would do so by providing enormous federal incentives for water supply, sewer plants, and other infrastructure whose actual beneficiaries would not be mom-and-pop businesses in small, isolated, and bucolic villages but rather large-scale developers of suburban housing, shopping malls, and business parks.[15]

But the federal funding the corporation requested did not come through, so this plan for a city of 80,000 on the shores of Greenwood Lake and in Sterling Forest's hills, with its water and sewer systems paid for by the U.S. taxpayer, died on the vine.

In late 1974, the corporation renewed its work on development of its vast holdings. As in its previous effort, the money came, not from City Investing, but from somewhere else—in this case, the Chicago-based Urban Investment and Development Corporation of New York, a national real estate investment and development firm headquartered in Chicago that was a subsidiary of Aetna Life and Casualty Company. City Investing was still pursuing its hope of capitalizing on the increasing urbanization in the "outer ring" counties of the metropolitan region and the expectation that migration to the outer counties would continue to accelerate. Developed land had increased by a third over the previous decade in this outer metro circle. [16]

And development in the Hudson Valley was being encouraged—for example, New York Governor Nelson Rockefeller had recently launched a plan to turn Stewart Air Force Base into a fourth jetport for the New York City metropolitan area, and Stewart, outside the city of Newburgh, was only 15 miles north of the forest: a quick hop by car and a single exit up along the New York State Thruway for the affluent suburbanites who were going to settle in Sterling Forest.

THE CORPORATION'S NEXT PLAN: STERLING ONE

Estimating the cost of development to be $200 to $250 million, the Sterling Forest Corporation returned to the town of Tuxedo with a request to build 3,900 dwelling units in three clusters on 1,300 of its Sterling Forest acres and additional commercial development. It was asking for a density in excess of what the town regulations allowed, which would require a change in the zoning laws. The new project was considerably less grandiose than the one proposed three years earlier, but would still increase Tuxedo's population from 3,000 to 13,000.

In presenting the plan it called Sterling One, the corporation laid out many of the themes that would prevail over the next two decades. Tucked into its proposal was the tacit recognition that only about 500 acres of the 1,300 acres in the northern portion could be built on with any hope of economic return—the land it was intending to set aside was generally too wet or too steep, or had too-thin soils, to make construction worthwhile or even possible. Moreover, of the 800-plus acres it proposed to leave as open space, much of it was in small fragments, ranging from 11 up to about 250 acres, and much of that would be "improved" into paths, playgrounds, ball fields—a far different landscape than the intact forest-and-wetland mosaic it would replace. And—emphasizing another theme, "tax-positive development," that it would frequently revisit in ensuing years—the corporation claimed that "Sterling One will pay its own way by providing a greatly expanded tax base that will more than pay for the increased cost of services. The increased revenues should be sufficient to provide for improved fire and police protection and for such amenities for the entire town as public swimming pools and other recreational facilities."[17] "[A]ny substantial decrease in the number of units," the corporation said, "would make the project economically unfeasible."[18]

Still another theme that survived into later decades was the claim that if the corporation was hindered from building its clustered development, "carefully planned to minimize adverse impact on the natural environment," somewhere down the road the land would be taken over by lot-by-lot-development, which would be much more environmentally destructive. Indeed, the corporation asserted that its proposed Sterling One was "absolutely the best way to use the land without ruining it."[19] City Investing clearly believed that its Sterling One was the best way to inject coordination into dealing with what was widely accepted as "inevitable" growth. "If not handled with a planned development approach," the corporation warned, "the natural growth in population will likely take place on an unplanned, haphazard basis, and will be a continuation of the scattered-site development which has characterised much of the area's urban growth in the last decade."

THE PEOPLE OF TUXEDO VERSUS THE CORPORATION

The corporation may have been sincere in its claims of good-stewardship goals, but the Sterling One proposal set off a fierce and acrimonious controversy among townspeople in Tuxedo and parallel struggles within and between the town's governing and planning boards. Many town residents worried that the development would leave a huge imprint on the community, straining road and school capacity, creating horrendous traffic congestion, and stretching fire and police capabilities beyond their limits. John Ronan, then president of the Laurel Ridge–Clinton Woods Association, commented, "The project will change dramatically and irreversibly the quality of life and the character of the town."[20] Residents were unconvinced by the corporation's assertion that development would pay its way and remained worried about the impact of expanded services on their tax bills. Tuxedo resident Sazz Crosby, head of the Tuxedo Conservation and Taxpayers Association, wrote, "We all know that a booming population requires more schools, more police, more fire protection, more road maintenance. Who will pay for this? We will! How? By increased taxes! We all know the problems of thoughtless development: sewage treatment, garbage, water supply, drainage, traffic, crime, drugs, and congestion. Who will take care of these matters and who will pay for them? Right again . . . we will!"[21]

Residents were troubled that any permissive town action on Sterling One could set a precedent for other large-scale developments in the future. The project's very name, Sterling One, suggested that somewhere down the line there would be a Sterling Two and a Sterling Three, which could eventually create a town of 100,000. It hardly helped that another large tract of land in Tuxedo was threatened with large-scale development—Tuxedo Estates, which would add 1,100 housing units and by itself more than double the town population.

In 1975, the town board rejected the Sterling One proposal—causing the corporation to flex its legal muscle and sue the town board, charging that the zoning law was improper and exclusionary because it would have allowed construction of only 2,300 units. Nevertheless, again in 1976 the town board turned down a variation on the project. Unfortunately, like local boards everywhere, but particularly in a "home rule" state like New York, where there is no regional planning body, the local board eventually capitulated to the pressure exerted by a powerful developer with the expertise and the money to sue and the interest in doing so. Notwithstanding its own rejections of the project and notwithstanding the recommendations of its own planning board to reject any change in the zoning, in May 1977 the town board amended the town zoning laws to allow greater density of housing, thus allowing the Sterling One application to proceed.

This move infuriated Tuxedo. Town residents accused the town board of negotiating with Sterling Forest developers in private, thus violating the new state open meetings law. The then-supervisor of the town acknowledged that three private meetings took place in the fall of 1976 but insisted that after the state's open meetings law went into effect in 1977, no secret meetings occurred. In June 1977, however, the Tuxedo Conservation and Taxpayers Association filed suit against the town board, charging that elected officials had ignored the widespread public concern about amending the town zoning and asked for support to make sure "the town government is to be controlled by the town residents, and that elected officials should represent not repress the substantive concerns of our residents."[22]

That summer Sterling Forest Corporation formally filed plans for its proposed Sterling One development.

Tuxedo Park resident Al Ewert, a lawyer active in the Sterling One fight, a slim and graceful man now with a full head of white hair and a no-nonsense lawyerly manner beneath his mild demeanor, recalls the events clearly. "Although the town board was the lead agency, the state recommended that they pass the review on to the planning board. And the town board did pass it on to the planning board, which was a critical miscalculation on their part! Because the town board lost control of the time schedule.

"In the November [1977] election, with feelings running high in Tuxedo, the Town Board essentially got voted out on this issue. It had had a 3–2 majority in favor of the development. But one of the Town Board members had run for supervisor. So that left a vacancy on the board, and it was split 2–2."[23]

The town's planning board meanwhile was moving ahead with its environmental review. As it happened, Sterling One was coming up under New York State's brand-new landmark environmental conservation law, the State Environmental Quality Review Act, or SEQRA, which required boards to take environmental considerations into account when they analyzed projects. Tuxedo was the first municipality in the state to consider a large-scale development under the new legislation, making it of interest to both the state attorney general and Department of Environmental Conservation.

"The state and the DEC requested an extension of time so they would have an opportunity to comment," Al Ewert recollects. "And the planning board granted an extension into January 1978. The town board lame duck administration, on the other hand, wanted to pass this thing before they went out of office, but the planning board's extension would extend the review for some time after the lame duck administration had gone out of office.

"So that set the stage for the December Massacre," Ewert explains. "The town board held a meeting and appointed itself to be in charge of the environmental review—in effect, the town board fired the planning board. Then they spent a few days on their own 'environmental review.' On December 28 the town board unilaterally approved the Sterling One application. They issued the permit for the Sterling One development and then went out of office. Of course the whole thing was ludicrous."

This approval, a giant step forward for the corporation's development proposal, was a huge affront to the many citizens opposing Sterling One—and, it turned out, an affront to New York State as well. Because the state was taking its new SEQRA oversight seriously, in January 1978, state Attorney General Louis Lefkowitz criticized Tuxedo's town board for accepting the corporation's "seriously deficient" environmental impact statement, which he said was "vague and confusing . . . replete with self-serving conclusory assertions based on the theory that what is good for the applicant must be good for the town and the region."[24]

That same month, the Tuxedo Conservation and Taxpayers' Association, the Laurel Ridge-Clinton Woods Association, and various residents of the town filed a lawsuit against the town and the developer, asking to have the permit annulled. Ewert, who was one of the attorneys to file the suit, recalls, "The first issue was that they didn't have an adequate environmental review and they didn't give the state attorney general and the DEC the opportunity to report.

"And the other issue was, that Neil Martineau, the person who cast the critical vote on the special permit, had a conflict of interest. Martineau was a vice

president of an advertising agency, Ogilvy & Mather, that did image development for the parent company of the Sterling Forest Corporation, City Investing.
During the public hearings Neil Martineau had announced that he worked for
City Investing but said he received no compensation as a result of that, he did
not work on the account. So, no problem.

"But we turned it around and said, 'You're talking about a project with half
a billion dollars' worth of real estate on the market and somebody has to do the
advertising and promotion work. And who better than the agency you're already
beholden to for passing the critical vote on your project?'

"The reason we were interested in the conflict of interest charge was that
there would be an election to fill the vacant board seat within a year's time, and
whoever was elected would have a critical vote on the project. And if we could
knock Martineau out on the conflict issue, he would not be able to vote on it
for the two years left to his term."

In July 1978, to the jubilation of development opponents, the state Supreme
Court threw out the town board's approval, a ruling confirmed in Appellate
Court a year later. The court wrote,

> Considering the breadth of this proposed $200,000,000 project, which
> will, when completed, essentially quadruple the population of the re-
> spondent municipality and probably impose equally proportionate de-
> mands in municipal services and the environment, this court finds that
> the hasty December 28, 1977 decision of the Town Board constituted a
> gross abuse of discretion which deprived state agencies and the public
> of their statutory right to a reasonable time period in which to consider
> the final EIS.[25]

Al Ewert summarizes the ruling thus: "This case just looked so bad, it just
had to be reversed."

Sterling One generated impassioned and bitter political battles in the town
of Tuxedo. In opposing Sterling One, citizens recognized that development of
Sterling Forest would have far-reaching impacts on their community. The Tuxedo Conservation and Taxpayers Association wrote, "All landowners have the
right to develop their holdings, but not to the financial and ecological detri-
ment of the communities in which they speculate." No one was more sensitive
to the problems of massive development than the Town of Tuxedo's embattled
planning board; in recommending rejection of virtually all of the corporation's
requested zoning changes, the planning board said, "The Master Plan states . . .
the most important goal is to protect and maintain the ecological environment
and continue the present Town character . . . the request [for project approval]

... appeared to us to destroy the cornerstone of the future development of the Town of Tuxedo."[26]

Nowhere was the hostility more acute than within Tuxedo Park, home of the affluent and politically powerful. Several prominent Tuxedo Park families were working on developments of their own in Tuxedo, and they took the community's opposition to Sterling as a personal affront. A number of Tuxedo Park opponents of the Sterling One development recall that for a time they were disinvited to Tuxedo Park social events. Ron Nowak of the *Greenwood Lake and West Milford News*, wrote, "Sterling One engrossed an entire community, divided it, held it under a microscope in ways that it, perhaps, was never scrutinized before."[27] Badly bruised by the infighting over Sterling One, many Tuxedo people chose to sit out later Sterling-related struggles in their community.

In opposing Sterling One, the people of Tuxedo were defending their own immediate environment—for some in Tuxedo it was not-in-my-back-yard (NIMBYism) in its most essential form. But the Tuxedo fight had a much broader context. By the late 1960s, many communities around the country had begun to realize that—contrary to the prevailing myth that development meant fewer taxes—the demands made by new development on schools, roadways, sewers and water supply, police and fire service would actually cause their local taxes to skyrocket. In short, municipalities subsidized growth by shifting the true costs of the development onto residents through increased taxation.

Some municipalities had begun to take steps to limit growth, like the eighteen-year timetable for incremental development of water and sewer systems established in the neighboring Rockland County town of Ramapo in 1969. Some cities increased minimum lot size to reduce the number of homes they would ultimately be supporting, while still others experimented with a variety of zoning code restrictions and other growth control measures.[28]

ORANGE COUNTY WELCOMES MONEY FROM SPRAWL

Ironically, while the battle over development raged in Tuxedo, two of the major corporations in Sterling Forest—Reichold Chemical and International Nickel—shut down their operations there and Union Carbide pulled out as well, selling its nuclear reactor to pharmaceutical giant Hoffman-LaRoche. IBM and International Paper stopped conducting research there. Partly because the oil crisis of the late 1970s reduced interest in development of the far suburban fringe, partly because Sterling Forest turned out to be not nearly as accessible as sites closer to New York City, in Bergen County, New Jersey, and elsewhere, and partly because the corporation was assessing the difficulty of steering its project through state and local regulatory processes and intense local opposition (and because for several ensuing years it still could not count on a majority on the Tuxedo Town Board voting its way), the Sterling Forest Corporation withdrew its proposal and put a temporary hold on further attempts at development.

Although plans for development at Sterling Forest were shelved for nearly a decade after the Tuxedo controversy, the atmosphere remained charged with various plans to intensively develop in the Ramapo River corridor just east of the forest[29] as well as in the wide swath of gently rolling landscape in the center of Orange County. The Sterling Forest Corporation was not wide of the mark when it sought to ride the expected crest of the wave of development as it hit Orange County. Orange, on the growth fringe of the metropolitan region, was seen as a key county. Its neighbor to the south, Rockland County, experienced its peak population increases in the 1960s and its growth leveled off during the 1970s. Orange was expected to overtake Rockland in both rate of growth and absolute population, and increase from 239,000 in 1975 to 346,000 in 1990 (its actual population in 1990 came to 307,000, fairly close to what had been projected a quarter century before). And because the population was continuing to move ever farther beyond the central city, the county's growth would continue despite the relatively stable population of the region as a whole. In effect, Orange County's population gain would be New York City's population loss.

In the mid-1960s, Orange County was still a fairly quiet and bucolic place with agriculture, in the central and western portions of the county, its major industry. But by the early 1970s, speculators and syndicates began buying up large tracts of farmland, in the widespread belief that windfalls from substantial development were just around the corner (and some investors also bought up land around Sterling Forest, in the expectation that they would benefit from any large-scale development there). Indeed, the Regional Plan Association's prophecy that Orange County was on the brink of suburbanizing was in the nature of a warning, but Orange County's development interests heartily welcomed the malls, warehouses, highways, and housing subdivisions that dominated the landscape in Westchester, Rockland, Bergen and other counties to its south—seeing in that future both a general prosperity and a significant boost to their own finances. "Paramus" was both a New Jersey town some 10 miles west of New York City and, with its interlocking highways and its superstore malls keeping homeowner taxes low, a paradigm for what Orange County could become if it encouraged development. Some in Orange County were particularly enthusiastic about Sterling One because they saw that development as an economic engine for growth—it could, for example, provide the water, sewer and roadway infrastructure that could spur development in southern Orange County. It was also at that time that New York State began development of Stewart

International Airport, which the business community welcomed as an engine for development in eastern Orange County.

Among the most ardent proponents of development in Orange County was Louis Heimbach, a onetime dairy farmer in the town of Wallkill, adjacent to Middletown, one of the county's three cities. A clever but taciturn and secretive man, as supervisor in Wallkill from 1971 to 1978 he oversaw the reworking of Wallkill's master plan and zoning to pave the way for large infrastructure projects and resulting increases in town population and commercial development. The two oil shortages of the 1970s were setbacks, albeit temporary ones, to the population influx Heimbach and his associates knew had to come and worked to encourage.

When Heimbach was elected Orange County Executive in 1979, he directed his energies toward positioning the county to welcome growth and launched plans for major county-sponsored projects, such as a reservoir and water supply system, and sewage treatment plants. His expansion of the county landfill to bring in downstate garbage and make money from tipping fees earned him the nickname "Landfill Louie" among his critics. These would be Orange County government's contribution to the effort to encourage development. Ironically, under Heimbach, who had run on a platform of fiscal responsibility, the county government expenditures soared.

CHAPTER FOUR

The Art of Launching a (Forest)
Preservation Movement, 1985–1990

PROTECTING THE APPALACHIAN TRAIL
IN THE 1980S, PIECE BY PIECE

ALTHOUGH, IN THE EARLY 1980S plans for development at Sterling Forest were on hold, the forest's proximity to a metropolitan center of tens of millions of people, making it a potential development bonanza, was also the reason planners, environment-oriented groups, and individuals far beyond Tuxedo had a stake in the tract. The forest's 20,000 contiguous acres were supplying high-quality drinking water to millions of people in New York and northern New Jersey and supporting major East Coast bird migration routes. Offering the very large blocks of forest needed to maintain a wide range of habitats and substantial wildlife diversity, the now largely undisturbed Sterling lands also formed the last substantial link in some 90,000 acres of largely protected and forested open space in the two states. It was this place that saw creation of the first sections of the historic Appalachian Trail, in 1923 and 1924. And this pristine natural environment was also of potentially great value to hikers, fishermen, birdwatchers, and hunters—millions of people within a one- or two-hour drive for whom places of solitude and recreation were becoming increasingly difficult to find.

With the Sterling One development proposal widely feared as a threat to the Appalachian Trail, in 1979 the National Park Service bought from the Sterling Forest Corporation 667 acres surrounding the Appalachian Trail corridor running east–west through the towns of Warwick, Monroe, and Tuxedo, in the northern end of Sterling Forest. Price: $496,000. This provided a narrow protective corridor as the AT passed through the northern portion of the forest, and also had the effect of splitting the northern end of the Sterling property off from the bulk of the corporation's tract. This purchase was negotiated by David Sherman of the National Park Service's Appalachian Trail Project. Sherman has been described as an important figure, with a wide range of political connections—and someone who was tuned into acquisition of Sterling Forest at an early date and continued to care about it. At one point, he walked the entire trail in order to personally annotate all maps the AT office used. Looking at the viewshed and extended corridor, he wrote all over the Sterling Forest-area maps, "this needs to be saved as viewshed."[1]

The Park Service also began acquiring additional parcels in the vicinity, in order to protect the trail between Greenwood Lake and Harriman Park. But protecting a segment alongside the trail itself did not provide real protection for the viewshed surrounding the trail.

Later, the Park Service also attempted to buy for the Appalachian Trail system additional Sterling Forest land adjacent to the Trail in Tuxedo, not far from Little Dam Lake. "It's an area we expect will be under considerable development pressure once the new intersection with the state Thruway is constructed at Sterling Forest," said project manager David A. Richie.[2] (Eventually, in 1988, the corporation sold 68 acres in the vicinity of Little Dam Lake for $10,000 an acre.)

Soon, the corporation made known its intention of selling the vast remainder of its property in its entirety; in 1985 and 1986, the corporation claimed it was negotiating with an unnamed buyer for purchase of all 20,000 acres, including the company's ski resort and conference center. Asking price: $50 million.

The forest was in limbo, as was, apparently, the corporation, which intended either a single large sale or some version of planned development; piecemeal development also seemed increasingly likely. And, whatever form the development would take, it was clear that local towns would be no match for ambitious developers with the money to get the permits they needed. For example, the Lynmark Corporation, headed by Governor Mario Cuomo's friend Sheldon Goldstein, proposed a 150-house development on its parcel in Sterling Forest, the former International Nickel property. Lynmark's parcel, a rocky wooded hill, was too small for the number of houses the company sought to build, so the plan required a zoning variance from the town of Warwick. After Warwick's zoning board of appeals denied the variance, Lynmark brought suit against the town. Faced with the lawsuit, the board capitulated and granted the company the variance; as part of the settlement, the developer agreed to pay the town's legal defense costs up to $30,000. In other words, remarked one observer wryly, "the developer agreed to pick up the legal defense costs … which the developer's lawsuit had caused the Board to incur."[3]

AS THE GRASSROOTS MOBILIZES . . .

Yet, as reports of development proposals and sales negotiations surfaced on the pages of local newspapers, notably absent were any deep pockets—government officials or private philanthropists—with visionary plans to protect Sterling Forest for the public good: seemingly, the time of Progressive Era sensibilities was long past. But in 1985 and 1986, the preservation of Sterling Forest took a giant leap forward with the singular and imaginative efforts of two people, Paul and JoAnn Dolan. Paul Dolan, then a thirty-six-year-old editorial manager with ABC's "20/20" television news magazine, was a volunteer for the New York-New Jersey Trail Conference, where his wife JoAnn was executive director. The Dolans had a summer house made of chestnut logs on the east shore of Greenwood Lake and, avid hikers both, had come to love the Sterling Forest lands right behind them. Writing letters to local papers, the Dolans said,

> [Sterling] Forest has been a source of beauty, enchantment, and excitement for thousands of people—hunters, hikers, fishermen and snowmobilers. Unfortunately, many of us took Sterling Forest for granted . . . in reality, only a small strip of land that contains the Appalachian Trail is now preserved—but there is now an exciting plan to save part of Sterling Forest . . . [New York] Governor Cuomo has proposed a new bond act for this November to help save some of the State's land for future generations—especially land like sections of Sterling Forest that are in reach for so many of us and our families.[4]

> Too often Warwick and Orange County do not get their fair share of government funds. We ask that any readers interested in helping or learning more about the idea write to us so we can mobilize support before it's too late.[5]

Paul Dolan is a compact man with a broad face and soft brown eyes, a beard now streaked with white, and thinning gray hair. A natural storyteller, his gift is putting a visitor at ease and drawing a listener into his vast world of interests. He has a powerful ability to persuade others to invest in his enthusiasms. Dolan says when he found out about the development proposed for the Sterling Forest he was "mad as a hornet—the idea that the forest would be ripped up seemed to call for trying to do something. I knew the governor, the media. I thought I had at least a chance to present the issues."[6]

The media-savvy Dolans undertook an ambitious effort to mobilize every group of players who might have a stake in Sterling Forest—citizens at the grassroots level as well as government agencies and the media. Paul Dolan organized the Greenwood Trust in 1985, including hikers, hunters, fishermen, snowmobilers, and environmentalists—the first serious effort to bring a broad public into the preservation effort.

At the time, his approach to land acquisition was to focus on a core 9,000 to 10,000 acres that would link Harriman State Park in New York with the Greenwood Lake State Park/Wanaque Wildlife Management Area and the new Monksville Reservoir in New Jersey. His proposed acquisition would protect the Monksville watershed along with the several-hundred-acre Atlantic white cedar swamp the Nature Conservancy had tried to buy several years earlier but without success, as well as the Sterling Ridge Trail, a north–south trail that connects the Appalachian Trail with the Monksville drainage basin.[7]

Dolan also floated the prescient idea of having various levels of government—New Jersey, New York, and New Jersey's Passaic County—work in partnership, and together with the federal government come up with purchase funds. Partnership, although a complicated thing to execute, had a number of things going for it. For one, the federal agencies were already involved in the area, with the Appalachian Trail, the New York State Thruway (part of the interstate highway system), and via several landfills in violation of regulations. Then, too, because much of New Jersey's reservoir water was coming from New York headwaters, New York was legally vulnerable if it allowed development that would degrade the water quality of its streams. And, as had been done elsewhere, a cooperative effort involving many government and private groups could make a purchase possible, whereas any single entity would not be likely to have sufficient funds.

To jump-start such a partnership, Dolan contacted officials of the three towns that contained Sterling Forest lands, the Palisades Interstate Park Commission, state park officials in New York and New Jersey, the New Jersey Department of Environmental Protection and that state's Green Acres program, as well as nonprofit organizations like the Nature Conservancy.

In the spring of 1985, Dolan hosted a tour that brought the Commissioner of the Palisades Interstate Park and representatives from the Nature Conservancy, the Regional Plan Association, the New York-New Jersey Trail Conference, the New York State Office of Parks, Recreation and Historic Preservation, the Trust for Public Land, and others to picturesque Little Dam Lake in Sterling Forest. Then, says Dolan, "We all came back to the cabin to work on a plan for preservation. I believe we did pop a bottle of champagne to kick off our campaign."

Out of this relaxed gathering of environmental leaders at the rustic Dolan cabin came a serious effort, a commitment to protect the land "for our children and our children's children." The Palisades Interstate Park Commission was an early supporter and in its 1986 annual report noted that "about 9,000 acres would lend themselves admirably for park and recreation purposes. . . . It would make a first-rate state park."[8]

At a meeting sponsored by the Regional Plan Association in January 1986, commissioners and planners from both states heard Dolan present his plan to preserve 10,000 acres of Sterling Forest land: 8,000 in New York and 2,000 in New Jersey. The project took off quickly in New Jersey, where that state's DEP officials, encouraged by hikers and environmental activists, quickly affirmed the importance of safeguarding the Passaic County watershed. Creeks from the Sterling Forest tract run into the Monksville Reservoir directly, and also indirectly, via Greenwood Lake, which drains into the Wanaque River. In 1980, City Investing had offered to sell to New Jersey a portion of the Sterling Forest tract that lies in that state, but at that time it was New Jersey that rejected the offer. Now, though, as officials became more aware of the need to protect water quality, the Passaic County project quickly became a high priority for New Jersey and gained support of both New Jersey Governor Kean and the North Jersey District Water Supply Commission.[9]

Spurred by Dolan's presentations at least in part, New Jersey moved expeditiously. At the March 25, 1986, meeting of the Greenwood Lake Watershed Management District, James D. Rodgers, planning director of the Passaic County Planning Board, promised to submit an application to the New Jersey Green Acres office to purchase the portion of Sterling Forest that was in New Jersey. The Garden State, which had been purchasing land since the 1960s through its Green Acres program, had previously acquired land to protect the Appalachian Trail and watershed area on both sides of Greenwood Lake. In August 1986, New Jersey allocated $2 million of Green Acres funding toward the purchase of 2,074 rugged and densely wooded Sterling Forest acres in West Milford and Ringwood, between New Jersey's Ringwood Manor and Abram S. Hewitt state parks. But over the next two years, negotiations between the Sterling Forest Corporation and New Jersey over purchase of New Jersey Sterling lands were fruitless. Passaic County was offering $2.5 million; the Home Group balked, saying it had paid nearly $3 million for the acreage back in 1970, and claimed the land was worth about $15.5 million. Finally, in November 1988, Passaic County, committed to protection of the watershed lands of the Wanaque, Monksville, Pequannock, and Oradell reservoirs and other impoundments in the Passaic Basin, seized the Sterling Forest land in New Jersey and arranged for commissioners to be appointed to determine what the county share for the acquisition would be. Richard DuHaime, a Passaic County freeholder who led the condemnation, said City Investing was "not at all interested with negotiations. . . . Their response to us was, 'We intend to develop the area.'"[10]

"It made sense for New Jersey to condemn its land because it was sitting right on top of Jersey's Monksville Reservoir," JoAnn Dolan observes. "If they didn't care what happened to their water, why should New York care?" [11]

Regarding this historic seizure of Sterling Forest land, Paul Dolan recalls, "The negotiations [to purchase Sterling Forest] were going nowhere. I knew the south portion of Sterling Forest, the portion in New Jersey, would be easy to develop, so I pushed hard for condemnation. Unlike the slow federal condemnation process, under New Jersey county law, public health seizure is a swift bold action and is a draconian power; the county attorneys hated the idea of seizure. So I was asked by the planning people to try to convince the attorneys. I met with Mike Glovin, then deputy county attorney, I showed him the water, I showed him the streams, we debated, debated, debated. Then he went to see the [Sterling Forest Corporation people]. And he was insulted, very insulted: they treated him like a local yokel lawyer, they treated him like a piece of garbage. And he got angry about it. At a board meeting addressing the seizure action, I calculated that the property was worth two to two and a half million (a stark financial miscalculation). So then they went ahead and seized it. The police drove up that day and posted signs—it was an irrevocable seizure."[12]

With the New Jersey acreage out of harm's way, the Dolans continued their grassroots organizing to acquire the rest of Sterling Forest. An annual Sterling Forest Day emerged from their coalition-building efforts. And ever energetic and optimistic, they began laying plans to help manage the expected Sterling acquisition in New York and devising ways to bring in tourist dollars. The New York–New Jersey Trail Conference was already scouting out where the hiking trails would go; and the Regional Plan Association was contemplating a land planning study.

But these usage efforts turned out to be premature. For one thing, New York, although it had the vast preponderance of the Sterling Forest tract on its side of the state line, did not have its sister state's urgent concerns about watershed, since New York's magnificent reservoirs, primarily serving New York City, were mostly in the Catskill Mountains, far away from the Hudson Highlands. For another, although there was money in New York coffers for land acquisition— New York's voters had passed the 1986 Bond Act, making $250 million available for land projects—there were many demands on this fund from throughout the large and populous state. And New York had just emerged from a successful but long and exhausting effort to acquire another major park in the Hudson Valley, Minnewaska.

So New York officials talked, rather than acted. By the end of 1988, seemingly everyone wanted to weigh in on the Sterling Forest issue. That fall, New York state, county, and town officials met several times; the group ultimately conferred with Sterling Forest Corporation in December 1988 in the office of County Executive Louis Heimbach. In his decade of county leadership and earlier, as a local town supervisor, Heimbach had long been an advocate of increased development in Orange County and especially in Sterling Forest. News reports suggested that while the working group members discussed with Home Group vice president David A. Wilkinson their interest in protecting water quality and environmentally sensitive areas and preserving important recreation opportunities, Orange County under Heimbach pushed mostly for preserving development opportunities.[13] But everyone, it seemed, was still spinning their wheels: As 1988 drew to a close, with various preservation advocates nipping at the heels of New York officials, the state had made no bid on Sterling Forest or even started an appraisal—a deal was nowhere in sight.

JoAnnDolan notes, "There was a lot of talk in New York. There were a number of meetings with the Palisades Interstate Park Commission, environmentalists, and the North Jersey Water District. New York was probably trying to figure out the strategy."[14]

. . . THE CORPORATION REINVENTS ITSELF

During this time of slowly building public interest in saving the land, the Sterling Forest Corporation responded with mixed messages, its ambiguity an outgrowth of both internal financial difficulties and a fundamental transformation of Sterling Forest's parent company and a whole new philosophy that emphasized assets management. The financial problems first surfaced in 1985, when City Investing decided to liquidate and divide the proceeds among the shareholders. CEO George Scharffenberger planned to retire at the successful conclusion of the liquidation and enjoy the $17 million he was to receive from the transaction. But the liquidation was a failure because some CI subsidiaries had no buyers.

The firm renamed itself the Home Group and came to include the wholly-owned assets that CI had been unable to sell but had to keep operational and actively managed, namely, some small insurance companies, Home Insurance, its financial services arm (named Home Capital)—and the Sterling Forest Corporation. Scharffenberger remained chairman of Home Group and the initial impression among preservation advocates was that Scharffenberger was "very supportive" of the idea of selling the forest intact for the public benefit.

But Scharffenberger also hired for top management several individuals with track records of high-level financial dealmaking—and what was later to emerge as an overall record of institutional assets looting. Brought in as president and CEO was Scharffenberger's friend, the flamboyant Marshall Manley, a top partner and head of the Los Angeles office of the national law firm Finley, Kumble,

Wagner, Heine, Underberg, Manley, Myerson & Casey, at the time the fourth largest law firm in the United States. Manley, who remained managing director of Finley Kumble, came East leaving behind him a trail of failed West Coast banks. One Los Angeles bank he founded in the early 1980s, the Merchant Bank of California, became the target of state and federal enforcement actions immediately after he left.[15]

Manley had played a reckless game with his own law firm: he and other senior partners had taken out enormous loans from Finley Kumble in 1985 and 1986 to pay the salaries and bonuses of the senior partners. The FDIC charged the bank with loose lending and collection policies and charged also that the bank's management had been encouraged to put "a large volume of worthless assets [on the books] to justify the payment of bonuses." Eventually, in a development highly unusual for a law office, Finley Kumble was forced to declare bankruptcy and close up shop, its monstrous $120-million debt partly due to the startlingly large sums paid to its partners.

With Marshall Manley at the helm at Home Group, the insurance company became the safe haven for several alumni of the failed Finley, Kumble law firm. Home Group took on Robert Washington as a director, Robert E. Thomson, vice president of government affairs and chairman of Sterling Forest Corporation, and Harvey Myerson, counsel; all were former Finley, Kumble staff. In addition, a large number of the officers and directors of Home Group were also directors of the Florida-based General Development Corporation, which was spun off from the old City Investing and became a major player in questionable land development deals in Florida. Complaints about GDC financial dealings brought that company to the attention of federal investigators, but not before Home Group offered to buy up the mortgages of GDC's complainants.[16]

The arrival at Home Group of the aggressive and flashy Marshall Manley as chairman and CEO suggested an effort to turn the Sterling Forest Corporation in the direction of becoming another GDC—a well-connected financial empire vertically integrated through construction, utility, finance, and real estate sales. Among the prominent people on the board of Home Capital was Jonathan Bush, brother of President George Bush.

Coincident with the aggressive new corporate stance, by the end of 1985 negotiations over the sale of Sterling Forest between the forest's owners and New York State and a group led by the Trust for Public Land, although close to an agreement, had ground to a halt. In 1986, the Nature Conservancy joined with the Trust for Public Land to negotiate a purchase—an offer likewise rejected by the corporation. Also aborted was an attempt by the Palisades Interstate Park Commission to explore the purchase of the forest and incorporate it into Harriman State Park.

Several newspapers then quoted Home Group as saying it now viewed the land as an asset worth $150 million, suggesting a heightened interest in developing and a growing reluctance to negotiate away its 20,000-acre asset.

In March 1987, only a year after Sterling Forest officials said they were close to striking a deal to sell the 20,000 acres, the corporation abruptly took the forest off the market. "We are sitting on an appreciating asset. It is not that we have to sell it. We have decided to do our own internal study of the possible uses for the land. We have decided we wanted to do it right."[17] And, in 1988, Home Group commissioned a consultant to conduct a market study of the site; its new idea was apparently to keep the property and do the development in-house.[18]

THE DEATH AND LIFE OF A THRUWAY EXIT IN TUXEDO

The corporation's intransigence had been greatly encouraged by official signals favoring construction of a Thruway interchange to be located just east of the Sterling Forest tract—the same interchange location City Investing had suggested in the early 1960s.

Governor Hugh Carey, Mario Cuomo's predecessor, had rejected that interchange on the grounds that it would merely be "an exit for a private developer."[19] Now, in mid-1985, the state legislature, responding to a request by Governor Cuomo, appropriated $5 million for design and construction of the new interchange, Exit 15A. The official argument was that local traffic was impeded by both traffic lights and a slow, winding and often dangerous stretch of Route 17M, the old road that parallels both the Thruway and the Ramapo River.

Most telling, though, the revived Thruway interchange plans promised to create an environment that would facilitate traffic flow from and to Sterling Forest and encourage development in the forest and neighboring Tuxedo. The Thruway interchange was a "cherished objective" of many Orange County officials and development interests, who wanted the interchange to stimulate the economy in its vicinity.

Governor Cuomo also wanted the Thruway exit, ostensibly to spur local economic development, more immediately because Cuomo's son Andrew was a business associate and counsel to Sheldon Goldstein, a builder with real estate interests in the Orange-Rockland area (his Lynmark Corporation had sought to develop a portion of Sterling Forest at about the same time) and a major campaign contributor to the governor. It turned out that it was Goldstein who had tried, without success, to buy the forest in 1986 after the governor persuaded the legislature to appropriate money for the exit.[20] Among pivotal supporters of the

Thruway exit: Congressman Benjamin Gilman, in whose district Sterling Forest lay, and his friend, Orange County Executive Louis Heimbach.

News of the Cuomo-Goldstein connection surfaced in the pages of the *New York Times* and the *Village Voice,* to considerable political embarrassment. In 1987, New York's Thruway Authority decided to suspend planning for the new Thruway interchange 15A; it cited "the inconsistency of this project with the possibility of state land acquisition . . . in the vicinity of the interchange." Specifically, the project would have required Palisades Interstate Park Commission to approve the sacrifice of Harriman State Park land for the interchange and receive other land in exchange. Of such a transaction, Robert O. Binnewies, then deputy commissioner for natural resources at DEC, has noted, "Approval by the PIPC for the interchange project would be required, a prospect whose chances were somewhere on a scale of dim to none."[21] This enraged the development interests and county officials who had pushed for the road project.

The Thruway Authority's discouraging words were reinforced at the end of 1988 by the state comptroller, Edward Regan, who issued a report that seemed to effectively deliver the coup de grace to the Thruway interchange.[22] Backers of the interchange had not demonstrated that it would promote economic development in the already rapidly developing Orange County, Regan said. The Regan report, emphasizing that the interchange would be likely to increase commuter traffic in the already congested New York City suburban ring, also noted that it was not needed—it would save only 84 seconds for northbound motorists. Moreover—in one of those public insights that would establish the parameters for the Sterling Forest negotiations for years into the future—Regan said the interchange would raise the value of nearby land, a situation that would drive up the price of the very land the state wanted to buy. He further noted that the exit could impede the efforts of other state agencies to preserve open space in the area.

Finally, the federal National Park Service announced that it intended to deny a key federal land exchange that would have been needed for the road's new toll interchange and would have made the exit possible. Quietly, behind the scenes, a state official had requested that the National Park Service deny the exchange, and that may have had much to do with NPS's announced intention of denying the land barter.[23]

Given the government agencies' extreme lack of enthusiasm for Thruway Exit 15A, the project seemed definitively dead, but, by 1989, the Sterling Forest Corporation, supported by local business leaders and politicians and regrouping under the name Task Force 15A, revived the matter. The corporation underwrote its own traffic study, which showed a bigger constituency for the exit than the 1987 Thruway Authority estimates. The study, conducted by a private engineering firm, suggested that about 380 cars per hour would now use the southbound on-ramp of the proposed exit during peak hours, more than twice what the Authority had projected for the year 2010. "The case we've made all along [for the Thruway exit] is much stronger now," said Christopher Dunleavy, then executive director of the Orange County Chamber of Commerce. But the traffic study's cars-per-hour analysis still kicked up a relatively low number, and by law, construction, operation, and maintenance costs must be recovered from tolls. While David Ardman, a spokesman for the Thruway Authority, professed interest in seeing the corporation's report, he reiterated that "the project remains on hold indefinitely."[24]

In the early 1990s, a new Thruway Exit 15A *was* built, but it was several miles further south, at the Ramapo Pass, and connected the Thruway to the new I-287, which belted New Jersey's suburban communities. After that, whenever the subject of a Tuxedo-area Thruway exit was revived, it was referred to as Exit 15B.

"CONVERGENCE OF CONCERN ABOUT STERLING FOREST"

In 1988, with all negotiations with Home Group stalled and worries about the forest's future escalating, and with the breakdown of negotiations between New Jersey and the corporation over New Jersey's purchase of Sterling Forest land in that state, the Regional Plan Association abandoned its carefully cultivated image as dispassionate oracle. In the fall it hosted a pivotal meeting at the offices of the North Jersey District Water Supply Commission in Wanaque, New Jersey, inviting politicians, environmentalists, and the Sterling Forest Corporation (although the corporate owners refused to attend). The RPA spoke out forcefully for coalition building, careful planning, and a range of preservation strategies. Acknowledging the difficulty of protecting a privately owned open space and watershed that straddled two states, three counties, five towns, and one village, and again calling for a plan that would protect the vital forest watershed, RPA said its major worry was that the corporation would subdivide and sell off the forest piecemeal. In a booklet it published, RPA wrote,

> The managers of Sterling Forest carefully preserved this natural asset and in the past have publicly asserted that only a small portion ... would be developed because of environmental constraints.... However, they now point out that the entire property has development value—although they do not necessarily intend to build on all of it. Consequently, the ultimate disposition of this property is in question.... Home Group is currently conducting an analysis of the real estate potential of this property ... RPA recognized that the property

was vulnerable since no master plan, addressing both development and preservation objectives, is in place.[25]

The RPA advocated for a single comprehensive conceptual framework and master plan for the property; at the same time it also proposed preservation of Sterling Forest lands as a link in a "Skylands greenway" connecting the Hudson and Delaware rivers. Such a greenway would be a buffer against encroaching development and contribute open space to a rapidly growing population.

In the same publication, RPA warned that,

> Although there has been an impressive convergence of concern about Sterling Forest, its future is far from clear. The worst case scenario would be development of the entire property in configurations which foreclose outdoor recreation opportunities and environmental protection (above all, water quality protection), habitat protection and scenic protection needs. If such a scenario were to unfold over a long period of time, its impact would be even worse because large problems which develop in small increments tend not to engender ample or timely public response. Given Home Group's long-term management history and public statements, there is cause to be optimistic that this will not happen.[26]

As preservation advocates criticized New York for not moving quickly enough on acquiring Sterling Forest, Paul Dolan again assembled representatives of government, planning, and water and land management groups to review progress in protecting open space near existing water supplies.[27] Pushing ahead for New York was Charles Morrison, who directed land acquisition planning for the New York State Department of Environmental Conservation (DEC). Morrison identified land in the hilliest western section of the forest as suitable for acquisition under the 1986 environmental bond act and delineated 11,400 acres he said the state was interested in protecting. The DEC began meeting with the Orange County Planning Department and the towns of Warwick and Tuxedo to develop a plan for land protection.

A NEW STRATEGIC ELEMENT: THE STERLING FOREST COALITION

Home Group's reluctance to undertake a master plan for Sterling Forest and its decision to go ahead instead with a market study of the development potential of the property sounded alarms among environmentalists and pushed environmental groups to work in concert. A new group, initially called the Sterling Forest

Liaison Committee and later known as the Sterling Forest Coalition, was headed by John Humbach. Humbach, an imposing man with unruly sandy hair, a trim beard, and a scholarly, reflective bent that seems to coexist somewhat uneasily with his energetic brand of activism, was a professor of law at Pace University. By his account, his interest in the outdoors came from taking his teenagers on weekend outdoor adventures and wilderness outings with the Appalachian Mountain Club, while his specialty in property law gave him an expert's niche in land preservation. Attending an AMC conservation meeting, he heard about the club's efforts to save Sterling Forest—and he was hooked. Paul Dolan, who wanted to drop out of the public spotlight, persuaded him of the urgent need for a strong, articulate leader to champion the forest. And soon Humbach was writing letters and arguments on behalf of the forest. As early as January 1987, he had became a prodigious advocate for the forest's preservation—for every general letter he wrote on behalf of preservation he tailored individualized versions for dozens of town and county and state officials, guardians of New Jersey's water supply system, congressional representatives, regional newspapers, conservation magazines, and his friends in official and unofficial positions high and low.

Says Humbach about his Herculean effort on behalf of the forest in the late 1980s, "I had a bunch of energy and I don't know where it came from—I was totally energized for a considerable period of time by the rightness of the issue. At first, it was that I was being the lawyer and Sterling Forest, as a forest, as an ecological community, was my client; I was protecting my client, kind of like a lawyer was appointed to protect an orphan, but then I really grew to have a very special affection for the forest itself, I recall it was more than just representing a client, but a lawyer representing a client with the feeling that the client was entitled to my time. And people we were working with played a part too, I was doing it for Enid [activist Enid Sackin], I was doing it for Paul, I was doing it for the people involved, Betty Quick and Charlie Morrison. So it was tremendously rewarding, not only because those people gave recognition but because I always thought preserving Sterling Forest was right. It wasn't a question of winning the battle . . . it was the right thing to do. All we had to do was tell people about it and they would see it was the right thing." [28]

In mid-1988, someone—Humbach can't remember for sure who—hatched the idea of bringing seven or eight environmental organizations together to pursue the Sterling Forest preservation effort, and in August representatives of about a dozen organizations met at the AMC offices in Manhattan. Deciding to form a coalition, they agreed with Paul Dolan's suggestion of Humbach as chair, a post the law professor was to hold for six years.

The fledgling coalition, with no officers, no treasury, and no bylaws, began meeting frequently. According to Humbach, the idea was to take the preservation debate public and educate people—especially the political leadership—about the importance of protecting Sterling Forest and water quality and containing Highlands sprawl.

In its first years the coalition met practically monthly. Neil Zimmerman, president of the New York–New Jersey Trail Conference, hosted the meetings. John Humbach and Paul Dolan took on the press, issuing letters and position papers, with Humbach doing research on water laws and other legal arguments for preservation. Robert Biddle, an activist with the New York–North Jersey Chapter of the Appalachian Mountain Club and an attorney in the New York City firm Davis Polk & Wardwell, lent invaluable assistance, ranging from providing large-scale photocopying to connecting with politically important people. Samuel Pryor III, of the same law firm, was also involved. Al Appleton, at the time head of New York City Audubon and later Commissioner of the New York City Department of Environmental Protection, was a key shaper of preservation strategy and arguments on behalf of conservation. Claudia Mausner of the AMC excelled in logistical support. Among the key players were a crew of Sierra Club activists—Enid Sackin, Jeff Tittel, Betty Quick, Jürgen Wekerle, Michael Vickerman, and Andrew Lawrence. Also active were JoAnn Dolan of the New York–New Jersey Trail Conference, Jennifer Melville of the Appalachian Mountain Club, and New Jersey activist Phil L'Hommedieu, who had long worked for preservation of the Highlands.

Affiliated with the coalition were activist groups, large and small, across the region: the Appalachian Mountain Club, the national and the New York City Audubon Society, New Jersey Audubon Society, the Adirondack Mountain Club, the New York Parks and Conservation Association, the Passaic River Coalition, the New Jersey Chapter and Atlantic (New York State) Chapter of the Sierra Club, and several local Sierra Club groups. "When we started, preservation of Sterling Forest looked like a long shot," Humbach recalls, "but for two years there was this group of stalwarts who every month came to meetings and kept the thing going." Rapidly becoming the central unifying force behind the preservation effort, the coalition argued forcefully against piecemeal development of the tract, rejecting the earlier concept of 10,000 or 11,000 acres and asking instead for protection of a minimum of 15,500 to 16,000 acres with about 2,000 acres for "carefully managed development" funneled into one area or two contiguous areas.

"The real argument was moral: saving Sterling Forest was the right thing to do," Humbach reflects. "It was the last remaining little piece of the great mid-Atlantic forest. It was on the doorstep of the homes of 16 million people. It was a key link of the greenbelt reaching from Connecticut to Pennsylvania.

"But the goal was purchase of the forest at a fair price and the value of the land for purposes of sale depended on the degree of development." For

Humbach that meant that the main value of the legal arguments was that they reminded the developer how the laws would limit the development density and thus how much less development could realistically be put there than the developer was claiming. "The purchase price was not to depend on an unrealistically optimistic vision of how much development could go there. So we brought up every legal consideration we could think of that was relevant."[29]

One of Humbach's most powerful and most widely disseminated legal arguments concerned the legal ramifications of a threat to water quality. New Jersey's drinking water supply reservoirs are directly across the New York border, and Sterling Forest's streams and creeks fed these vital water supplies; the burden of overdevelopment in this corner of New York would therefore become New Jersey's big problem. The AMC's Conservation Committee elaborated on Humbach's concerns, writing, "Even tertiary sewage treatment, the state of the art, is only partial treatment, and it places biological and chemical contaminants into the receiving waters . . . the streams flowing out of Sterling Forest will essentially be streams of partially treated sewage." The committee pointed out that there was no known economical way to deal with the nonpoint source pollution, such as road chemicals, heavy metals, and lawn applications associated with development. The best way to keep such pollutants out of the watershed was to make land-use decisions that avoided such problems in the first place.[30]

Humbach went even further, emphasizing that regulations preventing the degradation of water quality could stop all of Sterling Forest from becoming developed: "We had these streams going into a reservoir and there were laws governing stream quality."

The Appalachian Mountain Club also pointed out that while development in Sterling Forest had so far been limited, the development that had occurred did not bode well for the corporation's sensitivity to the environment. For example, a few New York University staff housing units had been located in the heart of an otherwise undeveloped area, requiring a mile-long swath of road through the forest. In another poor siting decision, a stand of old hemlocks had been bulldozed to build condos on stilts at the edge of Sterling Lake. And a residential subdivision had recently been approved right next to the Appalachian Trail corridor on Little Dam Lake. Overall, the corporation had allowed a fragmented and haphazard approach to development siting, imposing a "cumulative negative impact on the Sterling Forest landscape all out of proportion to the total acreage consumed."[31]

John Humbach also articulated other points intended to rouse the public as well; for example,

[U]nless the state is willing to exercise its power of eminent domain—a remote possibility at present—Home Insurance retains the final say

in the planning process, and normal profit incentives will drive the
decisions about [Sterling Forest's] future. Unfortunately, the best profit
strategy for the owner may not be the best overall plan for the Forest, for the neighboring communities, or for the people of New York
State.[32]

It was an urgent matter, said Humbach: the corporation was moving ahead
with development and, if the state waited too long, it could lose the chance
to preserve, essentially intact, the last large tract of open space in southwestern
New York State: "Construction projects can be successfully launched in many
places, but there is nowhere, and no way, to build a new forest." Humbach also
argued, "As the circle of dense development expands around New York City, the
pressure is growing to build in Sterling Forest and absorb its lands into the Orange and Rockland County suburbia. Ironically, however, the same population
pressures which create the demand for developable land also create a need for
expanded park and recreational resources for increasing numbers of users."[33]

Within the Sterling Forest Coalition there was much worry over how to
fund a Sterling Forest acquisition. It was clear that there wasn't enough state
money available to cover purchase of Sterling. The coalition understood that
acquisition would probably involve a constellation of strategies ranging from
outright purchase of land to conservation easements and acquisition by private
groups.

The coalition saw a need for having negotiating authority, underwriting a
legal defense fund, and fielding consultants. But because the coalition was not
an incorporated entity, the New York–New Jersey Trail Conference became the
logical choice for taking on those responsibilities.

In the spring of 1989, the Sterling Forest Coalition set up meetings with
every congressional delegate in the New York–New Jersey area, and every state
legislator, pressing for assistance with acquisition of the forest. At least one New
York state agency, the Office of Parks, Recreation and Historic Preservation,
opened up channels of communication with Washington to pursue the possibility of substantial federal funding.[34]

Early in 1989, activists had reason to be concerned about the dimming prospects for a state purchase. Neil Zimmerman, president of the New York–New
Jersey Trail Conference, warned that if a portion wasn't acquired that year, "all
would be lost": the pressure to develop was again heating up and the state was
running out of bond act money. The coalition began to think of urging New
York State to immediately acquire the partial purchase of 11,400 acres, an approach developed earlier by the DEC. And it issued a major position paper recognizing that some new construction in Sterling Forest was "probably inevitable"

and proposing permanent protection of 14,400 acres while leaving roughly 2,600 acres for carefully managed development. The worried John Humbach also wrote to the corporation, proposing that discussions begin on having the state acquire 4,500 to 5,000 acres in the northern section of Sterling Forest. If budgetary constraints were to limit the acquisition possibilities, the coalition's fallback proposal was that a partial condemnation of approximately 4,600 acres would protect the lands most at risk. But Paul Keller, DEC Region 3 Director, wrote back to Zimmerman with a hard-hitting demurral, saying,

> Acquisition of only a portion of the lands at this time might be perceived by some as resolving this matter, allowing continued development of Thruway Exit 15A and jeopardizing future efforts to complete the project as currently defined. At this time a campaign by your organization and its affiliates to put the pressure on DEC to move more aggressively appears to be the best course of action. You might also consider convening a 'summit meeting' of top level State agency representatives to assess the current situation and attempt to secure some further commitments.

THE CORPORATION STRIKES BACK

By 1988, Sterling Forest Corporation had experienced several losses that significantly affected the marketability of its Sterling tract. It had lost its easy-to-develop New Jersey 2,000 acres to county condemnation. It was continuing to lose land along the Appalachian Trail due to federal acquisition and condemnation—and as the trail corridor was widened and an increasingly broad swath separated the bulk of the tract from the most northerly strip of corporate-owned land, the corporation would find it harder to develop the portion of the tract north of the trail.

Another loss to the corporation was that the key New York political supporter of the corporation and the Thruway exit, Orange County legislator Richard Schermerhorn, was indicted for fraud; without Schermerhorn the corporation lost the New York support and funding for a Thruway exit directly leading to Sterling Forest land.

Faced with these major obstacles as well as a mounting barrage of unfriendly attention, at first the Home Group mounted an aggressive countercampaign to make clear who the owners were and who would see to the disposition of Sterling Forest. About RPA's prodding for comprehensive planning of the property the company said it had been working with towns to develop the area "the way the towns want it, not the way RPA wants it." About the Sterling

Forest Coalition, corporation president Marshall Manley said dismissively, "I don't know who they are. I don't know whether they've ever been on the property. If they have been on the property, they've been trespassing."[35] And the corporation imposed onerous restrictions on hiking groups' use of the forest trails.

Then Manley dramatically upped the asking price for the tract: he claimed the forest was worth "hundreds of millions of dollars"—the company's public stance was that the forest's value was $200 to $250 million—and said that despite the company's early assessment that the land was worth $150 million, that sum now would constitute an unacceptably low offer. And he laid out his plans for the property in a way that would remind the public that Sterling Forest was owned part and parcel by Home Group. First, he said, the company would review the market analysis and development plans, scheduled to be completed by early 1989. Only then would Home Group consult with town and county government officials. And only after that would Home Group consult with the state. And only after all those interests were weighed in would Home Group deal with the environmental coalition.[36]

The corporation's aggressive and hostile stance changed abruptly in early 1989, when Robert Thomson, who had come to Home Group the year before, became chairman of Sterling Forest Corporation while remaining as vice president of Home Group. Thomson, an associate of Manley's in the California financial empire, was also tainted by his close connection with several western bank failures: the Bank of Mammoth and the First Sierra Bank, which failed in the 1980s, and the Bank of the Ocean, whose nonperforming loans exceeded its net worth throughout the 1980s.

But the suave and stylish Thomson, a man acutely aware of the importance of public perception, had a different job here in the East: it was to cash in on a land, not a bank, asset. Thomson recalls asking Manley what he wanted to do with the forest—develop it or sell it. According to Thomson, Manley replied, "I want you to help me out and tell me how to get the hell out of this!"[37]

Among his other tasks, Thomson needed to alter the public's recent understanding of the Home Group as an aggressive corporation oriented solely to profits and uninterested in the sentiments of citizens in the Sterling Forest area. Under the direction of Thomson, the Sterling Forest Corporation became everyone's friendly neighbor. It presented an image of conciliation and compromise. It began an earnest and determinedly friendly political, legal, and public relations blitz that included mailings to all local residents, a phone survey of public opinion about the development, and full-page ads in local papers. That spring it also held a round of public meetings designed to explain the scope of its development to officials and interested groups. All were intended to encourage the approval of local governments and citizens for the corporation's development plans.

The Sterling Forest Corporation also scheduled public meetings for December 1989 and January 1990 to present a "list of planning principles" that it said it would use to shape its proposed development. And it claimed it would represent the interests of the various organizations that had expressed their vision for the forest's future. Spokesman David McDermott also said the corporation would be looking for "sufficient economic return to ensure the stability and continuity of the project."[38] But the actual list of planning principles did not appear until 1990.

Soon after, a new group, Citizens for Environmentally Responsible Development (CERD), came into being. Calling itself "a concerned group of Orange County citizens who are committed to the environmentally sensible development of the 18,000 acre Sterling Forest Community," CERD vowed to "watchdog" the growth process so that the forest would be "developed responsibly." It said that growth was inevitable and asserted that new growth could benefit the entire area—if it was "done right." The group sounded pro-environment, saying it was in favor of protecting important habitats, ecosystems, and wetlands, although it did not want another park, which "could easily lead to economic stagnation and a marginal local economy primarily dependent on the influx of weekend visitors and vacationers." It suggested that those people who would like to see Sterling Forest become a park or preserve were really outsiders, seeking to override local sentiment—CERD, therefore, was helping to protect community control.[39]

It soon emerged that CERD was receiving its funding from the Sterling Forest Corporation ("less than $10,000," the corporation said,[40] although later reports revealed that $48,000 in monthly installments would be going to CERD[41]). The corporate money enabled the group to run full-page newspaper ads created by the Sterling Forest Corporation's own agencies, supporting and promoting the corporation's development plan.[42] But the group lost public credibility with its very first ad, in which it failed to state that it received its startup money from the corporation. CERD soon had to admit that the Sterling Forest Corporation had provided funding for its activities.

For some, this has raised some questions about our credibility. . . . we are confident that our independence and commitment to our communities is clearly established. Because of the character and integrity of those involved with our committee, funding is not an issue here; the real issues are the master planning process, federal and state intervention in local decisions, protection of our environment, and reaching consensus on how to move forward.[43]

Before its exposure, though, CERD gathered some bona-fide county environ-mentalists like former county executive Louis V. Mills, who later reported how he had been tricked into signing on to what had been described to him as an en-vironmental group. Forest advocate Paul Dolan seized on the misrepresentation to frame CERD as "a cynical effort to take over the conservation effort."[44]

HEIMBACH BROUGHT IN AS DEVELOPMENT POINT MAN

At the end of 1989, Louis Heimbach, who had declined to run for another term as Orange County executive, accepted the position of president of Sterling Forest Corporation, effective January 1, 1990.[45] Thomson said he hired Heim-bach for his "top-flight" administrative skills—Heimbach fit Thomson's need to have someone to tend to the details. But obviously even more compelling, given Heimbach's wide and deep and long-standing connections in the Orange County business community and political circles and his unequivocal—even ideological—commitment to suburban development, was his ability to jump-start development. Heimbach's core constituency, the local business community, was generally bedazzled by the connections and apparent prestige of the Sterling Forest Corporation. And it was no feat for him to encourage the local political power structure to do everything it could to trigger the development of the in-frastructure needed to prime the pump for new business. Sterling Forest, Stewart Airport, and the Stewart buffer lands were his engines of growth: They would bring in outside money, and local real estate interests would be the conduits.

As of 1989, New York had made no bid on Sterling Forest or even started any on-site appraisal. Even the state recognized that the window of opportunity to buy Sterling Forest seemed to be rapidly closing. Robert O. Binnewies, at the time in charge of allocating the remaining 1986 bond act land acquisition funds at the DEC, said that money available for land acquisition from the state's 1986 bond issue was "almost completely committed," and that those commitments did not include any Sterling Forest land.

Under Binnewies, the DEC developed several categories of land acquisi-tion priorities. Its "A" list contained high-priority lands owned by willing sell-ers—acquisition of these was vigorously pursued. The "B" list consisted of other properties owned by willing sellers. And the "C" list included many desirable tracts owned by unwilling or hostile sellers. Sterling Forest was on the "C" list. Despite the efforts of several officials to raise Sterling Forest to a higher priority, Binnewies reports that "Sterling Forest ranked very high for all the right reasons except 'opportunity.'"[46] The "C" designation didn't mean that state priorities couldn't be shifted. But it argued against any sudden and heroic appearance by New York State at the bargaining table.[47]

In November 1989 a group of Passaic County New Jersey officials launched an effort to preserve Sterling Forest land in New York. Richard A. DuHaime, the freeholder who had been instrumental in saving the Sterling Forest land in Passaic County by exercising eminent domain, urged Passaic County residents to join the effort to save the forest and keep up the pressure on the corporation. "We just want to see our reservoirs protected," he said. "We'd like to get an agreement from [the New York towns of] Tuxedo and Warwick to help preserve the land. We feel we have to maintain the quality of life for our descendants." Countered Sterling Forest Corporation spokesman David McDermott, "I don't think that New Jersey should interfere in local government." [48]

THE PIVOTAL KOSTMAYER HEARING ON PRESERVATION SETS THE FEDERAL STAGE

In October 1989, Pennsylvania's Democratic Congressman Peter H. Kostmayer of the House Interior Subcommittee on General Oversight and Investigations of the Committee on Interior and Insular Affairs, at the urging of New Jersey Congressman Torricelli, held hearings in the Tuxedo Town Hall on the subject of Sterling Forest. The subcommittee had held previous meetings on the dwindling availability of open space in and around America's cities, towns, and neighborhoods. The scheduling of the Tuxedo meeting was an outgrowth of a dialogue that had developed between activists and Representative Kostmayer on national forest and local Appalachian Trail issues. Sierrra Club lobbyist Michael Vickerman, who was in Washington working on national forest issues, also found himself talking open space to Kostmayer; Vickerman mentioned the irony that while the East was in desperate need of forest preservation, the large and valuable Sterling Forest tract faced the bulldozer. The Sterling Forest Coalition's Bob Biddle also interested Kostmayer in holding a hearing.

Kostmayer, whose beautiful home district of Bucks County, Pennsylvania, was experiencing the same development pressures as the Hudson Valley, recognized that communities everywhere were facing tremendous dilemmas in trying to preserve open space. Kostmayer said he thought that for many communities it was already too late, but he knew the Sterling Forest area intimately and thought Orange County still had the ability to decide what its quality of life should be in the twenty-first century. His Tuxedo session was billed as an attempt to gauge the effectiveness of efforts to ensure open space in the highly urbanized corridor between Boston and Washington, and to seek a better understanding of the role to be played by the federal government. Partly, Kostmayer's hearing was to encourage some sort of rapprochement between the now highly polarized interests in the Sterling debate.

Appropriately enough, Kostmayer scheduled his October 2 hearing in Tuxedo, in the middle of the New York Highlands and adjacent to Sterling Forest. And the wide-ranging commentary inadvertently revealed an evolution of the thinking that had been going on about the importance of open space in the Boston-to-Washington corridor and the need to develop partnerships of government, the private sector, and business and industry to help save open space.[49] William Boyd, the president of Mid-Hudson Pattern for Progress, framed the situation for everyone when he said, "Sterling Forest . . . presents everyone with an interesting picture of a conflict of values. Certainly Sterling Forest is viewed from rather radically different perspectives by different groups." And not before or since has there been a meeting of laypeople—people not trained in planning but coming from particular interest groups—bringing such impassioned and well-articulated presentations about what the society envisions as its land-use goals.

It was the business community that presented a kind of collective philosophy of the need for responsible, environmentally sensitive development. The Sterling Forest project would become a model of its kind, business representatives said, allowing growth while preserving open space. Citizens could be assured that between the high-minded corporation and the oversight provided by local regulatory boards, the towns would ultimately get an environmentally sensitive plan and one good for the community as a whole.

"The Sterling Forest Corporation believes that growth can be achieved while preserving open space," said Robert Thomson, chairman and CEO of the Sterling Forest Corporation. "We are convinced that it can be achieved here. The size of our property gives all of us a tremendous opportunity to create a precedent-setting planned community development. We believe our history in managing the property . . . should demonstrate . . . that we are 'doing it right' and will continue to do so. . . . We are an integral part of the life of this area and have what I believe is a good, healthy relationship with our neighbors and local governments. I am confident that, working together, we can strike a proper balance between preservation and growth in the Sterling Forest community."

Roger Metzger, speaking as spokesman for Citizens for Environmentally Responsible Development (CERD had not yet been exposed as the corporation's front group), restated the corporation's assurance that development would be a very good thing for all, if it was done right, and that the Sterling Forest Corporation was up to the task. He said, "The Sterling Forest Corporation, which has owned and managed the property for over 30 years, seems to understand the values of our area. Its people have acted responsibly." The Sterling Forest Corporation, he said, had pledged to protect the area's scenic beauty and environmentally sensitive wetlands, to provide affordable housing and recreational opportunities. And it was committed to gradual development and to maximizing the amount of its land kept as open space over the long term. Metzger assured the Kostmayer committee that the corporation had welcomed input from local citizens and as it developed its property would continue to do so.

Developer George Boynton, a general partner in Tuxedo Park Associates, which owned and sought to develop 2,400 acres in Tuxedo, assured the committee that the local municipal review boards had an excellent track record and were capable of overseeing the development. "[H]ave faith," he said, "that these boards . . . will continue to demand good design, responsible and environmentally sensitive planning, and construction that meets the standards of local and State guidelines." Christopher Dunleavy, the executive director of the Orange County Chamber of Commerce, made a related point: "And believe me, the local officials are not going to just hop on anybody's bulldozer."

In any case, the business representatives said, the towns needed ratables for town improvements and job provision. Michael DiTullo, the president and CEO of the Orange County Partnership, a group soliciting development for the county, recapitulated the "tax-positive" assertions: The Forest could market its location for high-tech research facilities and provide more jobs and more ratables. Increased tax revenue from growth in the Sterling Forest Community would help improve the roads and provide more funds for schools and other government services. The project, said DiTullo, would "enhance, enrich and expand the quality of life."

And, according to developer Boynton, ratables were what the Town of Tuxedo needed badly. The town, he said, was suffering from a declining, aging population and lack of tax base. Struggling to keep businesses, schools, churches, and town services open and operating, it was in dire need of upgrading its water and sewer infrastructure, which were in poor shape. Ratables would be the only way to supply the large amounts of capital needed.

Anticipating the arguments of those who advocated for public ownership of Sterling Forest, Boynton asserted that government ownership of the land could not be a solution because what government would pay on its undeveloped lands would be only a small proportion of what private owners of developed properties would pay. "The Town of Tuxedo has already contributed far more than its fair share of open space to the public domain in the form of approximately 48 percent of its land area," he complained.

The environmentally sensitive development envisioned for Sterling Forest was offered as an excellent model for the modest growth and good planning throughout Orange County that the business community said it advocated. "Orange County must strive to be a world class competitor," said Mike DiTullo. "We must strive to create new wealth within the county, to increase our standard of living. Directed, selective and quality economic and employment development provides the resources (financial and human) for an area's quality of life." Added DiTullo, the long-range strategic plan was to direct growth into limited planned locations—"the ones best suited to providing access, infrastructure and other amenities."

Not only did the businessmen's testimony put them solidly behind what they viewed as the environmentally sensitive Sterling Forest project, it went further, calling for new socioeconomic policy, indeed, a new paradigm of land use that would reassess the whole idea that government efforts to acquire land was a public good. The most articulate exponent was William Boyd. Boyd criticized the committee for what he saw as its misguided focus on expanding the greenbelts around center cities. That approach, he said, was "passé": "Increasingly, the great commuting problem is how to move people within the county in which they live or between neighboring suburban counties rather than how to get people in and out of downtown . . . the people who live where the green spaces are available have their own priorities for the use of that land." For this dispersed post-sprawl population, Boyd added, the new emphasis had to be on mixing green spaces with desirable economic uses.

An accusation that had repeatedly surfaced in the decades of debate over the future of the Hudson Valley was that preservationists actually wanted to make Sterling Forest a playground of the city elite—Boyd was an architect of this accusation. "Some people view Sterling Forest as their potential 'playground,'" Boyd said, "a marvelous retreat from the day-to-day hectic pace of New York City. . . . Unlike others, we live in the Mid-Hudson, year-round. It is not our summer weekend retreat, it is our home—where we work, shop and live our daily lives."

Kostmayer Hearing: Open Space Is a Good Thing

The testimony from the environmental community took a broader tack, revealing an evolution of the thinking that had been going on about the growing importance of open space in the East Coast corridor and, to help save open space, the need to develop partnerships between government, the private sector, and business and industry. It also revealed the spectrum of thought about sprawl in the New York metropolitan area, suburbanization as a key problem for the late twentieth century, and the particular significance of Sterling Forest.

Subsidies, mostly hidden, made sprawl in rural areas desirable for developers. Developers of both business and housing sought rural areas, explained county environmental advocate Jürgen Wekerle, because such places had the potential for an inherently larger profit margin.

And our heavily subsidized highway system was a powerful engine driving sprawl by shifting growth from established cities to the countryside; our industry incentives helped to underwrite speculative office and commercial building booms in the suburban fringe, where building costs were still relatively low. Concluded Wekerle, rural growth distorted the allocation of our financial, social, and natural resources and shifted the costs and burdens from new development to other generations and other localities.

In answer to the argument that development added so-called ratables to the tax assessment rolls, thus reducing the tax burden on individual homeowners, the data showed something completely different: In actual fact, citizens suffer burdensome costs when development replaces open space.

In contrast, and contrary to the conventional wisdom, open space actually *subsidizes* the local tax base. The reason for this, of course, is that "open-space" uses of land—such as agriculture, forestry, or other traditional uses—created much less demand for local government services than did additional population.

"[O]pen space is one of the best 'ratables' that a local government can have as it makes little or no demand on services," said John Humbach. "Yet, the ratables' fallacy—one of the most enduring myths in local government lore—continues to be an obstacle to the preservation of open space."

In the two centuries since the founding of this country, environmentalists said, the country's open spaces had largely disappeared. The greatest need for open space was in urban areas near where most people live, yet it was precisely local open space tracts that were under the greatest pressure for being taken over by urban sprawl development.

By the year 2100, development would have encroached much further into lands north and west of New York City and its surrounding suburbs. For the people who would live in this future megalopolis, the availability of wild lands from the Catskill Mountains arching south and east to the Highlands would be an amenity beyond preservation would retain an area that is a remnant of our nation's original landscape. John Humbach was most eloquent: "The preservation of smaller parks inside the smaller cities in the past, the classic being Manhattan's Central Park, is a reminder of the foresight of earlier generations. We should do as much, but on a scale appropriate to our times and the massive super-cities which we foresee."

Lack of quick and easy access had until recently kept uncontrolled and unwise growth from taking place in the Highlands portion of northern New Jersey's watershed. But with the recent completion of Interstate 287, which brought new traffic right to the forest's doorstep, growth patterns would change unless safeguards were put in place.

Kostmayer Hearing: The Difficulty of Preserving Open Space

Sterling Forest, with its thousands of acres of forest-clad ridges, its lakes, swamps and meadows less than 50 miles from Manhattan, was especially at risk because it was just on the edge of the suburbanizing fringe. It was particularly important to save this particular forest, one of the region's very few remaining large properties still undeveloped and still in single ownership.

The difficulty of preserving Sterling Forest, John Humbach noted, was that the land was privately owned, and a private owner's objectives, especially for a large tract, do not coincide with the public interest. The company's management had a legal duty to stockholders to get the maximum financial profit from its forest asset and to consider all profitable development opportunities that the zoning allowed.

Sterling Forest Corporation watcher Jürgen Wekerle noted that the absence of significant development in Sterling Forest to date was probably due more to its inhospitable terrain and an inauspicious economic and political climate than to enlightened land-use management. And while up until now only 10 to 15 percent of the property had been thought to have financial potential, the owners were now claiming that new technologies could overcome the existing natural and economic constraints to allow the development of a much greater portion. No matter how sensitive the development, no matter how many wetlands and unique habitats were protected, the intensive development of the remaining areas would likely fragment and thereby eliminate much of the forest, along with its wildlife habitat, the timber operations, and hunting and recreation. After development, Sterling Forest would be just another wooded suburb no different from the hundreds of other wooded suburbs in the New York region.

Unfortunately, few tools were at hand to protect the public interest. The Orange County Master Plan, even when it espoused sound planning principles, had no enforceability and was ignored. In New York, as in many states, the regulation of land use is generally left to local governments—the much-vaunted "home rule" tradition—but small-town traditional zoning and subdivision regulations, which are primarily means to assure orderly development, simply cannot protect open space. This meant that preserving a large tract like Sterling Forest by means of land-use regulations would require extraordinary local effort and creative use of new planning tools. Even if local officials knew what they wanted to do, they wouldn't know how to do it—they lacked the rigorous training required. Moreover, part-time town boards and planning boards, no matter how dedicated, could not withstand the technical and legal challenges and general pressure exerted by development professionals and their arsenal of lawyers, engineers, consultants, and public relations experts. Lawsuits against local governments were a particularly heavy-handed weapon—they had become what John Humbach called the "nuclear weapons" of the land-use regulation process. Even though such lawsuits were seldom successful, just the threat of a lawsuit had a chilling effect on local decisionmaking.

Local government was simply no match for well-organized, well-financed developers who had millions of dollars to gain. Municipalities would need a full-time staff of experts to be able to combat the developers on equal terms, but most small towns depended on private consulting firms and outside attorneys to assist them in their regulatory work. These firms typically received a major portion of their business from developers and tended to share the development perspective. When a developer came to town with a big project and armed with vast technical and legal resources, local officials were simply swamped by technical data and legal claims.

Water quality was clearly identified as the most compelling reason to protect this last major unprotected tract in the Highlands watershed. Developers must be prohibited from putting a high level of development in the headwaters of the watershed because, no matter how well designed, the development would be in conflict with the need to ensure water quality. Government regulation would require a developer to spend more money to construct a sewage treatment plant for a higher level of treatment but almost certainly could not stop development.

Sterling Forest was a very special case, yet, environmentalists grumbled, despite an enormous grassroots push for the forest's preservation, public officials had shown little direct support. Indeed, with all the ferment about the issue, New York State had made no direct overtures for purchase, still had not come to the table with a real money offer, had not even decided how much land it wanted to consider for purchase, and, meanwhile, most of the money allocated in the 1986 Environmental Bond Act had been spent on other projects. The crux of the conservation position articulated at the Kostmayer hearing was that it would be a major policy error to give up Sterling Forest's existing natural amenities in the pursuit of development goals that unrealistically disregarded the inherent limitations on development—the same natural features that lent beauty and drama made it poor for development.

But New York's parks commissioner Orin Lehman put the state's lack of action in another perspective. Sterling Forest, he said, provided a case study of the type of problems that were increasingly confronting rapidly developing areas all over the state. Since the mid-nineteenth century, New Yorkers had supported state acquisition of open space and had set aside literally hundreds of thousands of acres. But rapidly rising land prices, particularly in developing areas, had made it virtually impossible to purchase outright all the land that the state desired to protect. "The root problem here is the classic one," Lehman said: "Too many worthy projects and too little state money."

Kostmayer Hearing: Urgency!

On the minds of many at the Kostmayer hearing was the urgency of preservation. New Jersey Representative Roukema said, "Regrettably the development pressure is growing on the owners of this tract. I understand their situation. They want a return on their investment and are bound and determined to have it. Clearly time is of the essence." Tuxedo resident Eric Nimke complained, "As environmental bond resources pass us by, 'development' demands are about to bid our objective out of reach, and possibly, out of existence." Without farsighted leadership—public leadership—the economic and environmental realities would inevitably take their course.

Hurry, they all urged.

Kostmayer Hearing: Need for an Enhanced Federal Role

New York parks commissioner Lehman, along with a chorus of the others who had come on behalf of the forest, called for well-coordinated, cooperative efforts involving all levels of government, environmental groups, and the landowners themselves. "The really tough challenge here, of course, is how to get all the different players to act in harmony."

But Wekerle was sanguine that once the real costs of development were compared to the costs of purchase of the forest, the economic benefits of purchase would become obvious and creative public–private solutions to preserve open space could be developed.

Many focused on federal intervention. The feds' primary role would be to help with funding a land purchase. But another vital federal function would be to create some coherence out of the competing claims on the land and the bewildering array of interested parties—the dozens of civic groups and thousands of private citizens, the two states, two counties, five towns, and one village, each with zoning, planning, environmental review, sewage treatment, and transportation interests. John Humbach conceded, "A regional natural jewel . . . may have to be protected by Federal action in order for it to be protected at all."

The Regional Plan Association's Hooper Brooks agreed that the federal government could make its vast technical resources and experience available in the purchase and planning effort and, in partnership with New York and New

Jersey, guide coordinated land-use decisions all along the state border: In these ways, Brooks envisioned the federal government as a major element in a model partnership to showcase the benefits of regional planning. Others suggested the need for a federal role in public education, to help move society toward a new land ethic stressing a sustainable future.

Sierran Michael Vickerman went much further: "In our judgment," he said, "Congress has a legitimate and proper role in shaping Sterling Forest's future, and we hope that these deliberations will encourage Congress to act quickly in developing a national open space policy that recognizes the need to preserve natural systems and traditional land uses near cities."

The Kostmayer hearing on October 2 revealed the fault lines in the community—especially that the underlying values of the business and the environmental interests were really too far apart to be bridged, at least conceptually. The business community advocated well-designed environmentally sensitive development. The environmental community objected that large-scale development in Sterling Forest, no matter how well designed, was not in the public interest. But the hearing undeniably brought new attention to the effort to save Sterling Forest, and moreover still viewed it as a bipartisan and nonpartisan effort.

The Sterling Forest Coalition used the occasion of the hearing and the renewed attention it brought to issue an action plan for the forest. The coalition's plan called for outright purchase of at least 14,400 acres, making sure any development would be concentrated along county Rte. 84, and strong efforts to enforce water purity standards for the Sterling Forest streams that fed New Jersey's reservoirs. At the time it seemed to the coalition that this was the best deal possible.

The publication of this position loosed a tidal wave of protests from environmentalists. After being buffeted by advocates' fury, the coalition did a complete about-face from its recommendation for partial purchase.

THE RECALCITRANCE OF BENJAMIN GILMAN

The Kostmayer hearing in Tuxedo had been greatly sought after by the environmental community, and they viewed its unfolding drama and the legitimacy it gave the environmental position as a great boost to their cause. Environmentalists had much less success in reaching an accommodation with their own representative, Republican Benjamin Gilman, whose district included Sterling Forest. The long-time congressman—like Louis Heimbach a native of the Orange County city of Middletown—was a close friend of Heimbach and other pro-development principals in Orange County, and a recipient of campaign contributions from Heimbach. He was also a staunch ally of the corporation and the only area congressman to support the forest's development. Gilman's aide Todd Burger said that the representative had been "skeptical about proposals for acquisition of land at Sterling Forest. . . . [T]he state hasn't done a good job managing the land it already owns. Also . . . [Gilman] thinks Sterling Forest has done a good job projecting the property."[50] Gilman originally opposed Kostmayer on holding the Tuxedo hearing, and succeeded in forcing its delay from the spring of 1989 until the fall. Although he had opposed the hearing in its planning stages, Gilman eventually decided to testify.

Representative Kostmayer used his hearing as justification for introducing legislation seeking federal environmental studies of the Sterling Forest area. The aim was to provide an evaluation, at a cost of $250,000, of the resources and land-use issues of the New York–New Jersey Highlands and the effects of development on the region.[51] The study, if coming to conclusions favorable to preservation, would at the least give leverage to officials seeking federal funding for purchase. But a comment in a *Bergen Record* article, "'[P]reservation advocates have yet to persuade the public that heroic action is essential" to save an invaluable forest resource suggests the current thinking in 1990–91.[52]

New York's Congressman Gilman, still recalcitrant on the Sterling Forest issue, declined to cosponsor Kostmayer's legislation; "To spend taxpayers' money on a study that is only duplicating other studies is a waste of money," he argued.[53]

In December 1989, New Jersey Governor Thomas Kean issued an executive order creating the Skylands Greenway Task Force. The object of the study was to look at the entire region as a resource and assess the impact development would have on the Skylands and on water supply. The Task Force was to make recommendations on how to achieve a greenway linking the region, which included the Wallkill River National Wildlife Refuge, Norvin Green State Forest, Hewitt State Forest, and Harriman State Park.

Kostmayer was supported by northern New Jersey representatives Marge Roukema and Robert Torricelli, both with a strong public commitment to saving the watershed for New Jersey's drinking water. Torricelli, an Englewood Democrat serving his third term in the House and an ardent supporter of forest preservation, had said he would back formation of a New York–New Jersey commission to preserve the entire 20,000 acres of the tract.[54] "I would like to preserve it all," he was on record as saying. "This is the last chance for the states of New York and New Jersey to plan for a greenbelt around the metropolitan area. It should have been done a century ago."[55] Torricelli had also written an op-ed piece that appeared in the *New York Times* going directly to the funding bottleneck at the state level. He argued,

[T]here is a broader public interest in Sterling Forest that must be considered when weighing its future uses. . . . this is an irreplaceable asset for the entire metropolitan region that is almost without parallel. . . . I am committed to persuading my New York and New Jersey colleagues to join me in pressing for an allocation from the United States Land and Water Conservation Fund to help keep Sterling Forest green. What has been lacking thus far has been a commitment from either Governor Kean or Governor Cuomo to work together across state lines to keep this regional asset from disappearing. . . . [W]ith the loss of land to uncontrolled sprawl accelerating at an unprecedented rate, there is almost no time left to take strong steps to secure the quality of life for our children and grandchildren.[56]

Again that June, Torricelli wrote an article for the *Bergen Record* espousing acquisition of the complete tract.

Torricelli's strong advocacy of preservation of the entire forest was a dramatic turnabout from a less ambitious position he had taken some years before—and some of that change was due to input from JoAnn Dolan. The Trail Conference director recalls a small group meeting to which key strategists had invited Torrricelli. "Bob got up and gave a presentation about protecting the watershed on the west side of the Sterling Forest tract. This was the idea: They were going to protect the west side watershed lands and this tract on the east side could be sold for development. They had this line on the map.

"So Bob eloquently made his presentation about preserving this watershed in the New Jersey section, and then he very nicely said, 'Does anybody have anything to add to that?' And I said, 'I do!' I said, 'Well, you talked about the watershed area, but the Appalachian Trail, which is a national scenic trail, runs right up north here, and this is all the viewshed for the Appalachian Trail, and development would literally destroy what tax dollars had paid for.' I couldn't just sit there and listen to a plan that leaves out the Appalachian Trail! In the past, Bob Torricelli had supported all federal Appalachian Trail legislation. In response, Torricelli's eyes literally bugged out. He got up and said, 'I want this whole thing protected—see what you can do,' and he walked out of the room.

"Something similar happened at a later meeting when Barney McHenry [Barnabas McHenry of the Wallace Foundation] gave a presentation to Kostmayer's aide Judy Noritake. Barney did his whole watershed protection presentation. And I did my same thing—it was like a repeat performance. The aide said, 'Oh, Kostmayer would never go for this unless we protect the entire piece. We have to protect the entire thing.' She had exactly the same reaction as Torricelli. Politicians immediately saw that the Appalachian Trail was a critical piece."[57]

CHAPTER FIVE

New Corporate Actions
Make Enviros Scramble

THE PARENT CORPORATION LOSES MONEY BIG TIME

UNDER ITS NEW WEST COAST MANAGERS, City Investing/Home Group entered into a series of risky financial speculations and acquisitions, the kind that, for some, defined the 1980s. Marshall Manley embarked on an acquisition spree that led toward the transformation of his insurance company into a financial-services bazaar: The company added a thrift and a brokerage firm, buying the Gruntal Financial Corporation, a brokerage house, in August 1987, and acquiring the Carteret Savings Bank of Morristown, NJ, in August 1988, besides adding several additional insurance units. The company's addition of Gruntal came only two months before the October stock market plunge, and its absorption of Carteret coincided with the unfolding of the nationwide savings and loan crisis, thus turning the insurer into what *Financial World* labeled "a financial services disaster-waiting-to-happen."[1] Was it simply that Manley's timing was off? Subsequent events suggest that Manley was repeating the maneuvers that proved so devastating to his old Finley Kumble law firm but so lucrative to its officers.

In 1989, the Home Group renamed itself AmBase and upped its focus on high-risk investments. It built its portfolio with more than $400 million worth of junk bonds (high-risk bonds) from Drexel Burnham Lambert and in addition lent Drexel $109.4 million. Environmentalist Jürgen Wekerle characterized the Drexel junk bond empire as a giant Ponzi scheme turbocharged by greed, price fixing, and insider trading. When Drexel went bankrupt in 1990, AmBase became its second largest unsecured creditor. Wekerle summed up this activity:

"The corporation managers cultivate an image of impeccable credentials while masking internal corporate financial maneuverings that have rotted faster than roadkill under an August sun."[2]

As a result of the Drexel debacle as well as poor earnings from its insurance companies and real estate holdings, the AmBase bubble broke. The company lost money throughout 1990 and by mid-year had to borrow $410 million from Chase Manhattan and a consortium of other banks to cover its losses. Wall Street responded accordingly: The price of AmBase stock, which had fallen steadily since its 1986 high of $31.50 a share, plunged precipitously—it fell to a pitiable 5/16 a share at the end of 1990, giving the corporation a year-end loss of $1.02 billion.

With the company's lenders forcing the issue, during the last half of 1990 a deal was negotiated to sell AmBase. In August, AmBase began purchase discussions with Vik Brothers International. But with shareholders angry at the low selling price and a pending lawsuit to block the sale, AmBase opened discussions with another group, an investment consortium composed largely of insurance executives, which looked like a better deal for shareholders. Under the terms of the $970-million sale, the investment group was to convey $507 million in cash and assume outstanding debt and, in turn, receive the Home Holdings subsidiary. All that AmBase could hold on to was the failing bank, Carteret Bancorp.

Now a consortium that included Trygg-Hansa SPP Holding AB, one of Sweden's largest insurance groups, held a somewhat downsized Home Holdings, consisting of Home Insurance, Gruntal, U.S. International Re (a reinsurance company)—and the Sterling Forest Corporation.[3] With this transfer of assets to Sweden, "Home Holdings" became an instant misnomer: Foreign Holdings, or perhaps Offshore Enterprises, would have been more accurate.

Even as the sale of the failed AmBase venture was pending, six AmBase directors took home $5.3 million from the company. Marshall Manley resigned as AmBase director in January 1991, but before his resignation received from AmBase $3 million plus the cancellation of a $4 million loan debt (he claimed the company owed him about $50 million under his employment contract). Stockholders finally approved the bargain-basement AmBase sale in February 1991.

Wrote Robert Hennelly in the *Village Voice*, "The Sterling Forest tale really reflects what has happened around the nation. Large tracts of land were held by the American captains of industry when America made things for export and lent the world capital. Today what we have for sale is our debt. Now, overseas corporations use U.S. corporate debt as entree into a depressed real estate market, where they can really buy American."[4]

NEED CASH? FLOAT A PLAN FOR 14,500 HOUSES

Sterling Forest would be first in line to bear the brunt of the maneuverings at AmBase/Home Holdings. In 1990, the Sterling Forest Corporation intensified its efforts to extract profit from its leafy, swampy asset. First, as noted, it added to its Sterling Forest management team a new president, Louis Heimbach, the high-profile former Orange County Executive, the power broker with powerful friends.

Then in February 1990, it launched a new development effort marked by release of a new report on development possibilities—a report summarizing months of research by nine consulting firms and covering the forest's topography, soils, water, habitats, and marketability and fiscal impacts. This "Initial Baseline Report" concluded that development would be possible on more than 60 percent of the land, and that the water sources on the tract itself could support about 14,000 housing units and more than 7 million square feet of office space; the forest's streams, the report said, had the capacity to accommodate treated wastewater from that level of development.

Unlike the Pereira study of nearly two decades before, which warned that only about 15 percent of the site could be developed, the work of the new consultants, Sedway Cooke Associates, rested on the assertion that the tract's problems could be mitigated. The California-based consultant held public workshops in the spring of 1990, with the aim of a final design plan by January 1991. The corporation did not equivocate when it said its detailed plan would be designed to maximize the number of people who live and work in the forest.[5]

In June, the corporation presented a preliminary development proposal for its entire parcel: 14,500 residential units in Tuxedo, Warwick, and Monroe, with industrial and commercial space, mostly in the Tuxedo portion, to be built over twenty to thirty years. "What we are looking for is a combination of a traditional New England town and the European mountain village," said Sedway Cooke principal Thomas Cooke. The corporation assured the public that three-quarters of the land would be kept in open space, but the maps showed that the plan, siting clusters of housing and commercial development throughout the tract, essentially fragmented the forest.[6]

"We knew what they were doing," recalls JoAnn Dolan, then director of the New York-New Jersey Trail Conference. "In the late eighties they took the land off the market and said they were going to do a plan. And it took about two years for them to show their plan. I think that their whole strategy was to actually begin to do the development. It's a standard ploy, developers put in roads and lighting, and then already the market value is escalated. What was shocking was that Sterling Forest Corporation *didn't* put in a road; for some reason they didn't do that. After the Sterling Forest Corporation did the plan, the sale price kept going up. I think the highest estimation of its value from the mouths of the Sterling Forest Corporation was $200 million. It went from $100 million to $150 million, to $200 million, then down again. They were doing the best they could to jack up the price."[7]

While most local officials kept silent about the new proposal, there were some signs that the renewed efforts at development were raising concerns among key public officials. For example, Mary McPhillips, a Democrat who had been elected Orange County executive to replace Heimbach, expressed grave concerns. She was already struggling with a host of costly and problem-riddled growth-related infrastructure projects bequeathed to her by her predecessor, including a jail, a landfill, a water supply project, and a malfunctioning sewer plant.

Also sharply critical of the developer's plan, especially the fragmentation of the forest, was Thomas Jorling, head of New York's DEC. Even though the state had not yet produced a cent for purchase, the DEC was consistently advocating acquisition of a larger unbroken tract. In August 1990, Jorling said,

> The corporation's plan presumes [that] development of significant portions of the property is the best use of this rugged and naturally scenic terrain. This may not necessarily be true from either an economic viewpoint or an environmental one. We believe that it would be desirable to present another alternative, one which would be more responsive to the open space and environmental resource values of the property. . . . [The plan is] inconsistent with the public's interest in ensuring perpetuation of the present and historic role of Sterling Forest as a large scale, quasi-public open space recreational park in proximity to the people of the New York City metropolitan region and the Lower Hudson Valley.[8]

Jorling also made this point at a September meeting between him and Sterling Forest Corporation's Robert Thomson. And the *Middletown Times Herald-Record*, the local newspaper, also reflected this awakening worry when it commented,

> Ambase Corp. . . . is in serious financial trouble. It is trying to unload Sterling Forest to raise funds. It is shopping the company and the forest in Europe, to potential owners who may be excused if they have little knowledge of Sterling Forest and why so many people want to see its open space preserved. . . . Sterling Forest Corp. has said it wants to preserve some 13,000 acres . . . A promise. But if a new owner puts a

higher premium on getting a bigger return for his dollar, old promises may not mean much.[9]

The development proposal, with its large glossy maps and extensive planning details, signifying that this time the corporation might really be serious about extensive development, underscored the need for decisive action. But John Humbach, chairman of the Sterling Forest Coalition, professed to being hopeful. With the new European owners having paid $507 million in cash, he surmised, they might be serious about selling their forest asset. New York was in a real estate slump, with a glut in both residential and commercial space, and the state might be the only game in town and might, moreover, be able to wrest a fair deal from the corporation

Nevertheless, the environmental community was nervous. Any purchase deal hinged on New York voters passing the state's 1990 environmental bond act, which proposed $800 million for land acquisition.[10] Given the uncertainty of the bond act's passage, the forest's advocates continued to hope that the federal government could be persuaded to contribute to a purchase. But in 1990, except for Pennsylvania Representative Peter Kostmayer, there was no federal presence in Washington advocating on behalf of Sterling Forest.

THE VERY FIRST FEDERAL MONEY — $250,000 FOR A HIGHLANDS STUDY

In the summer of 1990, forest advocates launched their campaign to enlist the federal government and began by supporting the modest $250,000 appropriation championed by Representative Kostmayer for a Forest Service Highlands study. In August, the Senate and the House of Representatives passed Kostmayer's provision *authorizing* the National Forest Service to study the Highlands, including Sterling Forest; Kostmayer said he hoped the study would eventually lead to government acquisition of the forest for preservation as open space.

Not informed of Kostmayer's authorization provision (a one-sentence insertion in the huge 1990 farm bill), an angry Representative Benjamin Gilman made a vigorous effort to defeat Kostmayer's subsequent request for an *appropriation*—that is, an actual financial commitment. Gilman was both genuinely irritated at Kostmayer's tactics and committed to forest development. He said that any federal study should wait until the forthcoming Sterling Forest Corporation's own report was completed and analyzed. He added legislative language stressing the rights of the private landowner. And again he said that government should not buy more land because government could not manage what it already owned.[11]

Gilman's continued stance against preserving Sterling Forest prodded even the politically cautious *Middletown Times Herald-Record* to challenge the lawmaker. The paper understood that the corporation's own report would by its very nature be self-serving: "By its own account, Sterling Forest Corp. is spending $5 million to provide a detailed study on what should be done with the land in question. It says it will be environmentally sensitive, but in the end, the suggestions will lean towards the corporation's objective—to make money," and it criticized Gilman's dilatory tactics, saying, "In Washington, the stall is often the best way to kill something."[12]

But Peter Kostmayer insisted that Gilman's efforts had not derailed the project, because the study was already on the Forest Service's list of fiscal 1991 projects.[13] Indeed, at the end of October, the Interior Appropriations Conference Committee did approve a $250,000 appropriation for a study of the New Jersey–New York Hudson Highlands. For the first time, Sterling Forest preservation was on the congressional radar.

The Kostmayer Highlands study appropriation required the U.S. Forest Service to examine the open space resources and land-use patterns of the New York–New Jersey Highlands region, including Sterling Forest, and outline strategies to protect the region's long-term integrity. Kostmayer garnered support from many of the region's representatives, including New Jersey Senators Frank Lautenberg and Bill Bradley and New Jersey congressional representatives Robert Torricelli, Marge Roukema, Robert Roe, Dean Gallo, and Richard Zimmer.

But Gilman continued to be a loud and powerful voice of opposition. An aide to Gilman said the Forest Service study was not well enough funded to do any more than critique the Sterling Forest Corporation's Sedway Cooke report. "As far as Mr. Gilman is concerned the USFS study is a waste of time and money," he said.[14] Gilman also criticized the work group formed to guide the Forest Service, which included both environmentalists and local officials. He said, "This is completely one-sided. Almost everyone in this group is opposed to development," and he asked for more business people. The Forest Service project coordinator, Joe Michaels, rejoined, "It's not about developers versus environmentalists . . . it's about my kids and your kids and what we all want for them."[15]

THE CORPORATION ENVISIONS
MURALS, FOUNTAINS, AND SOME TREES

At the end of March 1991, Sterling Forest Corporation unveiled the next iteration of its development plan resulting from its two-year, $7-million study. Under pressure from its parent corporation, Trygg-Hansa, to extract a sound profit from the forest, the corporation had largely stuck to its 1990 provisional plan. It did make a few siting concessions to public and environmental concerns—now it suggested 14,200 housing units (down from 14,500), clustered in five hamlets—but it actually upped its plan for commercial/retail space to 8 million square feet, a million-square-foot increase over its 1990 proposal. There were, in addition, a 250-room resort, three golf courses, and a ski center.

The new Sterling Forest plan was presented as cutting-edge planning via a return to the small-town concept of having stores, schools, parks, and offices within walking distance, or near a jitney bus stop, of the hamlets. Residential areas would offer a mix of starter houses, senior residences, and estates. Sterling Crossing, a traditional small downtown, would offer shops, theaters, apartments and offices. Sculptures, murals, fountains, and other art would enrich the streets and centers. Signage would be carefully regulated. Historic resources like the old Sterling Furnace would be restored. Each hamlet would have a distinctive architectural theme. Parking lots would be carefully landscaped.

Best of all, the corporation said, half of the 20,000 people who worked in the forest would also live there, thus keeping auto use to a minimum. The corporation also claimed that 75 percent of the land would remain as open space—and this was true, if you counted as open space the golf courses, ski centers, community parks, school fields, and buffer strips making up 7 percent of the total. The corporation's chairman and CEO, Robert Thomson, said at the time, "I like to joke that we are making other developers angry at us, we are setting such a high standard for them to follow." And Sterling Forest point man Louis Heimbach said, "From a purely academic perspective, this is a planner's dream. It is affordable, mass transit and pedestrian oriented, with a good jobs and housing balance."[16]

In touting the economic advantages of its proposal, the corporation described a community that would contribute $36 million in taxes over and above the cost of the services it would require: $6 million to three towns, about $17 million to the affected school districts, and $14 million to Orange County. The development, the corporation said, would create jobs and generate fiscal surplus through tax-positive development phased in over thirty years.

That spring the company launched a new media blitz. It took out numerous newspaper and magazine ads, aired radio spots, and held community forums and public information meetings. CEO Bob Thomson replaced its venerable logo—three trees and a stump—with a rounded and gently tipped leaf, reminding Heimbach and some staff of what they sarcastically referred to as "Casper the friendly leaf." It sent out direct mailings and conducted regular phone surveys.

A *Middletown Times Herald-Record* article reported,

Officials also take to the road several times a week to chat with groups of local residents—at coffee klatches, Chambers of Commerce breakfasts, town board meetings, Rotary Club luncheons . . . Thomson often wears open plaid shirts to public meetings and forums. . . . . the theme in its marketing campaign is that Sterling Forest is a local company whose plans will benefit the community. [17]

Nevertheless the corporation had developed its plan before it went out to town forums and citizen groups. The public was never given the option to make suggestions—especially suggestions of appropriate scale of development—but merely to react to a complex, essentially complete proposal. Many activists believed that their method of inviting local residents to informal discussion reflected a "politically correct" strategy to present a planned development to a community; the panels were seen to merely serve as a public relations tool for the corporation.

Everywhere the corporation went, it preached its development's tax positive mantra:

It's basic arithmetic. . . . Further development of Sterling Forest . . . will result in annual tax surpluses of nearly $17 million for the school districts of Tuxedo, Monroe-Woodbury and Greenwood Lake. These surpluses are the product of tax-positive development, which carefully balances a variety of housing types with a mix of commercial and retail development, to provide a diversified tax base. As a result, project revenues from further development at Sterling Forest will more than pay for educating and accommodating new students in our area—at absolutely no cost to current residents. . . . Sterling Forest Corporation will use "phasing" to ensure that along with each stage of residential development, there will be commercial development as well. [18]

Although the corporation never would abandon its tax-positive theme, in March 1992 it held a community forum at its conference center featuring tax and land-use experts not on its payroll. Contrary to what the corporation might have hoped, the eminent planner Richard Tustian told the audience that municipalities had never enjoyed tax surpluses from new development, even with huge federal and state tax-supported subsidies, and such subsidies, moreover, had not been available for years. [19]

Having dangled the "tax-positive" carrot, the Sterling Forest Corporation then brandished its stick, saying it could build its first phase of 6,000 units without the Tuxedo Thruway exit but it couldn't build the rest unless the state built the exit. Buoyed by the corporation's initiative, local business leaders beat the drums to revive their all-time favorite infrastructure project, which earlier the state had identified as not warranted by current traffic. The business community continued to see the Thruway exit, with or without the Sterling Forest development, as a way to prime the economic pump in southern Orange County. Although the state had shelved the controversial exit in 1988 because of lack of existing demand, and although New York's Thruway Authority steadfastly maintained that nothing would happen to create a new exit until after the Sterling development issue was resolved, each year since then Governor Cuomo had continued to request $5 million toward construction of the exit.

In May 1991, businessmen held a small pep rally at Tuxedo High School, with Congressman Gilman and other politicians coming out in support of the exit.[20] Simultaneously, the business community buttressed the corporation's talking points by arguing in public for "carefully planned growth" like that at Sterling Forest. Development pays its own way and benefits everybody, not just business, they said, by increasing property values and providing businesses that pay hefty taxes. Growth in Orange County was inevitable, they insisted, and the Sterling Forest development would "absorb" part of that growth to help prevent sprawl elsewhere in the county. And they claimed that Orange already enjoyed "controlled and directed" growth.[21]

BUT FOREST WATCHERS SEE A SWISS-CHEESE FOREST

The new development plan generated a small firestorm among forest champions, who repeatedly reminded the general public that the land was privately owned, that it was not secure, and, even more, that it was as close as it possibly could be to development. Lee Wasserman, director of the New York State Environmental Planning Lobby, a nonprofit advocacy group, said, "It is simply fantasy to expect that you could drop a city of 35,000 or 40,000 people into the last forested open space in the metropolitan region without forever destroying the magnificent ecological benefits it provides." New Jersey Representative Robert Torricelli said he would continue to fight for acquisition because "The only appropriate use for Sterling Forest is to leave it as nature created it."[22]

From environmentalists' perspective, a whole range of new headaches would unfold, now that the Sterling Forest Corporation was in Trygg-Hansa's Swedish hands. "The forest is almost a footnote in the balance sheet of the sale of the insurance company," fretted John Humbach of the Sterling Forest Coalition. "And really what we have now is the interests of foreign investors versus the public interests of the people who live in the region."[23] He worried publicly about the underlying impact on the forest. The plan might be a good plan, he said, but it was in the worst possible place. And, beyond the corporation's claim that 75 percent of the land would remain as open space, in fact the design chopped the forest into fragments and remnants, badly degrading the tract's worth as woodland habitat. "The specialness and glory of Sterling Forest is the size and extent of its essentially unbroken natural lands," Humbach argued, "and these would be lost to fragmentation as core forest lands become little more than buffering between the subparts of a new suburban landscape." Humbach noted that more than 100 separate areas of development would make Swiss cheese of the forest: "As a latticework. . . . it no more retains the open wild character of Sterling Forest than the wooded medians in the Thruway."[24]

Environmentalist Jürgen Wekerle warned,

> We cannot realistically expect the new corporate interests located in Stockholm, Bermuda and the Cayman Islands to advocate for our local economic well-being or for our regional environmental concerns. . . . With all the finesse of sharks feeding in a goldfish bowl . . . [the] ultimate strategy [of the corporation] is to exploit the speculative value of the land in order to harvest high-profit building permits. Those permits and subdivisions would then be spun off and sold to the highest bidders. The fate of Sterling Forest will thus be left to the actions of unknown developers. . . . We are presented with a financial mirage that will require massive public tax contributions. Or the corporation will fade into bankruptcy as did GDC in Florida. In either scenario, the public is the poorer for it.[25]

Wekerle was merely repeating what the corporation itself had described right up front and as long ago as 1967: It would spend millions on planning, public relations and obtaining state permits, then sell off the permitted lots to others.

Paul Dolan criticized the inability of Orange County officials to act courageously and with long-term vision for the region. County environmentalist Dan Miner dismissed the revival of the proposed Thruway exit it as "a very expensive public subsidy for private development . . . an economic development grant."[26]

Even officials were skeptical. The Greenwood Lake School Board listened to corporation president Louis Heimbach explain the plan's additional 2,500 houses in the Greenwood lake school district with a near-absence of commercial development to offset residential costs—without even a school site donated until the project's twentieth year. "I don't mean to attack you," Greenwood Lake Superintendent of Schools John Canzoneri told Heimbach, "but I don't believe [your] numbers."[27]

An Orange County resident, Joseph Fucci, panned the duplicity of the corporation:

> It does not take a mathematical genius to conclude that the Sedway-Cooke Plan, for all its size specificity and for all its purported and well-publicized environmentally sensitive 'principles,' has in fact taken the best case scenario of the carrying capacity of the entire 18,000-acre forest and crammed it into 4,500 acres. The claim that 75 percent of the forest is therefore being "saved" is, in my view, a blatant lie. If it is the intention of the Sterling Forest Corporation to develop the equivalent of the entire forest, then let it be said openly, so that any suggestion of duplicity may be dispelled. If Orange County does indeed require an additional 14,500 dwelling units with its concomitant increase in population equal to that of Newburgh and Middletown combined, then let 4,500 units go into the forest, if they must. The other 10,000 should go into Newburgh, Middletown, and Port Jervis, where quality housing is truly needed! [28]

Residents of Tuxedo also stepped up their efforts to oppose the plan, producing a newsletter critical of the corporation's plans. The Tuxedo Taxpayers Association took out two big ads in the *Times Herald-Record* warning that the corporation's foreign owners would raise local taxes and ruin the Tuxedo community. The Clinton Woods and Laurel Ridge Association, since the 1970s a watchdog for development in Tuxedo, phoned residents to garner their support and posted signs encouraging residents to attend planning board meetings.

In April 1991, the Appalachian Mountain Club, a member of the Sterling Forest Coalition, commissioned an evaluation of the corporation's economic analysis; its report, released that September, showed that the development could wind up not lowering taxes but actually raising them and shrinking services. The corporation, AMC said, did not account for the costs to the towns of Monroe, Warwick, or Tuxedo of the estimated 10,000 people who would work in the forest but could not afford to live there; estimated yearly cost: $2.4 million. The AMC disputed the corporation's estimate of the number of children for each household, which, it said, erroneously minimized the costs to the schools; another 600 students, which AMC said would be closer to national projections, would cost the three school districts an additional $4.6 million. AMC criticized the corporation for using school tax rates in Tuxedo that overestimated tax revenues. The corporation's overestimate, said AMC, was $10.5 million and the cost just to maintain current per-pupil expenditures in the Tuxedo schools was $8.7 million more. Thus, said AMC, the total additional costs would be more than

$33.8 million and would effectively wipe out the corporation's claim of total net revenues to the towns.

And, added AMC, this analysis didn't even figure in the costs that would spill over into other Orange County towns—costs the corporation had completely failed to include.

Finally, AMC reported, the project would be phased, and as long as residential development proceeded ahead of commercial development, the costs to the towns would outweigh revenues. If the project were never completed, the towns would be at risk for a long, long while.[29] "We want to make sure the towns have the opportunity to look at all the potential hidden costs of such a massive development," said AMC conservation director Jennifer Melville. "Sterling Forest claims this will be a boon, but I think in the short term and long term it won't be."[30]

Water quality, of course, was the chief problem, especially for New Jersey. New Jersey's Dean Noll, chief engineer of the North Jersey District Water Supply Commission, operator of the Wanaque/Monksville reservoir system, was concerned that development would heavily impact his state's water supply, which, he said, would "come down to us as treated sewage, which is certainly different from the water quality we're getting now."

John Humbach reserved his sharpest and most highly developed criticism for the development's effects on the watershed: The project would add five million gallons of treated sewage and additional nonpoint pollution from road salt, petroleum products, pesticides and herbicides coming from parking lots, auto, houses, and golf courses, and all running off into the mountain streams that feed New Jersey's reservoirs. The Pace professor of law had long argued that proposals to discharge tertiary treated sewage into Sterling Forest streams were quite simply proposals to degrade water quality. Now he insisted that even so-called state-of-the-art tertiary sewage treatment was only partial treatment and would leave most of the development's pollutants in the water. There was little likelihood that Sterling Forest could undergo significant development without degrading the water quality of streams flowing into the New Jersey water supply: "There may be ways to develop watersheds without serious declines in stream water quality, but we have not found them," Humbach said. Looking at the political ramifications, Humbach said, "Technologies are there, but the practical political ability to tax-and-maintain clearly is not." Of the highly sophisticated sewage treatment plants the new community would need, Humbach asked, "Will New York local officials be willing to raise revenues from New York taxpayers so that the waters going to New Jersey forever meet the standards of the comprehensive plan? To think that is politically naïve."[31]

Humbach had become especially interested in the issue of stream protection when, in 1988, he discovered that New York State had an antidegradation policy, linked to the federal Clean Water Act: protection of present quality and no further water-quality degradation. According to Humbach, this policy required that—regardless of a stream's purity classification—the regulatory agencies would have to put limits on development since development might degrade water quality. Argued Humbach, "even if these streams do have a "D" rating, the state has to honor its own antidegradation policy."

But the antidegradation policy was itself degraded—by the state's counterproductive stream designations. Right through the early 1990s, New York was in violation of the federal Clean Water Act by failing to protect high-quality streams flowing into New Jersey's reservoirs. Unfortunately, New York streams and rivers along New Jersey's northern border were given New York's lowest possible rating (its "D" rating, meaning not suitable for drinking and allowing sewage, industrial waste, and contaminated runoff to flow into them)—and this even though they were high-quality waters. In the 1980s, when New York had begun a stream reclassification process, New Jersey had asked New York to protect their shared rivers by adopting the federal policy and upgrading streams used for drinking to "AA," or pristine, quality. Such a New York upgrade would be consistent with New Jersey's use and classification. "New Jersey has adopted EPA's antidegradation policy—why can't New York?" complained New Jersey water engineer Dean Noll. Some years earlier, New York had agreed to abide by the request of Connecticut not to allow any additional discharge of sewage into Connecticut's AA drinking-water streams—New Jersey thought it was due at least as much consideration.

Humbach also applied to have the reclassifications upgraded for key Sterling Forest streams. New York had been considering giving the Ringwood and Jennings creeks a "C" designation, which would still have allowed discharge of contaminated runoff and treated sewage. In 1990 the DEC held a public hearing on reclassifying the Ringwood and Jennings Creeks, at which many citizens opposed DEC's proposal to reclassify these streams to Class C and favored a Class AA-classification. But DEC based its classifications only on "existing" uses, not on the current quality of the stream—contrary, as Humbach, noted, to the antidegradation policy. The DEC had not attended to this inconsistency and Humbach reminded activists it would be important to pressure the DEC to conform to federal law.

Nothing further occurred until the fall of 1993, when the DEC proposed to reclassify the two creeks in Sterling Forest to only a class A, and that for only 100 feet upstream from the New Jersey border. The agency argued that the higher designation for the 100 feet would force regulators to maintain rigorous standards upstream in order to assure that the water was of high quality when it reached New Jersey. But these "upgraded" classifications would still allow substantial additional pollution to be discharged into the streams. What was not clear, though, was whether the upgrades would prevent the Sterling Forest Corporation from building wastewater treatment plants discharging into Ringwood and Jennings creeks. The DEC was also proposing "Discharge Restriction Zones" that could change the way the corporation approached its development. Environmentalists seized on this DEC effort as an additional tool to resist the development, since stream upgrades would increase the cost of the project for the corporation.

The DEC did not upgrade its Sterling Forest stream designation and at the new-century mark New York was still in violation of the federal Clean Water Act governing nondegradation of streams.

Worries about the Sterling Forest water supply were intensified by an ongoing radioactive leakage problem in the old Cintichem nuclear reactor on the Sterling tract, a problem that came to a head at the very time the Sterling Forest corporation was trying to advance its development proposal. The Cintichem reactor, first put into service in 1961 by Union Carbide and later sold to Hoffman-LaRoche, was used until 1990 to make tracer and other imaging radiopharmaceuticals. In November 1989, Cintichem found a leak of low-level radioactivity in a storm-drain manhole that empties eventually into the Indian Kill Reservoir, a drinking water source for more than 100 households in the Laurel Ridge-Clinton woods development. Cintichem failed to report the leak to the town of Tuxedo until more than a month after it was detected, a failure for which the DEC fined the company $300,000. Cintichem said the amount of radioactivity leaking was minuscule, but, in February 1990, following heavy rains, the reactor's holding pond was found to have released 30,000 gallons of water containing radioactive iodine—twice as much radioactivity as permitted—into the Indian Kill Creek, a tributary of the Ramapo River. Investigators found another radioactive leak in the storm drain and later discovered that water that had flowed from the reactor site into the Indian Kill Reservoir, only 800 feet away, was slightly radioactive. The Nuclear Regulatory Commission ordered Cintichem to shut down its reactor until the company could prove that the leakage problems had been fixed, but rather than address its leakage problems, in April Cintichem decided to shut down its reactor permanently. In 1991, and again in 1992, the now-dormant Cintichem plant again leaked. Over two years, workers removed the 5-megawatt research reactor, the radioactive rods, 90,000 cubic feet of nuclear waste, and the water in the 100,000-gallon reactor pool. Soil under the labs was also found to be contaminated. The reactor was eventually cleaned up and dismantled, the labs demolished, and 220,000 feet of radioactive waste hauled away.[32]

ASKING THE FEDS FOR BIG BUCKS

While the Sterling Forest Corporation floated its plan and heard back from the public, the U.S. Forest Service unveiled a draft of its plan for the Highlands: its November 1991 draft "New York–New Jersey Highlands Regional Study" recommended limiting development on more than a million Highlands acres and creating a two-state regional planning authority to oversee area development activity. It singled out Sterling Forest for protection by public purchase, suggesting that the federal government supply 50 percent of the money, New York State, 40 percent, and New Jersey, 10 percent. This conclusion greatly buoyed conservationists and protection-minded politicians.

Several other studies, all urging protection of Sterling Forest, also came out in 1991 and the first half of 1992: New Jersey's "Skylands Greenway—A Plan for Action," the Palisades Interstate Park Commission's "Second Century Plan," and a report of the Hudson River Valley Greenway Council. Sterling Forest was also identified in New York's Open Space Conservation Plan, "Conserving Open Space in New York," as a critical tract that should be protected from development.[33] The consistent message: Sterling Forest was too valuable to be fragmented by development and should be conserved as watershed and open space, and federal and state public agencies should invest in its acquisition.

Money for Sterling Forest, however, was still not in evidence. In response to the obviously growing public concern about the forest lands, in the fall of 1991 officials from New York and New Jersey pledged to help get federal funding for acquisition of the forest tract. New Jersey Representative Robert Torricelli wrote to Governor Cuomo, asking for his help in obtaining New York state funds and urging the governor to consider taking the land by eminent domain if negotiations failed.

Robert O. Binnewies, now executive director of the Palisades Interstate Park Commission (PIPC) after his stint at DEC, took the lead in the effort to acquire the land. Although all three major sources—New York, New Jersey, and the U.S. government—were strapped for funds, Binnewies didn't see the acquisition as impossible. The PIPC worked on developing strategies, negotiating with the corporation, meeting with congressional representatives regarding federal help and with Governor Cuomo's staff to seek state purchase, and sparking serious discussion about funding for acquisition among New York, the North Jersey Water Supply Commission, land trusts, foundations, and individuals.

The emerging strategy was to seek funds from the hefty federal Land and Water Conservation Fund (LWCF). Established in 1965, the LWCF gets its revenues largely from offshore oil and gas leases. The fund's enabling legislation authorized Congress to spend a specified sum of money each year (in the 1990s the ceiling was $900 million per year) to enhance open space and recreational opportunities throughout the country. On average, though, less than half of the total revenues generated for the fund were actually being appropriated every year—despite a growing need for open space funding. In some years, Congress allocated considerably less than a tenth of the revenues for land acquisition, funneling most of it into the federal government's general fund. Still, over the years, the accumulation of unspent money in the fund had created a reserve of nearly $10 billion. Open space advocates in New York and New Jersey chafed at the fund's greatest use: to buy land in the West. Between 1988 and 1993, for example, California had received $248 million while New York had gotten only $9 million.

The Regional Plan Association also intervened, writing to Cuomo on behalf of acquisition. But the governor, widely credited for his urban and socially progressive initiatives, did not show a similarly well-developed sense of environmental protection. New York is broke, was all the governor's office could manage in reply. "The governor has always been interested in setting up some kind of mechanism for acquisition. But unless that's done, we don't see a way to fund. "[34] An angry representative Robert Torricelli countered, "We've all got budgetary problems, but we're all trying to do what we can to preserve the forest. New York has to accept some responsibility in this." Torricelli also lambasted Cuomo on his promotion of the Thruway exit: "If he can't help us, he shouldn't hurt us."[35]

Representatives Peter Kostmayer and Robert Torricelli continued their vigorous efforts to thrust the issue of Sterling Forest acquisition squarely into the consciousness of a spending-wary U.S. Congress, and then ratchet up the ante. In March 1992, buttressed by the draft U.S. Forest Service report recommending purchase of the forest, Kostmayer asked the House Interior Appropriations Subcommittee for $25 million from the Forest Service's Forest Legacy program. Congress had created the program in 1990 specifically to protect environmentally important forest lands threatened by conversion to nonforest uses, including residential and commercial development. With Kostmayer, Torricelli believed that Sterling Forest and Forest Legacy would be a perfect match. But the House appropriations subcommittee denied Kostmayer's appropriations request. Kostmayer and the New Jersey regional delegation then said it would take its request to the full committee, and would even lobby the Senate.

Kostmayer's continuing energetic efforts on behalf of preservation also renewed hostilities between him and Representative Benjamin Gilman. Gilman, the only regional congressman to favor Sterling Forest development, let it be known how much he resented Kostmayer intruding on his turf: "Perhaps he would best be looking at problems in his own district," Gilman fussed. Gilman responded to the Forest Service draft report with skepticism, doubted that government agencies could contribute to the purchase, and questioned the need for public acquisition at all, saying the corporation's development plan would provide all the protection the forest needed. He also advanced the bogus argument that keeping the land private would be the only way to keep the land on the tax rolls, eliding the fact that PIPC-owned lands pay taxes to the municipalities in which their lands are located.

In the spring of 1992, Gilman again went public in support of the corporation's plan for development, denouncing Kostmayer's $25-million funding proposal. Gilman's continued opposition was a major roadblock to federal involvement.

In the end, though, for Kostmayer the only thing more unwelcome than Gilman turned out to be the Forest Service. After the administration of George Bush, with its pro-business Council on Competitiveness, had finished scrutinizing the draft of the Forest Service study, the Forest Service unaccountably backed away from its pro-acquisition position. In June 1992, Kostmayer called a hearing of the subcommittee he chaired—the House Interior Subcommittee on Energy and the Environment. At the hearing, Forest Service spokesman Allan Schacht dropped the bombshell information that, rather than recommending total preservation, the final Highlands report would accept the option of large-scale development. At first Schacht attributed the complete turnabout to a response to public comment—but later said that the federal Office of Management and Budget objected to the cost of buying the tract in light of the huge federal deficit. Congressman Kostmayer blasted the Forest Service for caving in to OMB pressure and watering down the report.[36] Several environmentalists professed to see in this drastic turnabout the discreet hand of Ben Gilman who, as long-time chair of the House Foreign Affairs Committee, wielded a fair amount of clout at the highest levels of government.

New Jersey Representative Torricelli admitted that without the recommendation of the Forest Service it would be difficult to get the needed money. Nevertheless, in the halls of Congress, the preservation advocates, including Barnabas McHenry of the Wallace Foundation, Bob Binnewies of the Palisades Interstate Park Commission, JoAnn Dolan of the Trail Conference, and Ella Filippone of New Jersey's Passaic River Coalition, were pushing the regional congressional delegation hard in their effort to gain a House vote for an appropriation to the Forest Legacy fund for acquisition of Sterling Forest lands.[37]

At the end of June, the House Appropriations Committee overturned the earlier subcommittee decision to provide no funds and voted to authorize $5 million. And it required that New York and New Jersey provide a match. The allocation fell way short of the $25 million the New Jersey delegation requested.[38]

Meanwhile, New Jersey's Senator Frank Lautenberg was also weighing in with the search for $25 million to buy Sterling Forest and other key Highlands tracts. To his disappointment, the Senate passed a bill that included, not $25 million for Sterling, but only $15 million for the entire year's nationwide Forest Legacy Program.

By summer, both houses of Congress did pass legislation setting aside $5 million under the federal Forest Legacy Program specifically to help purchase Sterling Forest. But differences in the Senate and House versions still needed to be reconciled.

As this congressional drama unfolded, Representative Benjamin Gilman tried to appear as if he were open to some compromise over the issue of funding of the forest purchase. "If both the Palisades Interstate Park Commission and the Sterling Forest Corporation can come to some reasonable agreement, I won't be an obstacle to stand in their way," he said.[39] But an aide explained that Representative Gilman didn't fight the appropriation because the purchase plan wasn't "going anywhere. The $5 million will just sit there," since New York State didn't have any money to kick in. Gilman's opposition kept much of the New York delegation from strong support for preserving the forest.[40]

NEW YORK BARELY HANGS ON AS A PLAYER

In the November 1990 election, New York voters narrowly defeated the 21st Century Environmental Quality Bond Act. New York's urbanized downstate voters liked it, but upstate voters, fearful that the bond act would remove huge tracts of land from local control, voted against it by huge margins. This put a sudden halt to New York State's long and esteemed tradition of supporting land preservation. What made it worse, staff at DEC and the state Office of Parks were not especially enthusiastic about Sterling Forest, partly because they saw it as a big-ticket item and partly because the governor had not designated it as a priority. Given the loss of bond act money and the state's financial straits and its plans to lay off state workers and cut deeply into aid to local government, New York found itself at the very bottom of the list of possible sources of purchase money.

Still, PIPC's executive director Bob Binnewies continued to visit Albany to try to elevate Sterling Forest to the "level of success being achieved in New Jersey and Washington." A state acquisition team—Binnewies and other state officials—renewed discussion with the corporation's Bob Thomson "to see if an agreement-in-concept could be reached on acquisitions of enough contiguous acreage to allow for the creation of a new state park in at least a portion of Sterling Forest."[41]

Binnewies and New York's Park Commissioner Orin Lehman also contracted for two separate appraisals of the Sterling Forest property, with the cooperation of the corporation. Both appraisals indicated a land value of about $60 million, or about $3,500 an acre. Binnewies recalls that one of the appraisers reported that the corporation was overly optimistic in its projection of housing market share; his professional opinion was "that the time frame for selling 14,250 housing units at Sterling Forest would approach 70 years, not the 35 years projected by S.F.C. planners." This appraiser thought that a completed community would only materialize in the distant future, if ever, and concluded that the much-ballyhooed development plan was in fact riddled with problems. Writes Binnewies: "The appraiser's opinions hung silently in the air on the Parks-PIPC side of the table while Thomson and company continued to assert that they were sitting on a golden real estate egg, with emphasis on the gold."[42] And although state officials said they would not disclose the results of their appraisals while talks were ongoing, Binnewies did say publicly that the commission estimated the tract was worth $40 million—his figure a far cry from the owners' assertion of $150 million.

Two years after the bond act failed at the polls, Binnewies's efforts to keep New York as a player began to pay off: In 1992, he revealed that despite the large New York State fiscal deficit, New York officials were now indicating that the state would financially support the acquisition with $15 million and that Sterling Forest was high on the state's list of acquisition priorities.[43]

The Palisades Interstate Park Commission also emerged as the best agency to be steward of the forest, should it ever be acquired. Among several suggested options were the U.S. Forest Service and even the Mohonk Preserve, a private nonprofit conservancy in New Paltz, New York. But the big advantage of having the forest acquired by the bi-state agency would be that there would be no tax loss to Tuxedo—which would defuse one major objection to acquisition, taking the land off the tax rolls. Eventually it was clear there was no one else who could accept management of a Sterling Forest park except the Palisades Interstate Park Commission. That agency, established by interstate compact in 1937, is responsible for stewardship and management of twenty-three parks and historic sites in New York and New Jersey. Its vast Harriman State Park shared a common boundary with Sterling Forest.

But even as New York edged forward, Congress pulled back. Congress was in a budget-cutting mood. And over the summer of 1992, as a presidential election loomed, the Sterling Forest appropriation was battered by White House pressure to reduce spending. In September, negotiators reconciling House and Senate versions of a spending bill agreed to reduce the Sterling Forest allocation, from $5 million down to $3 million. Senator Lautenberg asserted that he was disappointed in the reduction but pleased that the region would receive some money. "It's a good start," he said. Representative Torricelli stated, "In this environment, it feels good just to survive. What's important is to have some money available to begin land acquisitions before the forest is destroyed." Environmentalist John Humbach said $3 million would be "better than zero."

David McDermott, director of community relations for the Sterling Forest Corporation, belittled the appropriation saying, "It's a very small sum, and it doesn't come anywhere near what we think the property is worth."[44] And, to those who were thinking of acquiring the tract piecemeal, McDermott said the corporation was not interested in that kind of sale.

Ultimately, in 1992, Congress appropriated the $3 million out of the requested $25 million from the Department of Interior's Forest Legacy Program, to be used in combination with matching funds provided by New York and New Jersey for acquisition of critical lands in Sterling Forest. And, after all that maneuvering, because the states failed to provide the necessary matching funds, the federal contribution could not be used anyhow. Regardless, the offering was taken as a sign that Congress recognized the significance of the land and the public support for its acquisition. Peter Kostmayer's work had been pivotal in moving the process forward.[45]

Forest supporters also recognized that acquisition effort was going to be long and hard, and the outcome uncertain. Bob Binnewies recalls that amid the great doubts about how such sums could be mobilized, both he and Barnabas McHenry had a belief bordering on pure faith that the money could be found. And it was McHenry, he recalls, who had the greater faith: When Binnewies "would start sputtering about the embarrassing lack of funds, or start venting about the slick style of the corporation, McHenry would smile, saying, 'Don't worry, this will happen.' On occasion, Binnewies would cast a sideways glance at McHenry, wondering what he might be smoking."[46]

DIVISIONS IN THE ENVIRONMENTAL RANKS

With so many different environmental groups and individuals trying to save Sterling Forest, differences over strategy were inevitable and unsurprising. With the dazzling prospect of $25 million in federal appropriations in 1992, New Jersey Sierra Club activists and a new Sierra Highlands Committee began making plans to work for a federally funded preserve along the entire Appalachian corridor, from Canada to Georgia, that would include Sterling Forest. This stance upset New York's Sterling Forest champions, who understood clearly that $25 million in federal funding—assuming it actually came through—would simply be disbursed into myriad projects from Maine to Georgia; little of the money, if any, would target Sterling Forest. And the New Jerseyans were promoting the idea of a National Forest along the Highlands tract, while New York activists, worried about the Forest Service orientation toward logging and resource exploitation, preferred alternative management—for example, the Palisades Interstate Park Commission, already a bi-state agency.

New York activists also worried about the message that was being presented to Congress, since any disparate bills introduced in the Congress would confuse the issue at best and most likely would delay or kill the whole funding effort. New York environmentalist and long-time Sierran Betty Quick, in a memo to the governing body of the Sierra Club's New York chapter, wrote, "Sterling Forest and nearby parcels represent the best opportunity for immediate and permanent preservation of any parcel of its significance and size ... in the entire North East ... we strongly support and applaud the efforts of Congressmen Peter Kostmayer (Pa.) and Robert Torricelli (N.J.) to secure federal funding for the study and for acquisition of Sterling Forest.... Until the future of Sterling Forest is clarified, any competing legislation and/or proposals to reallocate the proposed money for other projects—no matter how worthwhile—will dilute, detract, and ultimately sabotage the arduous efforts already undertaken."

The conflicts over strategy—to focus on Sterling Forest, to work on the New Jersey Highlands, or to work on the Highlands as a whole—bubbled over several times. In 1994, for example, several high-level environmental strategists had agreed about the overriding need to direct New Jersey funding into the Sterling acquisition; nevertheless, William Neil, assistant director of conservation for the New Jersey Audubon Society, wrote a letter that appeared in the *Newark Star-Ledger* flatly contradicting that conclusion. Neil quarreled with the idea that the acquisition of Sterling Forest should take precedence over efforts to acquire lands in New Jersey's Highlands, especially its watershed lands. "Seven New Jersey groups," he wrote,

> thought it was time we clarified the misplaced sense of proportion involved here, as well as the confusion over just which sources of New Jersey money ought to be used, if any, to buy land in New York state and under what conditions.... Sterling Forest [is] just 29 percent of the 60,000-acre watershed of the North Jersey Water Supply Commission.... The 25,000-acre New Jersey Wyanokie watershed ... lacks adequate zoning protection.... The $85 million available from [New Jersey's] '81 water supply bond act should be used to protect watershed lands in our state first, starting in the Wyanokie Highlands.[47]

Worried about the negative effect Neil's letter would have on government funding, PIPC's Bob Binnewies was outraged:

Sterling Forest should remain the number one NY/NJ Highlands priority. This priority affords the best chance for a major-scale success in
the Highlands as a whole, and provides a sharp focus, which hope-
fully will continue to merit the active support of NJ environmental
advocates, the media, and political leaders. If we agree that success at
Sterling Forest is highly important to overall success in the Highlands
Region, then accordingly, key political representatives should be so
reassured—preferably by New Jersey Audubon.[48]

Binnewies as well as a number of other individuals on the partnership went to
meet with Neil and the New Jersey Conservation Foundation's David Moore
to encourage them to fall into line.

JoAnn Dolan of the New York–New Jersey Trail Conference confirms this
rift: "There were a lot of environmental people in New Jersey, very divided.
David Moore was at the root of this, and Tom Gilmore of the New Jersey Audubon Society. They basically never supported the Sterling Forest acquisition, and
behind the scenes not only did they not support it, but they tried to undermine
it, they tried to undo the acquisition effort. It was pretty upsetting. Bob Binnewies wanted to get them on our side, and Jim Tripp, the guy in the middle, arranged a meeting at Dave Moore's New Jersey Conservation Foundation offices
and I remember going. And I found David Moore and Tom Gilmore so rude
to Bob, I couldn't believe how rude they were. And Bob was such an incredible
gentleman, he held it together but he was clearly upset.

"Jeff Tittel, Ella Filippone were way supportive, they understood we were
trying to protect the watershed of their New Jersey drinking water! It's land that
is a buffer for both states, they understood that. But David Moore saw it as a
territorial thing, if the money doesn't go to him, go to New Jersey, then it's use-
less, and he has to undo this. And basically he tried to get that $10 million [the
funding coming from New Jersey to acquire Sterling Forest in New York] to stay
in New Jersey. And as far as Tom Gilmore: these Sterling lands are neotropical
birdways, what does he think, the birds know where the border is?"[49]

A few weeks later the discord was smoothed over and a joint statement issued: The Highlands Coalition, the Sterling Forest Coalition, and the Palisades
Interstate Park Commission reaffirmed their solidarity in focusing on protection of Sterling Forest and lands in the New Jersey Highlands and working with
elected officials on funding these objectives.

Another ongoing point of contention was over the acreage to be protected.
The Dolans started their quest in 1985 advocating for 9,000 or 10,000 acres, as
did the Palisades Interstate Park Commission in 1986. In 1988, New York State
DEC recommended acquisition of 11,400 acres in the hilly western portion of

the tract. After the Kostmayer hearing in 1989, the Sterling Forest Coalition issued a paper recommending outright purchase of 14,400 acres and assurances
that any future development would occur along an existing road. And several
years later, in 1993, actual negotiations centered on a proposed partial purchase
of 13,000 acres, leaving some 4,500 acres for the corporation to develop.

Efforts on behalf of a partial purchase always grew from the "realistic" position that the fewer acres that were sought, the fewer dollars would be required
and the easier it would be to consummate a deal. But every partial purchase
proposal raised the worry that any such purchase would put so much money in
the hands of the corporation that it would then be able to develop the remaining unprotected portions much more easily and intensively. Thus, every proposal
for partial purchase fueled intense anger and anguish among many environmentalists, and some groups and individuals came out repeatedly, forcefully, and
unequivocally for purchase of the entire forest—this was especially true in 1993,
when serious purchase negotiations were launched (see chapter 6). None of the
partial purchase efforts went anywhere because at the time they were advanced,
no money was available.

Still another fault line involved the best arguments to use on behalf of the
forest. JoAnn Dolan, who was championing the Appalachian Trail corridor as a
key reason to protect Sterling Forest, recalls, "In about 1991 I called up Al Caccese and said, 'I really want to talk to you about Sterling Forest.' I asked to meet
with him to let him know what we were planning and what we were doing. Al
Caccese is a lawyer for OPRHP [New York's Office of Parks, Recreation and
Historic Preservation]. He did a lot of land deals, he was their top guy. So I see
Al and he's brought in Orin Lehman, the Commissioner! I said, 'You know, we
want to protect the watershed *and* the Appalachian Trail.' Al says, 'JoAnn, you're
going to ruin the entire plan—we're focusing on water. We feel we have a bi-
state water issue. If you start in on the entire thing, you may ruin everything.'
And I say, 'Al, I'm sorry, but I can't sit here and let this go. I can't sit here and not
defend the Appalachian Trail. So that's going to be our stand, like it or not.'

"We had to let OPR know where we stood. They were all convinced that
they could win on the water issue, and water alone. We basically made it very
difficult for OPRHP and PIPC in those days because we said, 'We're not going
to be quiet, we're going to be very clear that we have to preserve the Appalachian
Trail. I don't understand why it's going to be a liability, this is our national scenic
trail; everybody has spent tax dollars on it.' But they [OPR] were so convinced
they had their strategy, they didn't want to mess up their strategy. Here I was,
messing it up.

"I was worried: Jesus, was I doing the right thing? Oh God, What if I do
blow it? But I just kept hammering away."[50]

Other disagreements eventually surfaced as well: for example, there was a late-in-the-game power struggle between PIPC's Bob Binnewies and Bernadette Castro, New York Park Commissioner under Governor George Pataki. According to several watchers, Castro wanted to be in full control; she had political ambitions, she held the state purse strings, and she wanted the credit for New York's role. According to Robert Binnewies, she viewed him

> as a holdover from the Cuomo Administration, and was frustrated when she discovered that due to the design of the PIPC, deliberately fashioned so many years ago to provide for as much political immunity as possible, she simply couldn't give the Executive Director his walking papers, or demand that he by-pass the PIP Commissioner and report directly to her.[51]

Beyond these mundane skirmishes, the question of whether to undertake the larger task of preservation of the entire Highlands corridor was on the minds of many. Orange County civic leader, conservationist, and former county executive Louis V. Mills, in a memo to Bob Binnewies and Laurance Rockefeller, wrote,

> I've given additional thought to the central question you raised . . . as to whether we should fight publicly for a partial acquisition in Sterling Forest or make the bigger fight to preserve the Highlands as such. Until now, I approached this question by hoping to keep on our side the local interests who are pro business but would still like to see a large part of the forest saved. This may be all we can achieve, but I'm convinced now that we must fight the larger fight, which is the fundamental question of whether the greater metropolitan region is willing to meet the challenge of remaining a world class urban center surrounded by its superb green belt of forests, hills, and open space, or to let the opportunity go forever.[52]

The Regional Plan Association also grappled with the problem of scope. The RPA, which had been working on the concept of developing greenways and greenspaces throughout the tri-state region, was discovering that the idea of linear greenways was not sexy enough to grab the public's commitment and was not going anywhere politically. In the early 1990s, therefore, RPA abandoned its focus on greenways and began to look at specific large landscapes: Long Island's Pine Barrens, the vast New York City watershed, and the Highlands; the latter, it said, was deserving of regional park status. Sterling Forest, a major Highlands tract under threat of major development, became the catalyst that allowed dedicated RPA staffers Tom Miner, Rob Pirani and Robert Yaro to successfully make the case to the RPA board to push for stronger preservation throughout the Highlands. Following the Forest Service Highlands Regional Study, RPA and other members of the Forest Service study group, as well as other interested individuals, created a work group to promote action to protect the Highlands. Between March and July 1992, the work group developed a set of recommendations for Highlands conservation and development strategies.

A FOREST ON TWO LAUNCH PADS

If the forest preservation community was having trouble raising money in 1992, so was the Sterling Forest Corporation. The corporation's money problems were now global in scale. There were a spate of bank collapses throughout Scandinavia in the first half of 1992, one of which was Gota Bank AB, owned by Trygg-Hansa. Trygg-Hansa had acquired Gota Bank, the fourth largest bank in Sweden, in 1990. Gota experienced substantial losses in 1991, and in March 1992, Björn Sprängare, Trygg-Hansa's president and CEO, rejected the idea of injecting additional capital into the bank, and his generally negative comments caused Gota's stock to plunge. After a public outcry and Swedish government demands that Trygg-Hansa help save its bank, in June 1992 Sprängare changed his mind and committed to a bailout plan. But he withdrew the bailout two weeks later.[53]

By September, as a result of continuing financial problems, the Swedish government was forced to take drastic measures—it slashed expenditures and imposed tremendous interest rate increases on the central bank to prevent a devaluation of the Swedish krona. Trygg-Hansa's Gota Bank was in particularly bad shape—it suspended payments and was able to remain open only because the government guaranteed the bank's commitments to creditors and depositholders.[54] Largely due to the losses at Gota, Trygg-Hansa lost $1 billion in 1992. Trygg-Hansa had lost even more money than its predecessor AmBase, and lost it faster.

As the fortunes of the forest's owners plummeted, worry increased about the fate of Sterling Forest. To assuage the anxiety, Sprängare himself came to Orange County, assuring his listeners that his company was still healthy enough to support the development and reminding them that Sweden put a high value on environmental protection: "The plan is a good example of the possibilities to combine a modern planned development with protection of environmental assets that we all would like to preserve for coming generations," he said. Sprängare cast himself as environmentally sensitive and reminded his audience he had a doctorate in forestry—but neglected to mention that he had used his forestry experience to run a pulp and paper conglomerate in Sweden.[55]

The corporation continued moving toward getting its project approved, with corporate spokespeople holding informational meetings in the affected towns and with repeated appearances before the town boards. By the fall of 1992, the towns of Tuxedo and Warwick had both given preliminary "concept approval," which allowed the corporation to undertake the next level of planning and environmental studies.

By 1992, two powerful opposing efforts had been launched: the development plan put forth by the Sterling Forest Corporation, and the preservationist effort launched by environmentalists and carried forward, erratically, by federal and state interests.

CHAPTER SIX

Government Sees Green

THE PARTIAL PURCHASE PROPOSAL:
SELLING THE FOREST FOR SEED MONEY

BY THE SPRING OF 1993, THE STERLING FOREST CORPORATION had reached a point of serious negotiations with the Palisades Interstate Park Commission over the purchase of at least a portion of the forest. The corporation was spurred by what the *New York Times* called the "sour economic reality of the 90's . . . a sputtering economy that impoverishes both landlords and park preservers is forcing a new approach: compromise."[1] The suburban office market was overbuilt, so another business center was hardly an exciting financial draw. Sterling Forest Corporation head Robert Thomson said his company had been losing $2 million a year through taxes and maintenance and needed to exploit the property in order to bail out.

The Sterling Forest Corporation had to come up with cash, not just because of the sour real estate market, but also because the corporation's parent company, Home Holdings, was in deepening financial difficulty: In the first nine months of 1993, Home Insurance lost $100 million. In September, Home decided it would go public, hoping to shrink its debt and interest expenses and boost liquidity.[2] In December, Trygg-Hansa, Home Holdings' parent corporation, raised $127 million from an initial public offering of common shares in Home Holdings; while it hoped to garner close to $350 million, it, along with other insurance stocks on the stock market, was being stymied by concerns about rising interest rates.

Given the financial difficulties in which the corporation found itself throughout 1993 and given the real estate downturn, its ability to mount an expensive and uncertain development project now seemed less certain than just a few years before, and it apparently viewed development as its exit strategy—its next-best scenario if no single buyer emerged. The forest's foreign owners gave the go-ahead for Thomson and other corporation managers to negotiate seriously for purchase.

Bob Binnewies recalls that both Palisades Interstate Park Commission and the Sterling Forest Corporation explored how much land the corporation would be willing to sell and at what price. In April 1993, a deal seemed to be in the offing, in which the corporation would accept between $30 million and $40 million in cash in exchange for relinquishing 13,000 acres of the forest. This draft agreement would allow the corporation to keep 4,500 acres to build about 6,000 houses and 4 million square feet of commercial space—thus putting about half of the company's original proposed development on about a third of the original proposed built-on land.

Also included in the deal was something the corporation wanted badly: the state's commitment to build the corporation a new Thruway exit. The newspapers reported the partial-purchase negotiation, not knowing that, behind closed doors, Thomson was intransigent on the matter of a Thruway interchange. Thomson "wanted airtight assurance that the interchange would be constructed to funnel directly into the corporation's property," with the $10-million construction tab to be picked up by the Thruway Authority, not the corporation. The papers also failed to report that, as in earlier years, a new interchange remained "almost unthinkable" to the Palisades and state parks negotiating team because it would take a sizable chunk out of Harriman State Park.[3]

The local newspaper equivocated about the proposed compromise deal: "Finally there seems to be a reasonable solution at hand on what to do with Sterling Forest. . . . The corporation has drawn up an innovative plan." But, the *Times Herald-Record* mused, "The trouble with the plan is that it is too large for the area and it sprawls throughout the forest, tearing this unbroken stretch of wilderness into smaller pieces."[4]

To the environmental community, though, the deal was an unequivocal loser: too much money for too little land and too little public benefit. Many saw this as a purchase that would simply give the corporation millions of public dollars—enough of an infusion of dollars to allow it to maximally develop its remaining lands.[5] As a result of an agreement like this, Sterling Forest Corporation would be able to construct the lion's share of the 1991 development plan—the only difference was that now the massive construction would be on fewer total acres, making for a far denser urban conglomeration.

And because the construction would remain vast, the environmental impacts would also remain broad and damaging: The development would devastate the wilderness experience of the Appalachian Trail in the northwestern portion of the property, would jeopardize the quality of the waters flowing south into Rockland County and New Jersey, would still badly fragment the forest, and would cost surrounding communities hundreds of millions of dollars in schools, roads, and services. Moreover, in the corporation's original plan, the portions of the land not designated for construction would have had to have been set aside as undevelopable. In effect, therefore, this partial purchase plan would have government spend precious dollars to buy land the corporation couldn't build on anyway.

The proposed state gift of a Thruway exit particularly galled because it was such a glaringly misguided use of public money. By making development more attractive, the interchange would raise the assessed value of the Sterling Forest tract, which would make public purchase more expensive and therefore would weaken the public's land acquisitions options. The state, environmentalists argued, should not richly reward the Sterling Forest Corporation by pouring money into infrastructure unneeded by anyone except the Sterling Forest Corporation. And because the total costs of a new interstate interchange would come close to the purchase price of Sterling Forest, buying the entire forest, and saving water, air, wildlife and quality of life, would be far cheaper for the state than spending millions to pave over more land.

Ron Nowak, in the *Greenwood Lake and West Milford News*, wrote,

> Actually the money that may be appropriated for the purchase is really to buy a Thruway interchange and stage 1 of the development scenario which, let's be honest, is probably all the developers really wanted to build anyway. An interchange will make the centerpiece Forest hamlet that [much] more accessible to the outside world and not buying the northern portion of the forest will save face for everyone concerned: the developer who can now proclaim even more of the forest than the original 75% will be forever preserved while at the same time quenching the thirst it has to run jitneys somewhere, anywhere while making a tidy sum on the sale of the land; the Town of Warwick which will still get some of its promised ratables while not getting any of the school age kids; the Town of Tuxedo, which has taken the official stance that it needs a community-wide transfusion of new blood.[6]

The New York and New Jersey Sierra Club chapters and other environmental groups in the Sterling Forest Coalition instigated a new letter-writing campaign blasting partial acquisition and urging Governor Cuomo to support full purchase. Ed Morley, Conservation Chair of the New Jersey Chapter of the Sierra Club, wrote,

The Sierra Club supports full acquisition of Sterling Forest as its top Highlands priority. Although there has been discussion of a compromise that involves the public purchase of only 13,000 acres, the Sierra Club will vehemently oppose it for the following reasons.... Such a deal would publicly underwrite the funding we believe the owners lack, to begin the needless construction of up to 6,000 housing units and 1.2 million square feet of commercial space, all along the Appalachian Trail.... The compromise development would still degrade New Jersey's drinking water, the viewshed of the Appalachian Trial and fragment the forest ... this development could cost New Jersey up to $50 million for additional water treatment plants.[7]

In June 1993, when it became clear that no government money was immediately available, the Sterling Forest Corporation and the Palisades Interstate Park Commission broke off negotiations. "The hangup is that there's been no source of funding identified," said the corporation's Bob Thomson. But the hangup was not money alone: Jürgen Wekerle recalls that the publicly aired anger over the partial purchase agreement was instrumental in driving negotiators from the table.

By September 1993, the corporation was back to making its presence felt at local PTA meetings and elsewhere in the community. In Tuxedo, Thomson put a new minimum price tag on the forest purchase: $80 million.[8] Its ad campaign again filled local newspapers and the radio airwaves. "Planning for people," stated a newspaper ad early in 1993, describing how caring and community-oriented the corporation was and touting the corporation's intent to make preservation of open space its first priority. The ads were buttressed by a number of letters to the editors of local newspapers signed by CEO Thomson, underscoring the commitment to protecting open space, claiming that parent company Home Holdings was financially sound, and reiterating that the corporation was still a willing seller if government could come up with enough money.

But for every ad and every Thomson letter, it seemed, another letter from a citizen also appeared, disputing the corporation's claims of environmental and community sensitivity. Environmentalists also organized public meetings to inform the public about the hidden costs and massive public subsidies connected with the proposed development.

NEW PLAYERS IN WASHINGTON: THREE SUPPORTERS INTRODUCE KEY HOUSE LEGISLATION

With a new, Democratic, administration taking the helm in Washington in 1993 came renewed hope that the federal government would be willing to step in and commit to a portion of the funding needed to buy Sterling Forest, with New York and New Jersey to pick up their shares. In February 1993, a coalition of environmental groups urged the new Clinton administration to spend more than $1 billion from the Land and Water Conservation Fund to buy key parcels in New York, ranging from a third of an acre on the Fire Island National Seashore to 14,000 acres in the Adirondacks and including several key parcels along the Appalachian Trail.[9]

The new Interior Secretary, Bruce Babbitt, said one of his top priorities was expanding the national park system.[10] Conservationists argued that it was a good time to buy because the recession had kept land prices low. But, in 1993, with the economy sluggish and the federal deficit a festering political issue, spending for "frivolities" like land acquisition was not an easy political sell.

That spring, nevertheless, New Jersey Representative Robert Torricelli began working on the complex authorizing legislation for the Sterling Forest acquisition. The procedure to obtain federal funding is a two-pronged one, requiring both an authorization—permission to spend money—and an appropriation—the actual writing of the check. Thus, even with an *authorization*, it could take several years of *appropriations* to gather a pot of money big enough to buy a large portion of Sterling Forest land.

In May, New York Representative Maurice Hinchey joined with Torricelli to push for funding from the House Appropriations Committee and, surprisingly, a few weeks later, the two representatives were joined by New York's fiscal conservative and formerly adamant pro-development official Benjamin Gilman. The three congressmen committed themselves to obtaining $35 million from the federal Land and Water Conservation Fund to purchase 13,000 acres of Sterling Forest. Their proposed bill, HR 2741, would allow the National Park Service to transfer funds to the Palisades Interstate Park Commission to purchase and manage part of the forest. As Bob Binnewies explained,

> The rationale was that the PIPC, as an interstate agency functioning under a 1937 Compact approved by the Congress and President of the United States, could receive Federal appropriations. The interstate structure of the PIPC positioned it to receive funds from Congress, channeled through the Department of the Interior, that neither New York nor New Jersey could receive directly.[11]

The bill would authorize funding through 1999 but not actually appropriate any money—a separate appropriations bill would be needed to actually release funds. Still, passage of an authorization would allow PIPC to continue to negotiate with the corporation.

Especially noteworthy was the participation of Ben Gilman in this effort—was he changing his long-standing opposition to public acquisition? Now, at least, he was on record for preservation because, he said, the plan still allowed some development—and, of course, because at every town meeting his constituents had been telling him they favored preservation. "This is a new tack for Gilman," observed the *Times Herald-Record* in an editorial, "who for a long time kept saying the same thing about the forest—develop, develop, develop."[12] But Gilman, hedging his bets, was still calling on New York State to recommit itself to building the New York State Thruway exit at Sterling Forest.[13]

By mid-summer, the newspaper headlines were reading, "U.S. near Sterling purchase,"[14] and the unveiling of the Torricelli-Hinchey-Gilman bill moved Bob Binnewies to comment, "We're 95 percent of the way there." Torricelli crowed, "There is going to be a settlement. . . . The remaining issues are not of sufficient gravity to prevent a settlement."[15] Environmentalists, while expressing their continuing distaste for the partial purchase deal, then still on the table, were pleased. "This," said John Humbach tactfully, "is really a first step toward the eventual goal of preserving all of Sterling Forest and achieving a balance of development and preservation within the region."[16]

Meantime, New Jersey Congresswoman Marge Roukema, increasingly committed to protecting New Jersey's watershed, also introduced a bill, one asking for less money because she thought the $35-million price tag in the Torricelli bill was too high for Congress to swallow. Roukema's bill, aiming primarily to protect the New Jersey watershed, provided up to $25 million of federal funds available on a matching basis with state, local, and private funding. Roukema's bill was not intended to upstage the Torricelli proposal, but rather to reinforce it.

A key element of Roukema's bill was its intent to use a big portion of the funding to help reimburse New Jersey's Passaic County for its earlier 2,074-acre Sterling Forest condemnation purchase. In Roukema's bill, only the balance would go toward purchase of Sterling Forest. This aspect upset many New York and New Jersey environmentalists, who wanted new money to go toward new purchases, not for reimbursement of land already protected—"it's off the wall," one complained. But Passaic County's lawmakers applauded the Roukema proposal because their position was that if New York State land acquisitions were to benefit from an infusion of federal funds, New Jersey's Passaic County land acquisition should also.[17]

One potential sticking point of the pending Torricelli legislation was that Congress might have to approve a new bi-state compact because the Palisades Interstate Park Commission had not been specifically chartered to accept land (including Sterling Forest land) in New Jersey, except for a narrow strip along the Hudson River. To eliminate that problem before it surfaced in Congress, Ella Filippone, executive director of the Passaic River Coalition, "drafted legislative language that would extend PIPC land protection authority into the 1 million acre New Jersey Highlands Region. This change would allow New Jersey to make use of the interstate agency in efforts to protect its watershed."[18]

The New Jersey Assembly seemed likely to act on the new PIPC legislation, but Robert Littell, New Jersey's powerful state senator, another fiscally conservative Republican, loomed as a potential obstacle in that state's senate. "Filippone wasted no time," Binnewies has noted in response;

> She went straight to Littell with a concise, well reasoned presentation about the potential financial and environmental benefits of bringing the PIPC into the Highlands. Littell made one demand: he didn't want his county, Sussex, included in the legislation. Otherwise he gave it his blessing. In late April, 1994, the Assembly unanimously approved the bill that allows the PIPC to function in Bergen, Passaic, Morris, Somerset, Hunterdon and Warren Counties, New Jersey, a Highlands swath of hundreds of thousands of acres extending southwesterly from the New Jersey-New York border to the Delaware River.[19]

> To the amazement of many, Littell's Budget Committee unanimously approved the expenditure of $10 million in New Jersey funds for Sterling Forest acquisition purposes. So persuasive was his influence . . . that the full [state] Senate followed suit, voting in July, 1994, to support the appropriation. New Jersey was . . . ringing a signal bell for New York and the Congress that would be hard to ignore.[20]

The sense among preservationists was that, whatever form a federal initiative might eventually take, a bipartisan political will, critically needed in the Sterling Forest acquisition effort, was quickly taking shape. By September 1993, public support for acquisition had become a force to be reckoned with, and the campaign to save Sterling Forest had become an easy bandwagon issue for politicians of all stripes. That month, Secretary of the Interior Bruce Babbitt appeared at a press conference with New Jersey Governor James Florio and went on record as supporting the plan for $35 million from the federal government. The secretary had mentioned no source of federal funding, but "the fact that Sterling Forest is on Secretary Babbitt's radar screen is good news for those interested in preserving the land," said Torricelli spokesman Rob Henken.[21] As Bob Binnewies recalls, "The very fact that a member of the President's cabinet was even talking about Sterling Forest provided hope that the Clinton administration was about to join the bipartisan coalition in Congress to push forward the $35 million appropriations bill."[22]

Also that month, Governor Florio, running hard for reelection as governor of New Jersey against Republican Christine Todd Whitman, announced a shift in state environmental priorities from the shore to the Highlands; Florio's new plan started with a state grant of $250,000 to the Highlands Advisory Group that would mostly be used to create a database to help determine how much more land in Sterling Forest and the Highlands should be acquired. Florio supported a combined federal, state, and local effort to acquire open space in the Highlands; he said he was ready to work with the federal government to establish a national forest in the region and with Governor Cuomo to lay out an overall acquisition plan for Sterling Forest.[23]

In November 1993, New Jersey Senator Bill Bradley introduced Sterling Forest legislation in the U.S. Senate similar to the Torricelli legislation in the House; S 1683 was also cosponsored by New Jersey's other senator, Frank Lautenberg. "To allow this resource to be bulldozed would be a loss for the entire mid-Atlantic region," commented Bradley.[24]

THE PARK SERVICE GETS BALKY

Still, nearly a year after both sides said the deal would be done "any day," the federal bills to allocate $35 million were far from enactment, and in 1994 Sterling Forest was still vying with a backlog of many other tracts around the country for scarce federal dollars. There was a decided Catch-22 quality to the quest: The states of New York and New Jersey and private foundations declined to commit themselves to matching funds until a federal commitment was firmed up. But the federal government was reluctant to fund without knowing if substantial matching funding was in place. No obvious way to break the stalemate revealed itself.

At a hearing before Bill Bradley's Senate Energy and Natural Resources subcommittee in mid-May 1994, witnesses buttressed Senator Bradley's effort to authorize Sterling Forest funding via his S1683. Speaking at the subcommittee hearing, New Jersey Representative Bob Torricelli's comments set the term of the debate: "Certainly, with the billions of dollars we have spent to preserve land in the West, we can find $35 million to protect one of the last vestiges of open space in the Northeast."

However, in a seismic move that harked back to the U.S. Forest Service obstruction of three years earlier and that stunned forest advocates anew, the National Park Service announced at the hearing that it opposed the plan to put $35 million in federal funds toward the purchase of the forest. The Park Service told Bradley that his plan ignored other Park Service priorities, and that the

Service had never appropriated money to buy land that was outside the national park system and would not want to do so now, for fear of setting a "dangerous precedent." "With a current backlog in land acquisition of some $1.1 billion we should not divert what limited funds are available to acquire National Park lands to projects that are outside the system," stated Marie Rust, the Northeast's regional director of the National Park Service.[25]

The *Rockland Journal News* wrote, "Maybe the National Park Service is so blinded by the beauty of the California redwoods and Yosemite that it has written off the equally spectacular eastern part of the nation. How else can you explain the continuing bias against acquiring parkland, especially in Sterling Forest?"[26]

Rust's testimony was especially confounding in light of the previous support of funding shown by Secretary of the Interior Bruce Babbitt—no one knew if the reversal was a bureaucratic blunder or a political double cross at the highest level. Babbitt was a clear and strong supporter of open space, but the Park Service position indicated that he lacked consistent backup from his administration (or possibly consistent advice from his staff). There is some evidence that within Interior, Assistant Secretary George Frampton actively opposed the Sterling Forest appropriation, on the grounds that it was a "state" project and an appropriation would set a bad precedent. Bob Binnewies believes, however, that a federal appropriation for Sterling Forest probably would not take anything away from the Land and Water Conservation Fund: "To the contrary, timing for Sterling Forest seems to have fit nicely into the larger national effort to re-energize the fund and allow for a more equitable federal-state split of the money."[27]

Senator Bradley, though, remained hopeful that an understanding could be reached with the Park Service. The Park Service's stance generated a week of letters and phone calls from upset environmentalists and public officials; Gilman and Hinchey, along with other members of the New York–New Jersey delegation, rebuked Secretary Babbitt, writing, "You visited this magnificent tract of forest land yourself last fall, and quite clearly shared our sentiment that Sterling Forest must be protected from development."[28] Some viewed this obstacle, and others created by the National Park Service, as damning evidence that the agency that was steward of the Appalachian Trial really lacked vision and could not be counted on as a team player.[29]

Within a week of the congressional howls of protest, the Park Service did a drastic about-face and decided it was now prepared to provide $17.5 million toward purchase of the privately owned property. It now found it could justify using conservation funds for Sterling Forest because the money would be helping to protect the 6 miles of the national Appalachian Trail corridor that ran through the forest. Forest advocates saw in the change a decision at the Park

Service that protecting the trail corridor could be interpreted as protecting "a bulge in the trail that's as big as the whole woodland."[30]

The Park Service insisted on attaching strings to its expression of support: it would buy land adjoining the Appalachian Trail, with the Interior Department reserving the right to pay no more than 25 percent of the total purchase price for any Sterling Forest lands acquired. Park Service purchase would have made the deal unpalatable to the local towns of Monroe, Warwick, and Tuxedo because these towns, which together collected millions of dollars in taxes from the Palisades Park system, would not collect revenues from land newly acquired by the federal agency: "The mood of the New York–New Jersey Congressional delegations was that no new and restrictive Federal rules suddenly should be invented for Sterling Forest, when no such restrictions had been draped on other [Land & Water Conservation Fund] projects."[31] Negotiator and general troubleshooter Bob Binnewies made more trips to Washington to try to get these onerous new conditions removed.

The Park Service commitment of only $17.5 million was also seen as something of a setback by legislators and environmentalists because that level of funding would allow only a partial purchase. On the other hand, the Park Service's support, however grudging, also revived the momentum leading to a deal and created new expressions of commitment from both state and private sectors. For example, Joan Davidson, New York's Commissioner of Parks, now told Congress that New York was pledging $15 million from the state's Environmental Protection Fund.

By August 1994, the National Park Service and PIPC had reached a tentative agreement on the federal contribution. The Park Service agreed to drop its requirement that only a quarter of the purchase price come from the federal government. And it also backed down on an earlier demand that the forest be managed as a federal preserve.[32] Later in the month, Bradley's Senate Energy and Natural Resources Committee approved revised legislation authorizing $17.5 million, the House Natural Resources Committee was scheduled to approve Torricelli's similar bill, and the measure was expected to clear the full Congress before the October recess. With time running out for the 103rd Congress, lawmakers were not expected to actually appropriate any of the funds, but forest supporters were excited because the congressional authorization would also be sending a strong signal to the Sterling Forest Corporation that Congress was serious about preserving Sterling Forest. [33]

Alas, the two bills authorizing $17.5 million died without a congressional vote, joint victims of the 1994 end-of-session logjam and the congressional rush to adjourn in time to campaign for the upcoming elections.[34] Both Sterling Forest funding bills would have to be reintroduced at the start of the 104th

Congress in January 1995. "We're very disappointed that Congress did not get to this issue, but we're not surprised, given what was happening," said JoAnn Dolan, executive director of the New York–New Jersey Trail Conference.[35] Sterling Forest Corporation CEO Louis Heimbach said, "If the government still can get its act together, we are willing to sit down." Warned a tired and frustrated Bob Binnewies, who had put in months of feverish effort on the failed legislation, "Time is running out."

Yet experienced Washington hands told worried environmentalists that the overall plan—money from Washington, New York, New Jersey, and the private sector—looked like a viable approach, and predicted it would endure the political vicissitudes of the coming years. "This issue had bipartisan and very broad support. It is almost certain to pass in the next Congress," Torricelli reassured the grassroots.[36]

STATESIDE: NEW JERSEY FIRMS UP ITS COMMITMENT

Unequivocal commitment to preservation came from New Jersey first. In the summer of 1994, the legislature of the Garden State passed a bill that would have set aside $10 million to protect Sterling Forest, but that November newly elected New Jersey Governor Christine Todd Whitman made a smart move: She put a conditional veto on it. She said she supported the acquisition of the forest but wanted more than promises from New York and Washington—she wanted legislation. She firmly stipulated that equivalent or greater funding should come from New York and that federal funds should be available to match those from the two states, and she required New Jersey to withdraw its contribution if the forest was not purchased within three years.[37]

New Jersey's legislature agreed with Governor Whitman's conditions and in January 1995 passed an amended version of the bill. New Jersey's share would come, not from the state's Green Acres bond fund but from its little-used 1969 water conservation bond fund, which the governor's office had discovered still held $16 million in unused funds. "We are immensely pleased," said Palisades Park's Bob Binnewies. "We think the governor has offered a very constructive challenge to the state of New York and the federal government. We believe the results will be positive."[38]

By this time, New Jersey's Passaic County had already obtained clear title to the 2,074 acres of Sterling Forest land it had seized years before. As noted earlier, in 1988, Passaic County, committed to protection of its watershed, had taken the tract and waited for commissioners to determine what the county would have to pay for the acquisition. After that, the county's negotiations with the corporation dragged on and at one point the corporation asserted that the land, with its development already laid out as shown in the company's overall plan, was worth $20 million. The county sued the corporation, arguing that the tract had to be appraised as undeveloped land; the corporation countersued. The September purchase was finally negotiated in an out-of-court settlement: $9.3 million, or $4,484 per acre.[39]

STATESIDE: NEW YORK STATE CREATES
A NEW OPEN SPACE FUNDING SOURCE

At the end of 1993, even New York State, the conspicuous laggard in the funding campaign, scrambled for a seat on the Sterling Forest bandwagon. By the end of the year, Governor Cuomo expressed support for the idea of joint funding, and even earlier that year the state legislature had made it possible—in July, at the end of a marathon all-night legislative session, the New York State legislature had approved creation of an Environmental Protection Fund for land purchases. It was the apogee of a three-year struggle for legislation to enable the state to acquire open space—even without voters' passage of an environmental bond act. This landmark legislation allocated $25 to $26 million in 1994–1995 for land acquisition and other environmental actions around the state; within four years the allocation would grow to $94.5 million. Initial funding was to come from savings coming from refinancing state debts, sale of excess state properties and, eventually, from money collected through the real estate transfer tax.[40] Although other critical tracts would be competing with Sterling Forest for funding, the legislation offered at least the possibility that New York would come through with cash. Said Sterling Forest Corporation CEO Thomson, "It's the strongest possible source of money in the talks yet."[41]

In early 1994, as support for Sterling Forest continued to reverberate throughout the region, it prodded New York's Governor Cuomo to urge New York's congressional delegation to support the federal legislation that would authorize the $35 million. That spring, he also said he was including the forest in his list of parcels eligible for acquisition with funds from the state's new environmental fund, although he made no specific commitment. Later that spring he did include $9 million for purchase of Sterling Forest in his budget proposal. He was, after all, running for reelection.

THE DOWNWARD SPIRAL OF HOME HOLDINGS

Meanwhile, Home Holdings, the parent corporation of the Sterling Forest Corporation, continued to lose money. In the first three quarters of 1994 alone it reported an operating loss of $115 million. And its financial ratings declined.

That December, its parent company Trygg-Hansa fired its chief executive Bjorn Sprängare.

In late 1994, reporting third-quarter losses of $131 million, Home Holdings sought another quarter billion dollars in new capital. "Home Holdings . . . is one of a handful of once-powerful domestic insurers whose financial strength was sapped by fierce market-share competition in the 1970s," the *Wall Street Journal* reported. "With prices in the commercial liability market generally soft since 1987, Home Holdings has already pared back commodity-like businesses, beefed up higher margin specialty lines, brought in new management, cut expenses, sold itself to Trygg-Hansa and then, last December, raised $400 million in equity and debt." Prospects for new and renewal business looked grim. Standard and Poor lowered Home's ratings from triple B-minus, the lowest investment grade, down to double B-minus, the no-investment grade.

Analysts doubted that Trygg-Hansa could shine again given the disappointing performance of Home Holdings. "Home Holdings is a millstone for Trygg-Hansa . . . [it] has caused Trygg's net asset value to drop 22 percent since year-end 1993. . . . there is a major risk of the share price developing unfavorably over the short term."[42]

In December 1994, an investor group led by John J. Byrne, an insurance industry leader, offered to provide $420 million, in exchange for his investors getting 40 to 45 percent of Home Holdings. Byrne would become chairman of Home and his group would control five of Home's eleven board seats. The group would secure a new $170-million bank credit and issue new common stock to current shareholders for the remainder.[43]

But that same month, before the Byrne arrangement could be finalized, a rival group, composed of Zurich Insurance Company and an investment partnership led by Texas investor Robert Bass and Chase Manhattan Corporation, opened discussions with Home Holdings. Within weeks, Home Holdings had turned its back on Byrne's offer; paying a $12-million penalty to the Byrne group, it sold nine million shares to Zurich. The Zurich agreement created a powerful alliance between the Swedish Trygg-Hansa and the Switzerland-based Zurich Insurance.

Zurich intended to strip the assets from Home Holdings to take over only its healthy activities—essentially Gruntal and Sterling Forest—but not Home's liabilities. And Home would essentially liquidate itself, leaving its only business, said the *Times*, to "pay claims and decide the fate of the Sterling Forest Corporation."[44] In 1995, New Hampshire regulators approved a restructuring plan for Home Holdings, which was legally domiciled in that state. Under the plan, the new owner, Zurich, would take over many of Home's profitable property and casualty insurance policies, while Home would begin to disappear as it paid off claims and other debts. The plan was controversial because if Home ran out of money, the shortfall would have to be covered by state guaranty funds, which are financed by other insurers. In response to regulators' concern, Trygg-Hansa then agreed to provide nearly $300 million in reinsurance if Home ran out of cash.[45] Late into the 1990s, before the Zurich deal was finalized, Home Holdings was plagued by a series of financial setbacks, including its inability to pay policyholder claims and bondholder interest payments, and, in January 1998, it entered into Chapter 11 bankruptcy protection; this action, which eliminated much of Home's public debt and bestowed tax benefits on Home as well, also enabled Zurich to stay free of responsibility for Home's liabilities.[46]

Fortunately, Zurich Insurance, the company that took over Home, was a rich, successful, and ambitious conglomerate, with plenty of money to carry out its plans as well as an excellent credit rating. Expanding globally, Zurich was diversifying into businesses as disparate as tobacco (British American Tobacco, owned by British American Financial Services) and assets management. By the late 1990s, the Zurich Financial Services Group oversaw one of the world's largest insurance and asset-management empires.

These global deals swirling around the Sterling Forest Corporation were mirrored by a major change within. In August 1994, as forest advocates swarmed over Washington in search of federal funding, Robert Thomson was suddenly no longer CEO of Sterling Forest Corporation, and Louis Heimbach, who had been president and chief operating officer since joining the corporation, was promoted to CEO. Thomson apparently was unaware that he was to be eased out. He recalls a very short conversation with the head of Trygg-Hansa: Lars Nielsen simply notified him one day that the parent corporation had decided to make a change. Thomson's main function was as vice president at AmBase and, as AmBase withered away, so did most of Thomson's job. Thomson recalls, "I knew when I brought Lou on board that I was bringing in somebody who could replace me. Lou was an important local Republican in a state with a new Republican administration." Thomson soon went back out West, to practice law in Arizona.[47]

In short, major efforts toward acquisition marked the year 1993 and the early part of 1994: The Sterling Forest Corporation, now under foreign ownership and eager for a cash infusion, was negotiating seriously for the first time; the Palisades Interstate Park Commission spearheaded the deal discussions. Also for the first time, New York came along as a key player, with its new fund earmarked for land acquisitions and a governor under increasing pressure to take action, while New Jersey reiterated its long-standing commitment to acquisition. Even New York Representative Benjamin Gilman, long opposed to acquisition of the forest, acceded to constituent pressure—not only did he support preservation, he actually signed on as sponsor of a House bill that would funnel substantial money from the federal Land and Water Conservation Fund. These and a few other similar federal funding initiatives looked serious enough to give the negotiations weight. Despite environmentalists' worries about the key elements of the deal—especially the dangers of a partial purchase and revival of the proposal for a Thruway interchange in Tuxedo—the key players, buttressed by growing public pressure, had generated considerable momentum moving toward funding a purchase of the forest.

CHAPTER SEVEN

Turning the Grassroots
into a Fighting Force

STERLING FOREST COALITION MOVES TO THE REAR;
THE NEW STERLING FOREST RESOURCES IS LAUNCHED

ONCE THE FOREST HAD BEEN APPRAISED and the Palisades Interstate Park Commission had become the lead player, the Sterling Forest Coalition found itself in territory far beyond what its volunteers could handle. It was clear by 1992 that it would be necessary to nail down funding commitments to protect the forest, which was going to be tough and would require a concerted multiyear effort across the environmental spectrum, people pulling out all the stops, in New York and in Washington. JoAnn Dolan of the New York–New Jersey Trail Conference identified a number of expensive needs, including a legal expert to tend to the detail-filled environmental review of the corporation's project and provide a rigorous legal analysis, and expert witnesses to address and correct the forestry, wildlife, archeology, biology, hydrology, planning, transportation, and other aspects of the corporation's environmental impact statement. In addition, a staff person was urgently needed.

In late 1992, a new group began meeting. Spearheaded by JoAnn Dolan, it brought together advocates impelled by the understanding that only a highly coordinated and cooperative acquisition effort had a chance of succeeding. Attendees, appearing by invitation only, were primarily professionals or staff people on establishment environmental organizations; absent were many of the grassroots volunteers who had long been part of the Sterling Forest Coalition. Attending were JoAnn Dolan, Olivia Millard of the Nature Conservancy's Lower Hudson Chapter, Barnabas McHenry of the Wallace Foundation, Malcolm Borg,

115

publisher of the *Bergen Record* and a PIPC commissioner, Jim Tripp, head of the Environmental Defense Fund. Soon, Bob Binnewies, director of the Palisades Interstate Park Commission, Nash Castro, former director of PIPC, and others came on board. The group met at the offices of attorney Samuel F. Pryor III, senior partner of the prestigious New York City firm Davis Polk & Wardwell and chairman of the board of the Appalachian Mountain Club.

This elite new interim committee strongly supported continuing the effort to acquire the forest for permanent preservation. Sterling Forest, having attracted a few token millions of dollars of federal money, was now seen as a serious campaign deserving of no-nonsense professionals who were dedicated to getting "the best deal possible"—but a deal at all costs, even if it meant a partial purchase.

The Sterling Forest Coalition continued to meet and reiterated that it was for acquisition of Sterling Forest in its entirety and opposed to any deal for partial purchase. John Humbach, the articulate Pace University professor of law who had headed the coalition since its inception, understood that the effort had entered a new and more intense phase. He decided that after six arduous years, he had carried the Sterling Forest effort as far as he could.

Notwithstanding the smooth transition, a festering residue of resentment remained among some of the long-time volunteers, who felt they had been elbowed aside by a self-constructed committee of land-use and political professionals.

In early 1993, the new committee decided to try to fund a project manager, someone responsible for pulling together the vast and growing amount of information on land use and development in the Sterling Forest area and for interacting with residents of Tuxedo, Warwick, and Monroe to ensure that they would be kept informed about the development. The committee wanted to raise community awareness about the project and generate a public relations effort vigorous enough to counter the corporation's. The ideal candidate, the committee said, would be able to work well with a wide range of people, have excellent organizational skills, and be familiar with the issues and the many state, regional, and federal agencies involved—and be willing to work extra hours.

That spring, John Gebhards got word that the environmental groups were looking for a staff person. Gebhards, a long-time volunteer environmental activist in the Hudson Valley, was formerly a plant manager for Hercules Incorporated, but had decided to remain in Orange County when Hercules moved its local operations to the Midwest. Gebhards contacted JoAnn Dolan of the New York–New Jersey Trail Conference. Her hiring group had provisionally decided on someone else, but changed their minds after interviewing the energetic and charismatic Gebhards.

With $5,000 apiece from three organizations, the Open Space Institute, the Nature Conservancy and the New York–New Jersey Trail Conference, a new advocacy organization, Sterling Forest Resources, was born.[1] John Gebhards became director, charged with the entire grassroots organizing effort, taking over as well the grassroots connections established through the Sterling Forest Coalition. The lanky, bearded Gebhards came across as low-key, with a mid-westerner's affability; the Australian outback hat he wore everywhere gave him a picturesque outdoorsy look that made him the object of innumerable photos in the local papers. He was an indefatigable community organizer—eventually there was hardly a classroom, citizens' group, or organized hike in southern Orange County that failed to receive Gebhards's presence and message—and within months his *Sterling Messenger* newsletter was bringing up-to-the-minute news to citizens overwhelmed by the dizzying profusion of details about the forest deal.

During the maneuvering to get Congress to partially fund the acquisition, Gebhards worked overtime to get the public to pressure government, asking them to write early and often to congresspeople and the governors of New York and New Jersey requesting funding of the land purchase and to the National Park Service requesting additional funding to expand the Appalachian Trail corridor. He took over chairing the Sterling Forest Coalition meetings after John Humbach stepped down, seeking to improve the outward flow of information from the Public-Private Partnership and to energize and organize the grassroots. Gebhards also was instrumental in arranging for production of two videos arguing for protection of the forest. Created by filmmakers Anne Macksoud and Joby Thompson, both residents of Warwick, and released in December 1995, the videos juxtaposed vistas of the forest's clear mountain lakes and clear skies with views of densely built construction. Arguing in favor of protection was a cast of stars, from actor Richard Kiley to New Jersey Governor Whitman. A 10-minute version of the film was designed for busy lawmakers, while a slightly longer version was distributed to civic groups around the metropolitan region.

To pay for Gebhards and other emerging expenses, JoAnn Dolan began to raise money for Sterling Forest: "I wasn't sure where we'd be able to use it, in terms of purchasing. I set up a Sterling Forest Defense Fund. We had two major Trail Conference funding campaigns that were just for Sterling Forest. The Appalachian Mountain Club and other organizations couldn't do it—very few groups can devote a whole fundraising campaign to one particular project. The Trail Conference commitment to Sterling Forest was highly unusual. We could make decisions on a dime. We could get mailing lists in a day. The whole board let me do this. And I didn't spend a penny of it on the Trail Conference—that whole $200,000 went into the Sterling Forest project. It's so great to work for an organization that was committed to the project. And I figured as long as we were solvent, why not put it into the project?

"I raised $200,000 for Sterling Forest, all of it went for grassroots work. Much went to John Gebhards' group and also helped fund the Regional Plan Association and Environmental Defense Fund so they could get on with the impact studies. They said, 'We don't have any money.' I said, 'Well, here's some money so you can get started.' I gave $20,000 to Rutgers [University], got them involved in a forest fragmentation study, then Bob Binnewies paid a bigger part of that bill.

"But people did far more than I ever paid them for."[2]

THE PUBLIC-PRIVATE PARTNERSHIP TO SAVE STERLING FOREST

In the early fall of 1993, the interim committee transformed itself into a more action-oriented organization. JoAnn Dolan, astute at finding key people, asked Laurance Rockefeller of the Natural Resources Defense Council to head up the new effort; his stature in a much wider community would provide immediate legitimacy. The informal group—it did not even take minutes—came to call itself the Public-Private Partnership to Save Sterling Forest (PPP) and soon was meeting on a regular basis. The PPP presented itself as a "blue-ribbon" panel whose mission was to establish the high-level technical, legal, and political support that had begun to look essential for purchase of the forest—above all, that scenario meant negotiating a deal and amassing the funding. Within a few months, PPP had constituted itself with some of the most important powerhouses in the Northeast for fundraising, making political connections, and defending the forest against the possible blows expected from the state's environmental review process.

Besides Laurance Rockefeller, whose presence lent tremendous visibility and prestige, the partnership included Dan Ruzow, from the Albany law firm of Whiteman Osterman and Hanna and attorney Sam Pryor, a leader in the influential Appalachian Mountain Club. The attendees from official state circles included Carole Nemore, an aide in the New York legislature's Senate Minority Office, Julia Stokes, a representative of New York's Office of Parks, and, for a short while, a representative from New Jersey Governor Florio's office (he failed to win reelection in 1993).

The partnership formed committees focused on accomplishing specific targets: legal and technical committees to grapple with the environmental review; fundraising, to work on all the likely sources of money; and legislative committees to lobby in Albany, Trenton, and Washington. Among the partnership's hardest working members were Jim Tripp of the Environmental Defense Fund; Ella

Filippone, head of the Passaic River Coalition, the key New Jersey connection, and among the most dedicated and savvy of the environmentalists; and Olivia Millard of the Nature Conservancy's Lower Hudson Chapter.

Barnabas McHenry, a patrician New Yorker long involved in Hudson Valley issues, had important political connections and was a powerhouse of energy; he and Neil Woodworth, of the Adirondack Mountain Club, both offered important ties to the Albany power base. Sam Pryor, who became president of the Appalachian Mountain Club, was a politically active Republican with strong conservation values. Louis V. Mills, former Orange County executive and current president of the fledgling Orange County Land Trust, provided an important local connection.

David Moore, head of the New Jersey Conservation Association, was the prickly and outspoken environmentalist who had been effective in moving New Jersey conservation issues to the forefront but had introduced an element of discord in the partnership's effort by insisting the Sterling Forest acquisition was less important than the effort to obtain money for land purchases in the New Jersey Highlands. (Fortunately for the Sterling Forest effort, Moore rarely attended meetings and his coworker Wilma Frey was more supportive of Sterling Forest.)

By common consent Bob Binnewies, executive director of the Palisades Interstate Park Commission, by 1993 a veteran of the Sterling Forest acquisition effort, became the "taskmaster," handing out assignments to a receptive and willing cadre of workers. JoAnn Dolan, who worked closely with him, recalls the partnership as "a tremendous experience." "It was," agrees Rob Pirani of the Regional Plan Association, "pretty incredible teamwork." By general consensus, the fact that this association of high-powered individuals did not devolve into an intramural fight is due to the strong and effective leadership of Bob Binnewies. JoAnn Dolan says, "Paul [Dolan] had nightmares about losing Sterling Forest; but after he shook hands with Bob Binnewies, he never had nightmares again. Bob connects with people, and gets people to do more. He has respect for everybody."[3] After public hearings on the development were held in 1995, the partnership became the driving force in the high-level forest acquisition effort—it was the vehicle by which the bulk of national and regional organizations flexed their muscle in what JoAnn Dolan calls "the most coordinated effort that had ever been demonstrated to protect land in this region." By 1995, the Trust for Public Land (TPL) came on board, sending Rose Harvey to meetings and allowing the TPL's Washington DC office to become an important outpost; TPL's Alan Front became an invaluable asset in helping to interpret the forest's ever-changing fortunes in Congress. Later still, in 1996 and 1997, new faces appeared at partnership meetings: Carol Ash of the Nature Conservancy's Albany office, and two hardworking residents of the town of Tuxedo: Al Ewert, an opponent of the Sterling Forest development since the mid-1970s, and Mary Yrizarry, a veteran of environmental campaigns in New York City and the Hudson Valley.

At first, with Congress beginning to give Sterling Forest serious attention, PPP was thinking that $60 million could buy the whole forest. Trygg-Hansa, it reasoned, needed the money and was ready to sell; PPP felt it could plausibly request $35 million from the federal government and eventually receive $25 million, could get $5 million from New Jersey's Green Acres program, $10 million from New York state, and $20 million from the private sector ($5 million of which would come from New Jersey philanthropy). The group envisioned that the cheapest management result if the forest were taken as a federal park but managed by the bi-state Palisades Interstate Park Commission.

As time passed, it emerged that the partnership was running on a dual track—an "outsider" group that supplied lobbying support and raised over several hundred thousand dollars to fund expert environmental studies and an in-group that came to decide the most important questions, for example, to have TPL and OSI negotiate with the corporation.

ENVIRONMENTAL REVIEW OF THE CORPORATION'S PROJECT BEGINS

Meanwhile, efforts by the Sterling Forest Corporation to obtain state permits for the development plan it had put on the table in 1991 moved slowly but steadily forward. In early 1993, the courts settled a festering territorial dispute over who would take on the required "lead agency" responsibility for evaluating the impacts of the development on human communities and the natural environment—it was to be New York's Department of Environmental Conservation, not the local towns.[4]

With the lead agency controversy settled, the way was open for the environmental review of the full development plan presented by the Sterling Forest Corporation. In 1993, in accord with the state's environmental review law, the DEC held several "scoping" meetings in which, as a first step, it asked the public to identify its environmental concerns about the project and raise questions about how to reduce or eliminate the adverse impacts. Based on this public input, the DEC would then prepare a "scope of work" document that supposedly would reflect everyone's concerns—and indicate how broad a review the agency would require.

At the outset, JoAnn Dolan criticized DEC for not intending to hire independent consultants. "Responding chiefly to the work of Sterling Forest Corporation's consultants demonstrates a reactive, rather than proactive, approach to the issue of Sterling Forest by DEC," she pointed out. With money raised in its Sterling Forest Defense Fund, the Trail Conference had hired law firm Whiteman Osterman & Hanna to comment on the DEC's proposed scope of work and geared up to hire expert witnesses in various specialties who would review the environmental impact statement drafted by the corporation. JoAnn recalls, "The money paid for Dan Ruzow, who came from Whiteman Osterman & Hanna, to be our scoping lawyer. There was a meeting of [John] Humbach and Neil Woodworth, me, and [attorney] Phil Gitlen and his partner Dan Ruzow. And they said they would do this and they wouldn't charge what they usually charge, and I figured, 'Uh-oh I'm getting second rate here.' Which was totally wrong. Ruzow was definitely first rate: He had worked for DEC and was an architect of the state's SEQRA law. He had 'SEQRA' [State Environmental Quality Review Act] on his license plate!

"When Ruzow came to the DEC scoping meeting, there were [Ruzow's] colleagues, who had worked for law firms and were now employed by the Sterling Forest Corporation. They said, 'What are YOU doing here?' He points to me and says, 'I'm representing my client.' It was worth $10,000 just to make that statement to the Sterling Forest Corporation, that we were serious, we were not leaving, we were getting the best. And I think that really unnerved them.

"Then Ruzow said, 'I'm going to do something now that will pay off,' and he asked, through the Freedom of Information Act, 'Will I have access to drafts of the EIS before it comes out?' He didn't get an answer, but Dan came back to me and he said, 'Now it's on record, they have to give us an answer. If you say that publicly they have to answer.'"[5]

Within the scoping process was the legal requirement to identify the "reasonable alternatives" to the planned development. The corporation sought to set the terms of the discussion by identifying what it saw as the single alternative, which it termed "the future without the project": in this corporate scenario, the huge tract would be left open to eventual uncoordinated development by the investors who ultimately would buy the tract's 100 or so big and little parcels and subdivide them according to the towns' zoning. Bob Binnewies deemed this alternative "development" as in "development or slightly less development."

But environmentalists didn't think this was a realistic alternative at all and asked instead for a different "reasonable alternative"—public acquisition, which would leave the land as open space. This, they said, was the preeminent and most reasonable concept and had to be included in the environmental impact statement.

In addition, in responding to the DEC's call for scoping topics, environmentalists went beyond the public's environmental concerns about air, water, traffic, and habitat and submitted a host of new concerns specifically related to the larger issues of sprawl and public policy. Development projections indicated that Orange County could see an additional 50,000 people and 8 to 10 million square feet of commercial space within the next twenty years. But the Sterling Forest project, plus the county's plans for a large reservoir and water supply project for suburban-type growth, plus projects being planned around Stewart Airport, all depended on those same projections—that is, each project intended to capture most of the same growth. For government to underwrite infrastructure in Sterling Forest would only compete with the others.

Forest advocates urged the DEC not to shortchange the review of the "need" for the project—a key element of New York's environmental review process—and not allow the corporation to fudge the question of proving "need." Plenty of industrial and commercial building space was already available within an hour's drive of Sterling Forest, and, in addition, Newburgh and other nearby cities had vacant housing stock and urban renewal tracts aplenty—an oversupply fairly begging for rehabilitation. No market studies and no credible projections had ever been made to substantiate the corporation's development targets.[6]

The state environmental law also intended the review to include an evaluation of social and economic as well as environmental consequences. This prompted Jürgen Wekerle to call for an inclusion of the many obvious and hidden public subsidies, from UDC underwriting and IDA bonds to MTA improvements to subsidized mortgages. But, recalls Wekerle, the DEC was "bemused by my questions and in essence responded that the review would be as narrow as possible, [restricted] to issues within the property itself and focus mainly on quantifiable engineering issues. . . . Social and economic issues were thoroughly discounted. Specifically, they said that they at Region III have had little experience in being a 'lead agency' on a matter this complex, and they do not plan to evaluate economic and social issues which are too complex, too unfamiliar, and too 'political.'"[7]

The DEC's feeble responses to these larger issues of policy and oversight engendered widespread worry among forest advocates that DEC would be true to its bureaucratic mindset and would rigidly "go by the book"—meaning that it would not be particularly vigilant or wide ranging in its review. The New York–New Jersey Trail Conference reminded the DEC that New York law allowed the agency to consider the overall impacts of a project, and not limit itself to the narrow concerns of the permit requested. Sterling Forest was not a local but a regional resource and the DEC should take a regional approach. It also asked that the DEC, independent of the plan promoted by the corporation, identify areas most critical environmentally and those most appropriate for development; of the developable areas, DEC should then determine which areas should be developed first, which next, and so on.

And, said the Trail Conference, the Appalachian Trail was the resource most imperiled by the development. This great historic foot trail ran through the northern portion of the Sterling Forest Corporation's proposed project—the site of about a third of the planned development. The corporation's 1991 project plan would destroy the feeling of remoteness that trailside views provided and because a new community—two population centers, about 3,000 homes—was planned for within 300 feet of the trail; this would unavoidably degrade the trail itself. Worrying about complete obliteration of the wilderness experience in the northern portion of Sterling Forest, JoAnn Dolan wrote:

> More than anywhere else along the Appalachian Trail, the AT section in Sterling Forest and Bear Mountain-Harriman Park provides a unique "wilderness" recreational resource for the typically under-served urban populations. . . . And now, ironically, the area where the Trail first began in 1923 is currently the most vulnerable section along the 2,100 mile trail system.

> Sterling Forest Corporation's Stage 1 Plan stands to cause the greatest visual rupture along the entire Appalachian Trail . . . All of it is adjacent to the AT corridor . . . AT management for this section of trail will be nearly impossible; the pristine value of this prized section of trail will be forever destroyed; wildlife habitat will be severely impacted; viewshed damage will denigrate the trail experience. In Benton MacKaye's terms, the 'zone of sanity' closest to the nation's largest metropolitan region will be gone. . . . The Corporation's development plan . . . will forever destroy wildlife, viewshed, and spiritual experience for those traveling the Appalachian Trail in New York.[8]

The Trail Conference also attempted to pique the interest of the National Park Service, which did send a representative, Pamela Underhill, to the DEC scoping meeting in Tuxedo. The federal agency expressed its concern about the 3 miles of the Appalachian Trail that ran through Sterling Forest; development of such scope along the trail was "unprecedented," the Park Service said.[9]

Asking the National Park Service to "do everything in its power to take the lead in preserving this precious section of the AT," the Trail Conference proposed that the Park Service work to create a 4,000-acre Appalachian Trail corridor that included the northern portion of Sterling Forest as well as other lands.[10] And, in 1993, the Trail Conference hired land consultant John Myers as the key planner for the corridor. Myers would be mapping the corridor and studying the impact of the development plan south of the Appalachian Trail. JoAnn Dolan comments,

"I asked John Myers to look at all properties around the Trail. I have used that plan for grant proposals. I say, 'We're committed to protecting the corridor.'" Most important, this plan gave Dolan a basis for opposition to the corporation's development plan because, as she wrote to Sam Pryor in June 1993, "The development plan abutting the southern corridor of the AT stands to be the greatest rupture to the entire 2,100-mile Trail."

The Sterling Forest Corporation's CEO Robert Thomson put the best spin he could on this strong effort to counter the corporation's operating principles. "People around here see [the environmentalists] as a bunch of outsiders trying to tell the people of Orange County what's good for them," the California native said. "That they feel they need professional advice shows they know they face a difficult task trying to convince our neighbors that a development that saves 75 percent of the land as open space is bad."[11]

THE PUBLIC GETS ITS SAY

In February 1995, more than a year after the DEC's scoping sessions, the Sterling Forest Corporation submitted its 5,000-page "draft generic environmental impact statement" (DGEIS) on its development—a powerful milestone in a development that was inexorably moving forward. The document covered the projected impacts on ecosystems, traffic, clean air and water, towns' costs, and community character. The DEC ruled that the document was "complete," meaning that it was good enough to give it out for the public's review and comment. The corporation left copies of the draft statement in libraries and town halls in the southeastern part of the county and in the New York Public Library in Manhattan.

As with all such impact statements, the report reflected the concerns raised during earlier scoping, but it was written by the developer, thereby incorporating the corporation's underlying assumptions. The corporation's strategy was to contrast its proposed project, not against public acquisition and forest preservation, but against the uncoordinated growth that would follow if the tract were to be sold to hundreds of different developers.

Under the state's Freedom of Information Law, Sterling Forest Resources director John Gebhards was able to obtain an early copy of the report, even as it was being reviewed by New York's DEC and weeks before it reached the libraries. Making multiple copies of sections, he distributed them to individuals and groups having special expertise or concerns in particular areas. So that the community could respond adequately to the environmental review tome, Gebhards published a special issue of his *Sterling Messenger*, which outlined the environmentalists' main concerns. Attorney Jim Tripp, with the Environmental

Defense Fund and an active member of the Public Private Partnership to Save Sterling Forest, also worked on an analysis of the report.

As the public hearings on the DGEIS drew near, environmental groups urged the public to attend and speak. Strong public opposition could be key to limiting the development or even preventing it. "Public objections to the development could discourage governmental agencies from granting the permits necessary to build roads and bulldoze the mountainsides. Strong opposition . . . would also send a message to Washington, Trenton, and Albany that this land must be preserved," editorialized the *Bergen Record*.[12] Because development is an integral part of the review process in New York, because the law allows landowners to make a profit from the land they own, citizen challengers can only rarely discredit the idea of the development itself. To be at all effective in the review process, citizens are limited to challenging the developer on the developer's turf, at best winning mere alterations of the plan. Such adjustments—what the law calls mitigations—are based on what amount to technicalities: ways to reduce the impacts of sewage, traffic, demand for town services, and the like. "A mitigation merely acknowledges a risk and transforms it into a bureaucratically acceptable form," was the wry comment of Mike Edelstein, president of Orange Environment, a homegrown Orange County environmental group that had largely watched the Sterling Forest effort from the sidelines but brought a strong voice to the review proceedings.

But if the review formalities favor development, time and public opinion are on the environmentalists' side. If activists can delay the project, freight it with additional analysis and additional fieldwork, raise questions that cast doubt on the legitimacy of the whole endeavor, arouse the public to persuade officials to look unfavorably on permits, even create the legal basis for a lawsuit, then, it sometimes happens, a project loses momentum and the developer calculates that the plan is not worth the additional costs and rethinks the project's viability or takes it elsewhere. Delay and public opposition thus generally constitute the environmentalists' best strategy. In the case of Sterling Forest, to delay was also to extend the time in which the forest's public allies, like Torricelli and Babbitt, might work for federal funding commitments.

Anticipating this moment, the Public Private Partnership had turned to universities, environmental organizations, and paid consultants to gather facts. JoAnn Dolan affirms, "We had so much incredible testimony from scientists. Jim Tripp and RPA brought in experts on transportation and air quality. So we had scientists giving testimony who knew what they were talking about, which is very unusual."[13]

More than 700 residents attended the four hearings, held in June in Tuxedo, Warwick, and Monroe, with almost every speaker opposing development of Sterling Forest. The corporation's officers sat stolidly and impassively in the stiff hearing-room chairs, listening to hundreds of speakers hammer away at corporate claims that the development would be likely to have only small impacts on air quality, on the New Jersey water supply, on the Appalachian Trail viewshed, on population, on area traffic patterns, on the integrity of the forest, on the region's quality of life. The environmental community claimed that the environmental impact statement was rife with problems in the assumptions it made concerning the impacts on traffic, town finances, air quality, and population and returned again and again to its strategically strongest argument, the need to preserve the quality of the forest watershed and the inability to assure water quality if the developer's sewage treatment systems were to fail.

JoAnn Dolan remembers, "Dan Ruzow's request did result in the environmentalists getting early access to the EIS and enabled John Gebhards to do wonderful workshops based on the EIS material, and RPA and EDF to get an early look. We had a lot of time you don't usually get in such proceedings. So the EIS hearings were extraordinarily good, you didn't get that emotional sputtering. Instead you got testimony relevant to what the EIS and scoping document addressed. "The public hearings were packed with relevant comments. This had a lot to do with John's workshops, and that we had so much incredible testimony from scientists."

An environmentalists' consultant from Ad Hoc Associates in Salisbury, Vermont, elaborated on the earlier analysis that the corporation underestimated by 2,000 the number of children going to local schools and underestimated the number of residents by 4,500. She said the additional demand for services these new residents would generate would cancel out any anticipated tax benefits from commercial development. The Palisades Interstate Park Commission asserted that public acquisition of the forest would be financially beneficial to the towns, since the PIPC paid millions of dollars in taxes on land it managed; development, it stressed, would cost the municipalities far more in services than it would deliver in revenue. Other hired experts addressed impacts on the viewshed, on the endangered timber rattler, and on the need to preserve large blocks of forest in order to protect wildlife.

Speaker after speaker challenged the very methodology the corporation used to get its projections. "The DGEIS," said Orange Environment, "fails to present the kind of honest and integrative analysis that will allow decision makers to take the required hard look at the project." Tuxedo activist Mary Yrizarry observed that the Sterling Forest Corporation had completely developed its plan well before it instituted its town forums and citizens' advisory panels. Thus, she said, the public never had the option to suggest that the plan was too big and inappropriate for the entire region.[14]

Commentator Ron Nowak said what he gleaned from the corporation at the hearings was that the people who will inhabit the developed Sterling Forest are

> simply the best, most environmentally sensitive, non-breeding, clean human beings on the planet. They will ride jitneys instead of cars, create less waste than their counterparts on the outside, take up less space, create fewer children, and in general conform to the absolute but unwritten laws of society, such as if you buy a two bedroom house you will only have one child. Not only that, they will fail to see thousands of houses within a few feet of the Appalachian Trail, will agree that painting the houses in earth tone colors is the same as not seeing them at all, and will believe hundreds of thousands of gallons of treated sewage will not have any affect [sic] on New Jersey's drinking water. If you build it they will come. Unfortunately they won't disappear into a corn field at the end of the day like the ball players in "Field of Dreams." Or will they? Just about anything is possible if it's planned well enough. [15]

Said the *Greenwood Lake and West Milford News*,

> [I]t is hard to believe that the DEC could have certified this DGEIS as complete. It is impossible to believe that the DEC will somehow even agree that there is a way to mitigate the impact of this massive development on what is now a contiguous forest.... These hearings have been a reality check on whether the DEC is, in fact, really interested in environmental protection or interested in trying to find a self-serving way to allow development to begin. [16]

The Appalachian Trail Conference got a California company to do the viewshed analysis. Another Trail Conference presentation, with computer-generated views from the Appalachian Trail, showed how the viewshed would be devastated by the enormous development. The Regional Plan Association asserted that undeveloped open space was still the property's highest and best use.

Several speakers attacked the corporation's implication that it actually intended to build its plan; rather, they reminded the public of the corporation's own assertion that it was only in it to obtain the permits; then it would put its approved parcels—now much more valuable in the marketplace for having been given permits—up for sale to the highest bidders. In this scenario, there would in fact be little coherence to the construction that actually developed.

The expected strong criticism also came from the Environmental Defense Fund, the Sierra Club, the New York–New Jersey Trial Conference, the Appalachian Mountain Club, Sterling Forest Coalition, and the Passaic River Coalition.

About fifty additional people asked to speak, but the hearings were closed before they had their chance. Despite much grumbling, the administrative law judge, Daniel P. O'Connell, nevertheless ruled not to hold additional hearings. Following the hearings, and based on the many issues raised, the state DEC began to review the corporation's DGEIS with the expectation that it would take months of additional work before a "final" document could be produced.

In addition to the public hearings, a separate issues conference was tentatively scheduled for August. The months-long adjudicatory hearings that would follow would provide for expert testimony that could be cross examined, allowing for more in-depth evaluation of some information. But, on July 23, the DEC said the issues conference scheduled for August was adjourned indefinitely.

The 1995 public hearings were widely viewed as one of the high-water moments of the Sterling Forest preservation effort. Many activists who were involved recalled that the hearings, with the extraordinary presence of 700 citizens, were also a turning point, critical in convincing the Sterling Forest Corporation that it would encounter growing opposition to any development, including lawsuits, and most important of all, critical in convincing public officials of the powerful public interest in saving the forest and the need to find funding to achieve that goal.

CHAPTER EIGHT

Bounced Around in the
Washington Turf Wars

CONTRACT WITH AMERICA HOLDS UP CONGRESSIONAL ACTION

WITH THE SUSPENSION OF THE PUBLIC HEARINGS, the environmental community went back to lobbying Congress for money. But through most of 1995, it seemed that the country was going to repudiate environmental protection in a big way. In November 1994, for the first time in four decades, the nation elected to the House of Representatives a Republican majority, with many of the freshmen self-described antigovernment ideologues. Many of those representatives saw in their election a mandate to implement within the first 100 days of the 104th Congress Newt Gingrich's new program, called the Contract with America, an overt attempt to reduce the federal regulatory apparatus to a shadow of its late-twentieth-century self. Within the contract, with its emphasis on private property rights, tax reduction, and a diminished federal presence, was an agenda that would have ruthlessly dismantled long-standing environmental, health, and safety regulations.

As early as February 1995—in the Republican frenzy of budget cutting that affected many federal programs—the House Appropriations Committee moved to take back the $3 million in funds approved three years earlier for acquisition of Sterling Forest. "The new Republican Congress' belt-tightening efforts have made it increasingly clear that federal land and water conservation efforts face tough times—particularly in the Northeast. That could be disastrous news for Sterling Forest," the *Bergen News* reported.[1] And indeed, in July, Clinton signed into law a package of federal spending cuts that did eliminate the $3 million. Bob

Binnewies put the best face on this by saying, "That money was significant two years ago both financially and for the recognition of the project as a resource area. We've since moved beyond that first step in our fund-raising efforts."[2]

While the congressional juggernaut was intent on undermining government spending in the public interest, on April 24, 1995, Secretary of the Interior Bruce Babbitt was also back in Sterling Forest country, walking the Appalachian Trail in the company of preservationists and vowing to push for public purchase. Babbitt was dealing with his frustration with Congress by reaching out to the American people in hopes, he said, of "awakening a spirit across the landscape of concern and renewal." Babbitt had come east for a whirlwind five-state tour to attack what he called an attempt by Congress to dismantle a generation of successful environmental protection legislation. The secretary said the administration was "wholly in support" of buying Sterling Forest, and encouraged the public to maintain pressure on Congress. "Keep it up. This will be done," he said. But he also cautioned, "I don't want to raise your expectations too high. This year, Washington is a very unpredictable kind of place."[3]

On June 30, 1995, the U.S. Senate approved Senator Bradley's bill, the Sterling Forest Authorization Bill, now numbered S 719, which authorized $17.5 million to be used for the acquisition of Sterling Forest as public open space, with the funding to come from the Interior Department's Land and Water Conservation Fund. Representative Torricelli was impressed; he said the vote was extraordinary in "this anti-environmental Congress."[4]

Senator Bradley's bill was sent to the House where it received its House number, HR 400. Meanwhile, in the House, the similar bill sponsored by Representatives Maurice Hinchey, Benjamin Gilman, and Robert Torricelli, HR 1256, moved through the House Subcommittee on National Parks, Forests and Public Lands, but by mid-1995 had yet to reach the floor. Representative Marge Roukema's bill requesting $25 million was also pending in the House.

A fight was expected on the House floor, where members, many from western states, had been exercising their passion for budget-cutting and their bias against public acquisition of private lands: an early House budget proposal even included a drastic five-year moratorium on using the federal Land and Water Conservation Fund to buy any more open space. New York Representative Maurice Hinchey reassured environmentalists that the money could yet be forthcoming, despite such congressional efforts to reduce spending on park lands.[5]

"We know that we have a tough fight, but we wouldn't be trying if we didn't think we were going to succeed," PIPC's executive director Bob Binnewies said in June. But in the face of the Republican onslaught on the environment in the House, a discouraged Torricelli told the *Bergen Record*, "We may get [a spending bill] authorized—we probably will get it authorized—but getting it appropriated will be extremely difficult."[6]

By September, the National Park Service had not put the Sterling purchase on its priority list for fiscal 1996. The Park Service had agreed that the money could come from its Land and Water Conservation Fund, but by then Congress had tentatively decided to cut that fund by nearly half.

On September 28, 1995, James V. Hansen, R-Utah, the conservative chairman of the pivotal House subcommittee National Parks, Forests and Lands, held a hearing on funding the forest buyout. Governors Whitman and Pataki had sent a joint letter in support, and among those giving testimony were the National Park Service, New Jersey Representatives Roukema and Torricelli, PIPC's Bob Binnewies, New Jersey Senators Lautenberg and Bradley, Bernadette Castro, Pataki's Commissioner of the New York State Office of Parks, and others. The united New York-New Jersey delegation told the subcommittee that the land acquisition was necessary in order to preserve water quality for New Jerseyans. Sterling Forest Corporation CEO Louis Heimbach told the subcommittee that his company was a willing seller but said the corporation did not want a federal promise for money if it was not followed by a vote to actually spend it. "We won't be forced into a deal where we're held hostage by the promise of federal money," he said.

But for Sterling Forest advocates the hearing turned out to be a nightmare. For one thing, the Park Service made an unexpected request: that the proposed House bill be amended to limit federal spending to land adjacent to the Appalachian Trail—still another about-face for the apparently infinitely vacillating Park Service.[7] Too, the tenor of the hearing was hostile and sarcastic, as chairman James Hansen, a known apologist for mining and grazing on public lands, and other western congressmen were in no mood to spend money for the buyout, and were inclined to beat back the bill, as they had the year before. The *Rockland Journal-News* editorialized:

> These questions were from the National Parks, Forests and Lands subcommittee, which is dominated by westerners, budget whackers and property-rights backers, all of whom have long relied on the federal government through special-interest lobbying, to support the West. They have secured forestry rights on federal lands, they have threatened to sell off parkland; they have obtained funding for all manner of projects far and above what the East has gotten. Yet they have the gall to question whether this area . . . needs protection for Sterling Forest.[8]

The Hansen hearing became an opportunity for House Republicans, mostly freshmen from western states, to express their belief that the federal government owned far too much land as it was. As a spokesman for California Representative Richard Pombo saw it, "The Federal leviathan called the Interior Department is constantly seeking to expand its empire."[9] Maintaining water quality was not a federal problem, they said, and they were unhappy that it would be PIPC, not the federal government, that owned the land; besides, no price had been agreed to. Several referred to the bill as "pork" and derided its bipartisan supports.

The *Bergen Record* saw the congressional resistance as a high-stakes poker game. If Congress stayed entirely out of the picture, New Jersey and New York would have to underwrite the acquisition themselves. And Congress knew there was immense public pressure on the governors to acquire the forest.[10]

The congressional opposition worried officials of both parties in New Jersey and New York. Representative Hinchey fretted, "Particularly this new crop that was elected last year, somehow they have a very parochial view of the world. They have a very difficult time—really a seeming inability—to relate to the circumstances of other people in other parts of the country."

At the close of the Hansen hearing, it appeared that New Jersey Senator Bradley's considerable leverage might be the only thing saving the federal funding proposal: Bradley, who had announced that he would not be seeking another term in the Senate, let it be known that he would keep a "hold" on every piece of legislation in his Senate Energy and Natural Resources Committee until the forest funding authorization passed.[11] His tactic is not one generally used, because it weakens the collegiality that lubricates Senate work. But since Bradley had decided to retire from the Senate after 1996, he had made the purchase of Sterling Forest one of his chief priorities before his retirement, and the possible alienation of colleagues did not figure prominently in his thinking. Bradley's holds stalled many bills favored by western lawmakers who objected to the purchase of Sterling Forest.

NEW YORK WANTS IT TO HAPPEN

After Democratic Governor Mario Cuomo lost his bid for reelection as New York's governor, the Public-Private Partnership braced for the task of having to convince the new administration of George Pataki of the increasingly urgent quest for funds to acquire Sterling Forest. Yet Pataki, a native of the Hudson Valley, had a well-developed appreciation of the outdoors, and in early 1995, almost as soon as he took office, placed Sterling Forest on the state's short list of ten priority tracts eligible for funding under the state Environmental Protection Fund. This put New York State back into the funding package. In May 1995, Bernadette Castro, the new state Parks Commissioner, said, "Governor Pataki has authorized me to negotiate. He would like Sterling Forest to happen. We want it to happen. When we establish a fair market price, you will begin to see me lobby for this project. I've already started in Washington."[12]

When the New York State 1995–96 state budget passed, it included $18 million for land conservation, with Sterling Forest listed as a priority. In response to letters from constituents, State Senator Joseph Holland successfully pleaded for additional funding for open space acquisition to be allotted to the state's Environmental Protection Fund, making allotments for Sterling Forest available.

THE DIABOLICAL LAND SWAP PROPOSALS OF 1996

Into the fall of 1995, Senator Bradley's bill addressing the Sterling Forest funding authorization was being held at House Speaker Gingrich's desk. Noted the *New York Times*, "The region's Republicans in the House, meanwhile, have made heroic efforts on behalf of the forest, especially Benjamin Gilman of New York and Marge Roukema of New Jersey. They need to keep pushing to get the measure through the House this week."[13] The *Bergen Record* assigned responsibility to New Jersey's governor: "As [Governor Christine Todd Whitman] rubs elbows with her fellow Republican [Newt Gingrich], she'll twist his arm as well. As speaker Mr. Gingrich has the ability to bring a key bill on Sterling Forest to a vote by the full House. . . . the governor can help the House speaker see the light on the forest."[14]

In mid-December, though, Speaker Gingrich's support went, not to HR 400, but to a wild new land-swap proposal. The new plan, concocted by freshman Republican Representative William Martini of Clifton, New Jersey, proposed selling at auction 56,000 acres of federally owned Oklahoma grassland and using a portion of the proceeds to help New York and New Jersey buy Sterling Forest. The idea was supported by Oklahoma Representative Frank Lucas, and the western Republicans viewed it as a reasonable, "budget-neutral" solution. But strongly opposing it were environmentalists, not only in the Northeast but from all over the nation, who worried that the scheme would set the troublesome precedent of requiring the government to sell some public lands in order to purchase others; the Arapaho and Cheyenne tribes of Oklahoma, who insisted they had a claim to some of the grasslands dating back more than a century; hunters and Oklahoma wildlife officials who cherished the tracts as prime hunting lands; and the Interior Department. Representative Maurice Hinchey interpreted: "Gingrich knows it will fail. He supported this plan because when it falls apart he wanted to be able to say he offered something." Hinchey concluded it was more about Washington politics than about acquiring the forest.[15] Freshman Martini had pushed this idea without consulting Marge Roukema or the other New Jersey legislators, and they were furious.

In an editorial the *New York Times* said, "[T]he House bill to which [Gingrich] has given his blessing is a politically tortured and environmentally unsound approach to a problem that the Speaker could solve much more cleanly."[16] The House plan to sell public Oklahoma lands in order to buy Sterling Forest lands died by the New Year: intense opposition at home caused Oklahoma Representative Lucas to drop his support of the legislation. Senator Bill Bradley reiterated his intention of holding dozens of unrelated pieces of legislation hostage in the next Congress unless Gingrich supported the House version of his bill.

Representative Marge Roukema, who felt she had been "blind-sided" by the land-swap proposal, continued in her own steady way to apply pressure. In mid-December, she prodded the Interior Department, which then identified Sterling Forest as a national funding priority in an appropriations bill that passed the House with an unspecified amount of money coming from the Land and Water Conservation Fund; again she wrote to Gingrich, in a letter signed by thirty-seven other members of the New York–New Jersey congressional delegation, to ask for $17.5 million for outright purchase of the forest.

The PIPC's Bob Binnewies said Congress was "within millimeters" of getting a funding bill passed. Marge Roukema was slightly less optimistic, but thought her letter signed by her colleagues and asking Speaker Gingrich for approval of funding was having a positive effect.[17]

DOUSING THE CONTRACT WITH AMERICA BRUSHFIRE

Environmentalists renewed pressure to get the public to write to their elected officials in support. Nineteen-ninety-six was an election year and, said grassroots organizer John Gebhards, politicians were going to be listening to the public. But, early in 1996, the bill authorizing $17.5 million toward the purchase of the forest was still being opposed by House committee chairs Don Young and James Hansen.[18] Many influential western members of Congress opposed adding more land to the federal inventory. On some level, they also wanted to even the score with eastern members who blocked pet western pro-development legislation. And the most radical Republicans were intent on cutting back on environmental protection of all kinds. In the ideological war being waged in Congress, EPA and the Interior Department had been operating without a final budget, and Interior was still being hung up by disagreement over what policies it was to adhere to.

But what began to be clear in 1996 was that the Republicans' intransigence on the environment was coming back to haunt them. Their Contract with America eventually began to trouble all sorts of citizens nationwide; the Congress was besieged with millions of letters and phone calls from constituents who had not had an anti-environment outcome in mind when they pulled the Republican lever in the voting booth in 1994. The yearlong effort of environmental groups around the nation to raise public awareness about the Republican effort to dismantle decades of environmental protections had begun to bear fruit; Americans were increasingly unhappy with the Republican zealots who sought to slash environmental programs.

"Our party is out of sync with mainstream American opinion," wrote Republican pollster Linda DiVall. Polling revealed that by large majorities Americans were not pleased with GOP efforts to cut budgets for environmental enforcement and indicated that the Republicans had an image problem with the public on environmental issues. The League of Conservation Voters awarded Gingrich a failing grade on the environment. President Clinton had spoken at length about the environment in his 1996 State of the Union address, saying that by voting to cut environmental enforcement, Congress was capitulating to the interests of corporations at the expense of the public health. Republican moderates complained to Gingrich that the party "had taken a beating this year over missteps in environmental policy" and asked him to lead the way in backing down from the Republican effort to emasculate environmental protection.[19] It was a resounding irony that Sterling Forest—the East Coast's most important conservation issue in decades—had landed in the lap of the man who had masterminded the flamingly anti-environmental Contract with America.

On January 31, the New York–New Jersey Republican delegation met with Newt Gingrich, with Marge Roukema and the now-chastened freshman Bill Martini making the case for preservation of the forest. The meeting seemed to bear fruit, enabling Gingrich and the eastern representatives as well as Alaska's Don Young and California's Richard Pombo to reach accord on the outlines of a package that would include funding for the forest.

Unfortunately, the Gingrich–Young–Pombo agreement still left unsettled the specifics of what else would go into the environmental bill, how much money would be allocated to Sterling Forest, or where the money would come from.[20] The Democrats did not see the accord as necessarily a good sign for forest funding: The Senate had already passed Bradley's serviceable bipartisan Sterling Forest bill with no objectionable swaps, and a version of that bill remained locked up in House committee. The Republicans could show their genuine commitment, said New Jersey Representative Bob Torricelli, by simply releasing that bill. A Senate aide expressed surprise that Gingrich would think that a wholly new House version could possibly pass the Senate in a straightforward and expeditious manner.

Immediately the new Republican proposal was introduced. The new plan would tie funding for Sterling Forest to other environment-related provisions, although the critical ingredients—the environmental specifics—had still not been made visible.

By the end of February, those new Republican specifics began to emerge: Funding for Sterling Forest would be included in an omnibus bill, which would link it to a provision that would open 4 million acres of magnificent federal redrock wilderness lands in Utah to pipelines, communications towers, dams, bulldozers, and other commercial development. It was clear that Representative James Hansen, chair of the National Parks, Forests and Lands Subcommittee, was demanding this-for-that in order to win the votes of moderate northeastern Republicans for his pet Utah plan.

Outraged Utah environmentalists called the proposal "unfixable," and Sterling Forest Resources' John Gebhards said the Utah link "will almost certainly meet the strong opposition of environmental groups around the country. If they put Hansen's bill in the omnibus bill, that will kill it as far as we're concerned." Interior Secretary Babbitt said he would recommend a presidential veto if Sterling Forest were packaged with a Utah wilderness giveaway.[21] The *Bergen Record* editorialized:

> Incorporating the Sterling Forest proposal into a larger, as yet undetermined environmental bill is a dubious proposition. The bill would have to start from scratch in both houses, and there's no guarantee it would pass—let alone win Mr. Clinton's signature. . . . the best course for the New Jersey delegation is to continue to press for the existing Sterling Forest bill. . . . Here's why. The main reason congressional Republicans are even considering money for Sterling Forest is that for almost a year, Senator Bill Bradley, D-N.J., has put a hold on some 40 bills coming out of the Senate Energy Committee. He says he won't release the bills until the House moves on Sterling Forest. That's not a bad position to bargain from.[22]

A scant two weeks later, Speaker Gingrich suddenly repositioned himself as what the *Bergen Record* referred to as "Sterling's odd savior" and made an historic pilgrimage to Sterling Forest on a sunny, cold, and slushy March 4, 1996.[23] Using New Jersey's beautiful Wanaque Reservoir as backdrop, and later traveling to the Ringwood, New Jersey, section of Sterling Forest, the repackaged Gingrich declared that funding for Sterling Forest should not depend on the sale of any other environmentally sensitive lands and affirmed his support for purchase of the forest in its entirety. He pledged to end the deadlock that had blocked public purchase. "I'm for saving all of it," he said, to applause. "We are going to pass a bill this year. We are going to get it through and to the president's desk." Although he did not offer any clear proposal, he did mention selling federally owned Housing and Urban Development land across the country. A New York state official said preliminary talks were under way to look at yet another possibility: selling Governor's Island in New York City in exchange for buying Sterling Forest.[24]

Of the Gingrich remarks John Gebhards allowed, "It was a stronger statement than we anticipated." Even Sterling Forest Corporation president Louis Heimbach professed to be encouraged. Said Heimbach, "It's a different viewpoint from what we've heard before."[25]

In mid-March 1996, Republicans in the Senate arrived at a new strategy to force passage of Bradley's dozens of holds: They would bundle them together and pass them en masse. Senator Frank Murkowski of Alaska vowed to introduce a Senate omnibus measure like Gingrich's, which would include funding for Sterling Forest and have a number of other good provisions but would also include surrender of millions of acres of Utah wilderness. The *Times* referred to this as "legislative extortion, holding [Sterling Forest funding] hostage to a truly destructive Utah lands measure."[26] Clinton threatened a veto.

Senator Bradley said he was prepared to forestall a vote by filibustering. "We're going to fight this until hell freezes over and then we're going to fight on the ice," said a Bradley spokesperson.[27] Leading the Democrats in turning back the proposal, Bradley said, "You wouldn't sell your family heirlooms in order to pave your driveway, and the Senate decided that it could not sacrifice such precious Utah lands to dig mines, build roads or drill oil wells." Continued Bradley, "What I want to preserve is the possibility for silence and the possibility for time that exists only in the wilderness." Snapped Utah's Republican Senator Orrin Hatch, "We know what silence and time is. They don't even know what wilderness is. We do. We've got plenty in Utah." While Bradley argued for broader protection of the redrock canyons, Hatch objected to eastern senators dictating land-use policy to the West.[28]

On March 25, 1996, Bradley and six Democratic allies began their filibuster against the controversial bill, now known as the Omnibus Parks and Recreation bill. Bradley spoke on Monday, as well as on Tuesday and Wednesday mornings. Senate leaders attempted to limit the debate and shut down Bradley and the others on Wednesday morning but fell nine votes short of the sixty votes needed to cut off debate. After that, Majority Leader Bob Dole of Kansas withdrew the entire bill from consideration—it was "tabled indefinitely."[29]

The western delegation, which had been outmaneuvered, was angry. Despite the bad feeling, Marge Roukema, a seasoned lawmaker, remained optimistic about the prospects for Sterling Forest funding. She knew western lawmakers were furious at Bradley anyhow, for his yearlong effort to block their pet Senate bills. But she thought a Sterling Forest bill was going to pass because there were "a whole lot of Republicans who want to establish their environmental credentials."[30]

Roukema was right on at least the "furious" part: The westerners were angry. They weren't through with Bradley, either. In April, over in the House of Representatives, Utah's James Hansen announced he would acquiesce to the wishes of Gingrich and move out of his House subcommittee the bill that had been stalled there since the year before—Bradley's straightforward Sterling Forest funding bill. Representative Robert Torricelli, who knew a thing or two about the House, remained skeptical: "This markup is a charade purposefully destined to fail," he said. And indeed by the time the subcommittee had finished tinkering with it they had created bizarre legislation that would have designated the forest as a "wilderness area" and would have required New York and New Jersey to block off two major roadways, tear down power lines and buildings, and ban vehicles. "Oh my God, that's so funny," said a staffer for California representative Richard Pombo. "We threaten to do stuff like that all the time. But then we back off, because it becomes very rude and very offensive."[31]

In early May 1996 the Senate did pass its major omnibus parks bill, but missing entirely were two key and controversial provisions: one that would have sacrificed Utah wilderness to private commercial development; the other, the Sterling Forest funding provision.[32]

BACK TO THE NEGOTIATING TABLE

Even before the DEC "issues conference" adjourned in the summer of 1995, purchase negotiations with the Sterling Forest Corporation started up again. JoAnn Dolan suspects that negotiation had again become possible in part because the environmental community had so thoroughly and effectively criticized the company's environmental impact statement that the corporation saw that it was going to encounter significant opposition to its development and was not going to find it easy to obtain the permits it needed. "Of course, I can't prove this, but I think that given the overwhelming response from communities, plus the scientific facts, that developers were not jumping at the door. I think the Sterling Forest Corporation did talk to some developers who did back out, who saw that for whatever reason Sterling Forest wasn't something to get into.

"I would imagine that the [environmental impact statement] also provided a lot of backup for the state to see it was a worthy project to pursue: it provided the state with an extraordinarily credible project from a scientific—from every—point of view. The public hearings gave the state the political backup for us to say to Governor Pataki, 'You give us a state park, and people are going to love you. People don't want this development, they don't see this as an economic boon, they see this as a small disaster economically. If you let this get developed you're going to have some very angry constituents.' And so the public response to the [environmental review] gave a political platform for Pataki to move on.

"So what probably happened was that after the environmental review was done, the state was knocking on the door to talk with the developers, and the corporation was always out there for the right price."[33]

By 1995, the Sterling Forest Corporation had yet another owner, the Swiss-based Zurich Insurance, and Zurich seemed agreeable to the negotiation of the price, terms, and conditions for a sale. Real estate in the outer suburbs remained in a slump and at least one source was quoted as understanding that the forest's owners wanted a quick cash sale.

At the end of 1995 and in the early weeks of 1996, a new round of serious negotiations quietly got under way between the Sterling Forest Corporation and two of the conservation groups authorized to make deals—the Open Space Institute (OSI), which protects public land in New York, and the Trust for Public Land (TPL), a national group that buys environmentally sensitive land or holds it until a government agency can acquire it.

The PIPC's Bob Binnewies has a clear recollection of how OSI and TPL emerged as the negotiators on behalf of the forest:

> At one of the early P.P.P. meetings, I sought out Rose Harvey and asked her whether the Trust for Public Land would be willing to join with The Nature Conservancy, Open Space Institute, and Scenic Hudson to form a private-sector negotiating team that would work with New York and New Jersey to hammer out a purchase price for Sterling Forest. Harvey said yes, but ground under the negotiating team concept shifted when Heimbach made known to Bernadette Castro that any purchase discussions must be draped in strictest confidentiality, and that the PIPC, in particular, was not welcome at the table. Ms. Castro thereupon turned exclusively to the Trust for Public Land (TPL)'s Harvey and the Open Space Institute (OSI)'s [Kim] Elliman to negotiate with Heimbach, sending them off for the next several months on a behind-closed-doors odyssey about which those left on the outside could only speculate. Harvey and Elliman recruited Steve Horowitz, a talented attorney with the law firm Cleary, Gottlieb, Steen & Hamilton, to provide what proved to be thousands of dollars of donated pro-bono counsel for the team. . . . "Grinding" was the best word to describe the process . . . the shades were drawn. Harvey and Elliman stopped attending PPP meetings.[34]

Not surprisingly, recalls Binnewies, "the rumor was out that Heimbach was a very tough and adept negotiator. Heimbach was being paid to defend corporate interests to the hilt, and he was not about to give away anything."[35]

SALES CONTRACT FOR 90 PERCENT OF THE FOREST

In mid-May 1996, following nine months of secret negotiations, the governors of New York and New Jersey announced agreement on a purchase price, and in June Sterling Forest Corporation signed a letter of intent indicating its willingness to sell. The deal brokered by the Trust for Public Land and the Open Space Institute was for 90 percent of the forest—some 15,280 acres—for $55 million. The area to be purchased included all the land visible from the Appalachian Trail, all the land important to the New Jersey watershed, and all the land considered critical to wildlife habitat. The land would be administered by the Palisades Interstate Park Commission.

A sales contract was set to follow. The deal required a down payment of $5 million from private sources within three months—not a problem to the environmental community since $5 million had come through the Scenic Hudson Land Trust and the Open Space Institute in 1995, each contributing $2.5 million of their funding from the Lila Acheson and DeWitt Wallace Fund for the Hudson Highlands, established by the founders of the Reader's Digest Association. The new contract gave the buyers two years to get the full financing. Interest was to be paid in the second year if the contract had not been executed. Legislation needed to be passed in the next New York State legislature to arrange for payments taxes to the towns of Warwick and Monroe; Tuxedo already received such taxes for land in the PIPC system. Assuming $17.5 million would come from the federal government, and $10 million each from New York and New Jersey, $12.5 million was needed from private sources, local governments, or, perhaps, additional money from the states.

Sterling Forest Corporation's chairman Louis Heimbach said, "We are very very pleased to be a part of this. We always said we were a willing seller under fair terms and at a fair price. . . . it was the right thing to do and we are good corporate citizens."[36] The 2,220 acres that would remain in the corporation's hands, at least for the present, included the ski resort and convention center. Louis Heimbach said the remaining 2,220 acres would be subject to a new series of negotiations after the contract was signed.

Some environmentalists welcomed the agreement. Rob Pirani of the Regional Plan Association said the deal turned the metropolitan area's largest privately owned tract into the key parcel of a bi-state greenway. Observed Pirani, "Sterling Forest is the jewel of the New York–New Jersey Highlands. It's the cornerstone of creating what we hope will be contiguous open space from the Delaware River to the Connecticut border."[37] Rose Harvey of the Trust for Public Land, one of the negotiators, justified the partial purchase by saying, "we asked ourselves, do we walk away if we cannot save every last acre, or do we reach a compromise that achieves most of our environmental goals? We got the best protection we could, given the money available to us."

Many, though, remained distinctly uneasy about the fate of the remaining land and the details of the agreement, which were still largely unknown. Rockland County environmentalist Geoffrey Welch said, "I would be completely overjoyed instead of just joyed [sic] if they had bought the entire parcel."[38] Even the *Middletown Times Herald-Record* worried:

> This small parcel of land [the acreage not under contract] prompts the most questions in this big deal. Sterling Forest Corp. had proposed building . . . 13,000 housing units, schools and related commercial development. . . . That is not possible under the announced deal, which is a big relief. Orange County does not need a new city. But the corporation still has plans for 3,000 units of housing on the 2,000 acres, along with considerable commercial development. . . . The best solution would still be for 100 percent of the forest to be preserved . . . let not the 10 percent get overlooked in the current euphoria.[39]

As more information leaked out, forest advocates grew increasingly unhappy. Wrote environmentalist Jürgen Wekerle, "The Devil is in the details and much of the details of the compromise deal are still in flux or are unknown. We remain committed to the preservation of all 17,500 acres, which can best be accomplished by total public acquisition. To that end we remain committed to lobbying for public monies to provide necessary funding."

The ink had hardly dried on the purchase agreement before the Sterling Forest Corporation was already planning the development of the lands that would remain after the purchase. As environmentalists had warned, Sterling Forest Corporation was intending to use the public purchase dollars to fund a substantial development project on the lands it had held back. Louis Heimbach wrote to the town of Tuxedo proposing to develop and reminding the town that it intended to benefit from the "transfer of development rights" that the sales contract had stipulated: "We propose to develop on some portion of the other 2,000 acres we have agreed to limit our development proposal to a maximum of one dwelling unit per acre, or a maximum of 3,000 units." The corporation asserted that since its project was now smaller, it would not have to start anew with a completely new environmental impact statement: "the pending SEQR proceedings will, of course, continue."[40]

BACK TO THE WASHINGTON MELEE

As of May 1996, though, it was unclear that Gingrich would be able to deliver the western Republicans, given their insistence on opening up Utah wilderness to development.[41] Ironically, the popularity of the idea of funding the Sterling Forest acquisition was partly what was defeating the actual legislation: Congress kept trying to tie the idea of Sterling funding to other, less popular programs. And as each of these in turn got shot down, so did the Sterling Forest funding. And, of course, there were those diehard anti-environment Republicans:

> A bill authorizing Federal money to help acquire the forest from developers remains blocked in the House by some western Republicans, who are holding it hostage until they gain support of their own anti-environmental agenda to raid public lands in the West. . . . Despite the hopes of some Republicans to lure voters concerned about the environment, the party is clearly split over these issues. Mr. Gingrich's pledge on Sterling Forest has received nominal backing from Representatives Don Young of Alaska and James V. Hansen of Utah, Republicans who play powerful roles on issues affecting the Interior Department. But they are holding up the possibility of quick action by making unrelated demands. Joining with other western Republicans, they are angry that Republicans from the Northeast, particularly New Jersey, have not supported their efforts to curb the Endangered Species Act and use environmentally sensitive public lands for mining, logging, grazing and other activities. . . . Both Mr. Gingrich and Senator Bob Dole are talking a lot about how much they want to protect the environment. Sterling Forest offers an excellent chance for them to put their principles into practice.[42]

As if to remind eastern legislators that the westerners still had the upper hand, Hansen said western congressmen now intended to link Sterling Forest to another anti-environment bill: this one would give ranchers greater grazing rights on publicly owned lands, a proposal widely opposed by environmentalists nationwide.[43]

Despite the lack of authorizing legislation, the legislators writing the next federal budget, likely impressed by the newly signed purchase agreement, thought 1996 would be the year in which Congress would provide an actual monetary appropriation for Sterling Forest: In early June, the House Appropriations Interior Subcommittee inserted $9 million in the Park Service budget for fiscal 1997 to help fund the purchase of the forest, the money to come from the Land and Water Conservation Fund once Congress passed authorizing legislation. And the lawmakers agreed to request an additional $8.5 million in the following year's budget. Subcommittee chairman Ralph Regula, a Republican from Ohio, said Sterling Forest was a very high priority: "We're very concerned about having clean, safe drinking water. We have to preserve the sources of this water and Sterling Forest is a crucial watershed." And although the National Park Service, the designated funding source, had only $100 million to spend on forty proposed projects, the House Appropriations Committee decided that Sterling Forest would be a top funding priority.[44] The House's new support for the appropriation suggested that the anti-funding contingent might be softening its stand.[45]

The other prong of the federal approval, the contentious authorization bill, remained stuck until mid-summer. On July 26, as the August recess beckoned, lawmakers working on the authorization in the House struck a new deal, linking federal funding for Sterling Forest to a measure called the "Snowbasin land exchange." The new bill, HR 3907, would authorize the federal government to give 1,320 acres of Utah public land to the private owner of the Snowbasin resort, acreage needed for the 2002 Winter Olympics in Salt Lake City; in exchange, the owner would give 4,100 acres of nearby private land to the U.S. Forest Service.[46] Representative Hansen called the deal a "very good piece of legislation. . . . I think they should have Sterling Forest."

Predictably, environmentalists in Utah were distraught; Lawson LeGate, southwest regional representative for the Sierra Club, said supporters of the Snowbasin provision were using the Olympics as an excuse to develop pristine mountain forest land. "This land-exchange proposal is designed to give a wealthy developer, who is also a big Republican contributor, a prime piece of alpine land that should stay in public ownership," he said. But Representative Torricelli reminded environmental advocates, "In this Congress, this is the best deal we're going to get." Legislators expected a vote on the bill before the August recess.

The looming election was putting pressure on the House as nothing else could: There was a growing fear that the Republicans would be blamed if the federal contribution for Sterling Forest failed to materialize.[47] By voice vote on July 30, 1996, the House passed HR 3907, which contained authorization for Sterling Forest funding and the Snowbasin land swap.

The bill also contained a provision, added at the last minute by Alaska's Don Young, that required the federal government to buy back a mineral lease from native Alaskans. Maurice Hinchey said, "To purists like me, it's unfortunate that they had to attach things to it . . . the committee chairman couldn't resist the temptation to tack on things that are a lot less clearly in the public interest."[48] A spokesman for the Interior Department wasn't sure the president would sign the bill because, he said, Clinton wanted a clean Sterling Forest bill, one without the Utah and Alaska land bills attached. But, said Interior, "time is running out to preserve Sterling Forest and we're very much aware of that. Every day it's not preserved it gets a little bit closer to being lost."[49]

As the *New York Times* noted, HR 3907 was a relatively clean Sterling Forest bill not too heavily encumbered with harmful precedents for national environmental policy. Moderate Republicans including Marge Roukema helped keep Speaker Gingrich focused on the issue. In the end, reported the *Times*, "it was the Speaker who stood up to the Western Republicans holding Sterling Forest hostage to their pet projects."[50]

TIME IS RUNNING OUT

Something new and positive was in the congressional air, but the problem was that after Labor Day, Congress would only be in session for about three weeks before adjourning for the 1996 campaign trail, and something still had to come out of the Senate. Activists shifted into overdrive to convince the Senate to get legislation passed. Because the bill passed by the Senate in April 1995 did not include the Utah or Alaska provisions, the Senate needed to take up the new House version, either to reconcile its earlier bill with the new House version or to pass the House bill itself.

New Jersey's Senator Bradley became the Snowbasin bill's chief sponsor in the Senate but a handful of senators put holds on it, trying to use Sterling Forest as a bargaining chip to prompt action on their own favorite land-deal legislative demands. The *Bergen Record* reported that "Supporters fear the demands, if met, would prompt still others to demand their legislation be added, eventually weighing down the bill until it sinks. More than 50 land bills are caught in House-Senate gridlock, and the time available to pass them is running out."[51] A Washington-based Congress watcher was frustrated and gloomy. "Getting it through now in its current form is unlikely. If there had been a quick resolution of the holds, this would have moved. But the clock has ticked down too far."[52] Some were worried that animosity toward Senator Bill Bradley and his committee's holds could derail the measure. "You remember what Bradley did?" asked a spokesman for Senator Frank Murkowski. "Now he wants this? He can get in line."[53]

With the Snowbasin bill on hold in the Senate, environmentalists worked feverishly to keep up pressure on Congress. The strategy was to ask for both of the viable bills authorizing funds for Sterling Forest: HR 3907, passed in the House but stalled by Senate holds, and the bill passed by the Senate the year before, called S 719 in the Senate but still awaiting action in the House as "HR-400 as amended." The latter, if passed by the House, would not need to return to the Senate but could go directly to the president for his signature. Kathy DeCoster of the Trust for Public Land's Washington office put together a list of groups who would contact members of the New York and New Jersey congressional delegation during the August break. Contact every senator, supporters were told; they are key to getting holds removed in the Senate. Contact House members to press speaker Gingrich to make good on his promise of protecting Sterling Forest. Contact the governors of New York and New Jersey. Contact congressional leadership. Just get them to pass anything that authorizes Sterling Forest! DeCoster's message was:

> We should not choose one legislative vehicle over another since we cannot control the House and Senate floor schedules. The message: The question of which bill passes is not important; the important thing is to see that Sterling Forest funding is authorized. It is up to the NY/NJ delegations and the Congressional leadership to find a way to do this. . . . Time is running out and the funding level hangs in the balance with very little of a positive nature to show the appropriators yet. . . . It is expected that the Interior Appropriations bill will be among the first items considered on the Senate floor in September with a House-Senate conference occurring soon thereafter. Therefore resolution of the funding authorization will likely occur in mid-September 1996.[54]

When Congress returned after Labor Day, the bill HR 3907, weighted down by senators of both parties who wanted to add their own projects, seemed destined to sink. Of necessity, therefore, attention shifted to yet other options not nearly as straightforward. The first was the previous year's bill, HR 400: House Speaker Gingrich could bring it to a floor vote under a procedure in which it could not be amended. The *Bergen Record* commented, "Mr. Gingrich pledged earlier this year that Congress would come up with the money to save Sterling Forest. With the speaker's tremendous clout, the measure would stand a solid chance of getting enough votes to pass."[55]

There was yet another long shot: a larger, omnibus parks authorization bill that would contain a variety of bipartisan, noncontroversial provisions. Bob Binnewies recalls, "Senators were exercising all sorts of parliamentary privileges, slowing legislation, blocking legislation, speeding legislation, ignoring legislation, hooking on amendments to the most popular bills. Somewhere in this flux, surfacing from time to time was the omnibus package."[56] "If [the omnibus bill] happens, then Sterling Forest would be out of the woods. But that's an enormous long shot at best, and so much hangs in the balance," lamented the *Bergen Record*.[57]

The omnibus parks bill soon stopped looking like a good bet, when, as in the final frantic days of the 104th Congress, legislators began littering it with anti-environmental measures. The Sterling Forest provision and a few other good ideas, said the *Rockland Journal-News*, risked "being used as bookends to hold up more questionable ones."[58]

Still, by September 25, both House and Senate leaders announced their agreement on an omnibus parks bill package to preserve more than 100 natural areas. Congress deleted some of the worst anti-environmental provisions, such as grazing on public lands and development in Utah wilderness areas. President Clinton sent a letter to Gingrich and Senate Majority Leader Trent Lott, warning that he would veto any version that included clearcutting in the Tongass National Forest in Alaska, allowing companies to sponsor national parks, or allowing oil development on Alaska's North Slope. Alaska's Senator Frank Murkowski refused to take out the parts the administration found objectionable. Sterling Forest was now caught in a tug-of-war between Clinton and Murkowski.

On September 28, after intense and bitter negotiations, the House passed, 404–4, a nationwide omnibus parks legislation that included the Sterling Forest funding authorization and lacked the provisions objectionable to the White House. The compromises included two provisions the administration didn't like but that everyone expected would not warrant a veto: one would exempt some Florida beachfront properties from a coastal barrier islands protection program, and the other was the Utah Snowbasin swap.

In addition, on that same highly charged day, the House also passed a budget bill that included the $9 million appropriation for the Sterling Forest purchase.[59] Anxious to hit the campaign trail, House members left for home, leaving the Senate still in session. On the last day of September, the Senate also signed off on a budget that included an actual appropriation of $9 million for Sterling Forest and $8.5 million awaiting appropriation in the 1998 budget—if indeed that august body would actually pass its authorization.

However, the authorization legislation for the weighty omnibus parks bill that had been passed by the House remained stuck in the Senate. It had come down to a single hold, that of Alaskan Republican Murkowski, who refused to relax his grip on the broad package. Now Murkowski was seeking to get the administration to go along with his own bill for extending timber sales to the Ketchikan Pulp Company for fifteen years. For decades the company had been turning timber from the Tongass National Forest into pulp. The contract was to otherwise run out in 2004 and the company said it would close the pulp mill unless the timber contract was extended. Because the omnibus parks bill affected parks and public lands nationwide, held hostage along with Sterling Forest were the San Francisco Presidio, a tallgrass prairie preserve in Kansas and the Craters of the Moon Park in Idaho, as well as dozens of other parks, trails, and historic battlefields. "We don't know if we're going to be able to get it done, or how, or when," said Majority Leader Trent Lott, "but we're going to keep trying."[60]

Facing Murkowski's stubborn refusal to drop his hold, Senator Bradley intervened one more time, brokering a deal in which the administration agreed to allow the Ketchikan Pulp Company to log for two more years after closing its mill. With Murkowski sufficiently satisfied, the Senate passed the omnibus parks bill authorization by voice vote on October 3, literally in the session's last hour. It was the Senate's final act before adjourning, and it was Senator Bill Bradley's last deal and his last vote on his last day in the Senate. "This non-controversial bill . . . got caught up in controversies involving other lands bills," said Bradley. "But in the end, common sense prevailed." "The price of new parks," said the *Times*, "is two more years of logging in a national forest."[61]

"Congress couldn't have gone out on a brighter note," said Alan Front, a vice president for the Trust for Public Land. "We are gratified beyond words that Congress has formally and finally recognized the national importance of Sterling Forest." And Sterling Forest Corporation's Louis Heimbach said, "Obviously we're very happy."[62]

The laudatory reviews came thick and fast. New York's Governor Pataki said the acquisition would be "one of the state's most significant conservation achievements of this decade—and will be the largest single land purchase for state park use in our history." Representative Hinchey said, "Protecting Sterling Forest has been a bipartisan, community-wide effort to ensure the survival of a naturally beautiful area in the midst of one of the most densely populated areas in the world."[63] Hinchey also praised Bradley for doing "an absolutely fantastic job. He inserted himself personally, holding hands with some people who had been personally unpleasant to him. He was able to put that aside."[64] The *New York Times* saw Bradley and Gingrich as the heroes in the end-of-session dealmaking. "Mr. Gingrich . . . persuaded his colleagues to strip the bill of several items certain to invite a Presidential veto. . . . Mr. Bradley brokered an agreement that the bill would go forward in exchange for [the Alaskan logging agreement] . . . that will give Mr. Murkowski a little something to show his logging constituents back home." The *Bergen Record* identified dozens of people who deserved credit, including New Jersey Governor Whitman, who pledged $10 million at a time when "support was thin," and especially New Jersey's legislators Torricelli, Bradley, Lautenberg, Roukema, and Martini, all of whom helped

get Gingrich to make good on his promises. And the *Bergen Record* concluded
that it was once again fashionable to be an environmentalist and predicted that
the environment would emerge as an important election issue in the wake of a
two-year Republican campaign to roll back major environmental protections.[65]
The *Rockland Journal-News* said, "Gingrich's involvement, which included arm-
twisting western leaders not so environmentally conscious, is testimony to the
first real Republican push for the environment since Teddy Roosevelt led the
way for this nation in such matters at the turn of the century."[66]

President Clinton signed the Omnibus Parks and Public Lands Management Act of 1996 in an Oval Office ceremony on November 12. The signing of
the bill started the Sterling sale contract clock ticking: there were only twenty-
four months to come up with the rest of the $55 million. Now that $9 million
had been appropriated in the federal budget, the forest's supporters intended to
see that the remaining $8.5 million was included in the next year's federal bud-
get. Because spending of the entire $17.5 had been authorized, no one expected
much opposition to the additional appropriation. Another hopeful portent was
passage of the New York State Clean Water-Clean Air Bond Act in that November's election, which allocated $100 million for land acquisition. The federal
funding, along with funds from New York, would trigger the availability of $10
million from New Jersey. With that and the $5 million from the Wallace Fund,
$42.5 million would be available. At the end of 1996, preservationists anticipated
they still had $12.5 million to raise.

CHAPTER NINE

The Open Space Movement
Saves a Highlands Jewel

AS JANUARY 1997 OPENED, President Clinton began his FY 98 budget, which included an appropriation of $8.5 million toward acquisition of Sterling Forest; the president's early and clear commitment served as a significant boost to the funding cause. Marge Roukema, House representative from Ridgewood, New Jersey, said Sterling had become a symbol of a renewed environmental consciousness in Congress and she thought that despite cuts needed to balance the budget there was "good reason to believe that this will have strong bipartisan support again this year."[1] And indeed, in March, when New York and New Jersey officials visited the House Interior Appropriations subcommittee to reiterate the need for the additional funding, they got what New York parks commissioner Bernadette Castro said was a "warm and fuzzy" response. "It is supported by the speaker," said subcommittee member Charles Taylor; "he has indicated he would like it considered for a very high priority."[2]

On February 18, 1997, the Open Space Institute and the Trust for Public Land formally signed the purchase agreement to buy Sterling Forest. The Sterling Forest Corporation's normally controlled CEO Louis Heimbach was uncharacteristically exuberant, "The rubber hit the road this afternoon," he exulted.

Although the contract called for a closing within two years, the conservation groups said they hoped to take title within a year, because 7.5 percent interest on any outstanding payments would be imposed starting the second year. The $5-million down payment promised by the Lila Acheson and DeWitt Wallace Fund for the Hudson Highlands came through in early March 1997. Also in March, the New Jersey legislature voted to forward the $10 million it had committed for the purchase to the Palisades Interstate Park Commission and, within weeks, Governor Whitman signed the legislation. It was an historic event: New Jersey's governor signing over funds to buy land in New York. The Palisades Commission agreed to put the money in an interest-bearing account, which after a year would provide an additional half-million dollars. And also in March, New York's Governor Pataki announced the first allocations from the $1.8 billion Clean Water/Clean Air Bond Act voters had passed in 1996; at the request of the contract negotiators, Pataki provided an additional $6 million toward the purchase of Sterling Forest, making New York's total contribution not $10 million, but a welcome $16 million.[3]

The government largess signaled the need for intensive fundraising in the private sector, but $6.5 million was not an insignificant hurdle. Donations of $5 to $10,000 were coming from individuals, hiking clubs, preservation groups, and businesses. Over the 1997 summer, four young cyclists pedaled the 3,600 miles from Seattle to Bear Mountain, completing their trek on August 6 and delivering $5,000 in pledges. One school in New Jersey raised $158, another, $1,035. In mid-August, the New Jersey-based Victoria Foundation, which funds open space and other environmental projects in that state, donated $1 million.

The Interior Department's overall budget request, including the $8.5 million Sterling Forest allocation, went to the House and Senate on October 1 and was approved by both houses of Congress on October 28.[4] For a short while a presidential veto seemed possible: The administration was worried the Interior budget contained other items that would prevent the Forest Service from carrying out its land management plan in the Northwest. But Clinton did sign the spending bill on November 14, thus providing a quiet but happy finale to the long and tortured history of federal funding for Sterling Forest.

Through the fall, as the one-year purchase deadline approached, the conservation community remained $5 million short, but on December 9 the Doris Duke Charitable Foundation announced that it would donate just that sum. The Duke grant came from a foundation created after an intense, four-year battle over the $1.5 billion estate of the "reclusive and eccentric" tobacco heiress, settled in 1996. "Great day!" exclaimed Bob Binnewies, "it's like climbing a mountain and suddenly we got to a pass."[5] "There was a lot of nailbiting," said Christopher J. Elliman, president of the Open Space Institute. "There's enormous relief and gratitude. It is a fitting and remarkable end to what has been a remarkable story."[6]

CONTRACT COMPROMISES MAR THE DEAL

The details of the purchase contract remained undisclosed. Sterling Forest Partnership's John Gebhards said, "Although we don't know all of the details of the contract, in principle we support this purchase and we thank TPL and OSI for their many hours of hard work to reach this agreement."

For the first few months of 1997, environmentalists remained on edge about an arrangement that kept from the public the details of a contract that involved more than $43 million of public money. Starting in the spring of 1997, they began to learn more about the contract details, and what they discovered then and later they found profoundly unsettling. First, the contract would allow the corporation to log the forest extensively until the entire transaction was complete. Much more disturbing, the corporation had been able to retain limited water rights to Blue Lake and Sterling Lake in the forest, with the total use of two million gallons per day, for future development or for sale to outside developers and utilities. That meant it would have the water needed to build thousands of housing units and millions of square feet of commercial space on the 2,220 acres it had not yet agreed to sell.[7] That Sterling Lake water remained in the hands of the corporation was in the opinion of RPA's Rob Pirani the worst concession. "Sterling Lake is a recreational jewel that could have been a swimming lake," he said. "Not enough people pushed for retention of the lake."[8]

To comply with the contract stipulation that there be no net transfer of water out of the Wanaque Reservoir watershed, for every gallon of fresh drinking water the corporation withdrew from Sterling Lake, it would be required to pump a gallon of sewage effluent into the south-flowing Ringwood Creek, which feeds the Wanaque. The corporation also retained the right to discharge sewage effluent eastward into the Ramapo River, just upriver of the people in Rockland County and New Jersey who drank Ramapo water. The complexity of allowed water export-import purchases and sales muddied the picture of how these watershed stipulations could be honored.

The deal also allowed the corporation enhanced density rights, so it could build 1,000 additional housing units on the tract it had not sold.[9]

These revelations about the contract buttressed the fears expressed by environmentalists years before that a partial purchase would give the corporation too much money and the public too little benefit. Now it seemed as if the contract negotiators on the land preservation side had not been able to match the hard-nosed corporate negotiation team. And, too, the push to make a deal happen had put OSI/TPL negotiators under a lot of pressure to come through with something tangible, even if the contract was not perfect.

The contract also made glaringly clear the effect of transferring public money to the corporation: it would enable it to fund development. Congressman Hinchey understood all too well that the contract failed to protect the forest: "I go to bed at night worrying that we have helped capitalize the very development we did not want built in the first place," he said. Michael Edelstein, the shrewd leader of Orange Environment, assessed it this way:

> Playing smart poker with a mixed hand, Heimbach sold off the least buildable lands that would not have been permitted for development anyway, while retaining 2,000 acres of prime land and earning $55 million with which to develop it. . . . Development there would likely be of high density and cause most of the growth-related problems of the original proposal.[10]

New Jersey had special reason to be worried: The Garden State had been a major player in the Sterling Forest purchase out of concern for its water supply. Now it appeared the public dollars would be encouraging development whose wastewaters would be flowing into both northern New Jersey drinking water sources, the Wanaque-Monksville Reservoir watershed and the Ramapo River.[11]

Disclosure of the Sterling Forest contract details greatly unnerved New Jersey representative Marge Roukema: "We were told the development would not affect the Ramapo," she worried. "We got approval from the environmentalists." In an action some interpreted as a sign of New Jersey's discomfiture, Governor Christine Whitman of New Jersey temporarily withheld payment of the $10 million it had pledged toward acquisition of Sterling Forest.[12]

Out among the grassroots, fear was widespread that Sterling Forest State Park was being fatally compromised even before the public got to see it.

NEW YORK AND NEW JERSEY GET THEIR NEW PARK

On August 14, 1997, the $5 million down payment provided by the Lila Acheson and DeWitt Wallace Fund for the Hudson Highlands was signed over to the Sterling Forest Corporation and, as per contract provisions, in exchange the Palisades Interstate Park Commission received the first Sterling Forest parcel, 1,400 acres in the northern section of the forest.[13]

On February 5, 1998, the Open Space Institute and Trust for Public Land closed on the next tract of 12,880 acres and on February 12 the governors of New Jersey and New York, along with representatives of leading environmental and open space groups, held a press conference in historic Bear Mountain Inn in Bear Mountain State Park to celebrate the occasion. Facing the inn's massive stone fireplace and with the Hudson as backdrop, Rose Harvey, senior vice president and regional director of the Trust for Public Land and a key contract negotiator, remarked,

> This is the first regional park purchased since World War II and this was the best public-private partnership ever gathered in this country.... Protection of Sterling Forest is . . . a beginning. It's a model of land protection efforts we can and must replicate in the future. We see Sterling Forest as the keystone of a future New York-New Jersey greenbelt that will cross municipal, regional and state boundaries, and create a wild preserve at the edge of the nation's largest metropolis.

New Jersey Governor Whitman said, "Saving open space is the right environmental choice, the smart economic policy and one of the best things we can do for families." New York's Governor Pataki remarked, "This is not a closing but an opening to acquire other parcels that are sensitive. This is just a very important beginning. It's a great day. There will be more such great days." He emphasized his commitment to the purchase of open space and indicated his continuing interest in negotiating with the Sterling Forest Corporation for the remainder of the forest.

With public acquisition of the Sterling Forest acreage, its management was turned over to the Palisades Interstate Park Commission. A draft interim management guide was to be the basis of management policy until the commission could develop a master plan. The emphasis was on continuing traditional low-impact uses of Sterling Forest: hunting was to be allowed (but not in the portion designated as the 1,500-acre Doris Duke Wildlife sanctuary in the northern portion of the forest and not along the Appalachian Trail corridor). Fishing and hiking were permissible; biking, camping, and ATVs were not.

In the late 1990s, a team of scientists from the New York State Museum set to work to catalog the biological diversity of the forest. With the hills in private ownership and with some areas not much disturbed for most of the century, many habitats had reestablished themselves. The forest has a mix of species, from both southern and northern domains of the Appalachians. The researchers identified some 1,100 plant species in the park—almost two-thirds of all the known plants in the Hudson Highlands. Of these, twenty-six are on New York state's endangered or threatened lists. Ongoing work indicated that the new park was at the heart of the most species-rich area of amphibians and reptiles in the entire state, with forty-one species and in particular nearly a quarter of the state's timber rattlesnake dens.

THE CORPORATION STILL BANKS ON A PIECE OF THE ROCK

As transfer of the first large tract neared completion, the corporation continued to negotiate with the conservation community over the next 2,220 acres.
Louis Heimbach warned that whoever bought the remaining Sterling property
would have to pay considerably more than the $3,600 per acre that formed

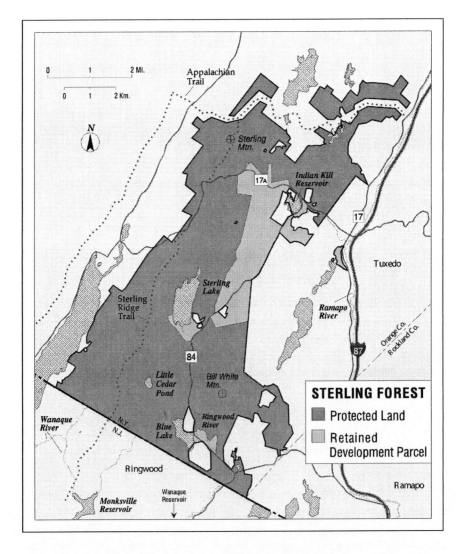

FIGURE 5. *Sterling Forest protected land and retained development parcel circa 1998. Courtesy
of the Grant F. Walton Center for Remote Sensing & Spatial Analysis, Rutgers University.*

the basis of the 1997 deal. Throughout 1997, the corporation declined to accept negotiators' offers as high as $25 million, or more than $11,000 per acre, for the smaller parcel. And although the corporation meanwhile continued to assert that it was willing to sell those acres, at the same time it was pursuing a major new land-development plan, with the assistance of Sasaki Associates of Boston, to build thousands of residential units and several million square feet of commercial and light industrial space.[14] As before, the corporation planned its greatest density of development in the headwaters of both the Ramapo and Wanaque watersheds, the most environmentally vulnerable area within the watershed. Long-time activist Mary Yrizarry said, "[Heimbach] is playing hardball. He sold the main part of the forest and saved the soul for himself."[15]

In April 1998, the developer presented a new project plan to the Town of Tuxedo. Every household in the town received its full-color 14-page brochure describing 1,344 homes, 300 units of assisted senior living, two golf courses, and half a million square feet of commercial development, all on a 1,500-acre strip along County Rte 84. Its large number of senior housing units was no act of altruism: federal Housing and Urban Development money was now subsidizing senior housing.[16]

The Sterling Forest Corporation said it planned to apply for a Planned Integrated Development (PID) zoning approval. The PID zone uses a system of density credits to give developers points for providing open space, senior housing, and other desirable concessions. The Town of Tuxedo, struggling to update its regulations governing large development proposals, slapped a moratorium on PID applications.[17] The town's new PID law passed in late December and in the new framework the corporation's development would be only minimally limited, to about 1,600 units. The corporation was to come before the town board in February 1999 with a revised plan.

Not coincidentally, during those same momentous months of 1998, the controversial Thruway exit at Tuxedo, which had figured so prominently in the Sterling Forest controversy and had been presumed dead years before, arose once more from the ashes. Only six weeks after the partial purchase of Sterling Forest had been completed, Rockland County's State Senator Joseph Holland announced that he was trying to convince Governor Pataki to allocate $500,000 for a study to evaluate anew the feasibility of such an exit. Holland was thinking ahead to 1999, expecting to ask for $10 million to actually start building the interchange. The senator complained, "I'm running into problems here in Albany. The governor isn't crazy about it and I don't know why. We're trying to convince the governor throughout the budget process. We just spent for Sterling Forest park land. This would allow people to get into it."[18] But Governor Pataki vetoed a budget item that allocated $250,000 for the Thruway exit study.

In 2001, however, the Thruway Authority granted $250,000 for a new interchange feasibility study. As mentioned earlier, law governing the authority requires construction, operation, and maintenance costs to be recovered from tolls, so the feasibility study's conclusion—that an exit was feasible but would not be self-supporting—would seem to have halted the proposal yet again.

Relieved at Pataki's veto and the more recent unpromising study results, environmentalists nevertheless remained wary that the road interchange might still reappear: The Thruway exit at Tuxedo was by design essentially an engine to induce growth and, even with a big part of Sterling Forest protected, it would still be such an engine, greatly increasing traffic to the Highlands on the western flank of the Ramapo Valley, encouraging sprawl development in the Town of Warwick, and potentially fueling construction of a four-lane highway slicing through the forest.

In March 1999, the Sterling Forest Corporation came back to the Town of Tuxedo with yet another development proposal for the land it still owned. This time the corporation proposed fewer residential units than a year earlier but still envisioned two golf courses and nearly half a million square feet of commercial space, much of the development intended for areas bordering the new Sterling Forest State Park.

The formal filing of this application sparked a feverish renewed push for public acquisition, and a frustrating déjà vu effort. A new round of negotiation opened, with the corporation on one side of the table and the Palisades Interstate Park Commission and Open Space Institute, acting for New York State, on the other. Negotiators saw this as the last chance to save the remainder of the forest. Grassroots letter writing resumed. New Jersey activists sent petitions containing 7,000 signatures to the New York governor, and a thousand more came from alerted New Yorkers.

Behind-the-scenes negotiations went on through 1999. And on February 7, 2000, nearly two years to the day after the first large tract of the forest was saved, the state announced that a contract had been signed to purchase approximately 1,100 acres of the 2,220 acres still in the hands of the Sterling Forest Corporation. Also negotiated was a conservation easement on a 250-acre parcel that would remain in the corporation's ownership as a golf course. The state also took the occasion to announce its purchase of 659 acres from New York University (a transaction completed later in 2000) and 209 acres from a private landowner. All three tracts were to be added to Sterling Forest State Park.

To complete the 1,100-acre purchase from the corporation, New York committed to contributing $4 million of the $8 million purchase price, New Jersey promised $1 million, and the Clinton administration committed $2 million in Forest Legacy funds—a near-instantaneous election-year move that provoked

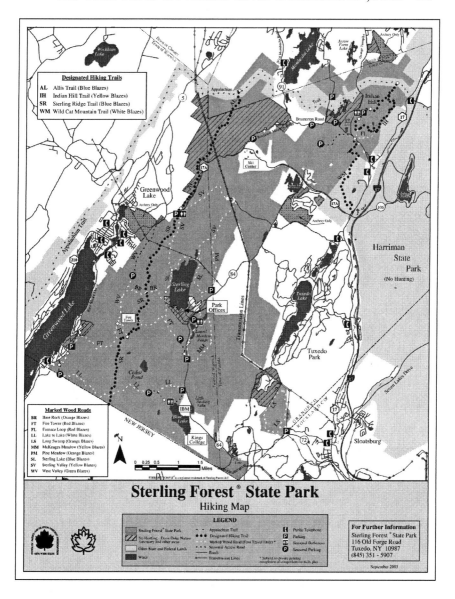

FIGURE 6. *Sterling Forest State Park hiking map (2003). Courtesy of the Palisades Inter-state Parks Commission.*

Table 1. Sterling Forest State Park Acquisitions

Parcel	Size (Acres)	Date Acquired	Cost	Seller	Buyer
Sterling Forest Corporation	1,400	August 1997		Sterling Forest Corporation	New York State, Sterling Forest State Park [Palisades Interstate Park (PIP) management]
Sterling Forest Corporation	12,880	February 1998	$55 million in 2 payments	Sterling Forest Corporation	New York State, Sterling Forest State Park (PIP)
Sterling Forest Corporation	1,000			Temporarily retained for credit for transfer of development rights	
Sterling Forest Corporation	500			Temporarily retained pending receipt of town building permits on its other land	
Sterling Forest Corporation	1,065 in two parcels	December 2000	$7,890,000	Sterling Forest Corporation	Open Space Institute/Trust for Public Land, conveyed to Sterling Forest State Park (PIP)
Sears Hunter	209	December 2000	$610,000	Private owner	Open Space Institute/Trust for Public Land, conveyed to Sterling Forest State Park (PIP)
New York University/ Eagle Mountain	659	December 2000	$860,000	NYU	Open Space Institute/Trust for Public Land, conveyed to Sterling Forest State Park (PIP)
Indian Hill	490	May 2002	2,250,000	Private owner	Scenic Hudson/Orange County Land Trust, conveyed to Sterling Forest State Park (PIP)
Arrow Park	144	May 2002	$750,000	Arrow Park	Scenic Hudson/Orange County Land Trust, conveyed to Sterling Forest State Park (PIP)
Totals	18,347				

Sterling Forest Area Lands Not In State Park

Parcel	Size (Acres)	Date Acquired	Cost	Seller	Buyer
Appalachian Trail lands	677				
Passaic County	2074			Acquired by eminent domain	Passaic County
Arrow Park	80	Spring 1996		Arrow Park	Held by Orange County Land Trust
Totals	2,831				

a round of joking both cynical and elated, since the struggle to obtain the first infusion of federal funds had lasted a decade. Negotiators set about finding a final $1 million to wrap up the deal, and by the end of the year 2000 the money was acquired.[19] The new tracts, together with an additional nearby 1,500 acres that the state had acquired in the intervening two years and an additional 600+ acres purchased with fines levied against local polluters, brought the Sterling Forest State Park to nearly 19,000 acres (see Table I), with additional protected parcels nearby.

Even with these major public additions, acquisition of the remaining Sterling Forest land remained a goal of forest protectors. The Sterling Forest Corporation, now greatly diminished, was still looking to make money from its remaining 571 acres. And it was still publicly proposing its now-standard formula—golf course, houses, commercial development—in order to either develop or ratchet up the purchase price as high as possible. The environmental community continued to characterize the corporation's development proposal as a "hole-in-the-park," since its high-intensity development would be virtually entirely surrounded by the new forested wild park. As of this writing, the fate of this remaining tract is still up in the air, the environmental review process is under way, public hearings have been held, and the Sterling Forest Partnership and individual activists have needed to raise tens of thousands of dollars to pay for experts to testify about the adverse environmental impacts of putting a development in the midst of an important but fragile ecological community.

CHAPTER TEN

A New Vision for Land Preservation

HOW PRESERVATION PREVAILED

THE STERLING FOREST CORPORATION WAS NOTABLE for its single minded twenty-five-year quest in search of the maximum return for its large forest tract. Former corporation chairman Bob Thomson recalls telling his boss Marshall Manley that there were only two potential ways to divest of the forest: government purchase or development. "But government had no money, so we had to act like a serious developer. That would give environmental groups the ammunition they needed to go to the government for money. I did publicly describe this as a two-track approach; or as Lou Heimbach repeatedly said, 'We'll exchange their green for our green.'"[1]

But in government, preservation of Sterling Forest was initially opposed by New York's Governor Cuomo and Representative Ben Gilman and by the Orange County power structure—all of whom bought into the prospect of more development on the suburban fringe. Moreover, political authority over the forest was so confused—spread as it was over five townships in three counties, several state agencies in two states, and with a water supply system in New Jersey depending heavily on privately owned land in New York—that changing the course of the collective ship of state became an overwhelming task.

Paul Dolan recounts a number of the key strategies that helped to slow down the momentum of the Sterling development. The condemnations—the Park Service's condemnation of the land tract near the Little Dam Lake, and New Jersey's condemnation of the 2,000-plus acres in Passaic County—brought development plans to a halt in two potentially highly profitable locations. Halting development of a new exit of the New York State Thruway—including New York's own state bureaucracy itself helping to sabotage the governor's intentions for an exit at Tuxedo—put another substantial obstacle in the way of development.

Dolan himself played a key role in getting a broad-based grassroots effort launched: a series of roundtable lunches of business leaders, legislators, and environmental leaders to bring together stakeholders in forest preservation, and open-house grassroots events such as the annual Sterling Forest Day.

The success of the grassroots effort initially was rooted in the canny strategizing of the Sterling Forest Coalition: the coalition hammered away at the corporation, preventing it from free access to the resources it most needed to do its development; water, of course, was key, followed in importance by the location of the Appalachian Trail, bisecting some of the most developable lands.

The coalition's successor, the Public-Private Partnership to Save Sterling Forest, was a model for how to approach a large project with complex requirements in the way of funding, public pressure, and political action: by bringing together high-level professionals, high-visibility community leaders, and prominent citizens with important political contacts. Overall, said Paul Dolan in 1999, "in classic social action the tendency of groups is to self-destruct. The Sterling Forest effort was one of the few I've ever seen where people kept relinquishing power. John Humbach of the Sterling Forest Coalition sensed when it was appropriate for the Public Private Partnership to come in. The Partnership in turn knew the role of the grassroots groups. It was a permeable wall. In part this is a credit to Bob Binnewies. . . . In a world of short-term goals and short focus, Sterling Forest was a 14-year battle—if you include Sterling One, a 25-year battle. Most foundations and government entities work on a two- to three-year cycle, and they fail. The lesson is: clear goals, and a long time horizon." [2]

Finally, public officials, first in New Jersey and eventually even in laggard New York, were swayed by the loud public chorus, the thousands of people who, even if they had never walked the Sterling Ridge Trail or seen the Atlantic white cedar swamp, expressed a powerful need to save the last large undeveloped tract in the metropolitan region. It was, as Paul Dolan observes, "a unique example of vision from the bottom up." The public clearly and viscerally understood the argument that saving Sterling Forest was the morally right thing. Sterling Forest was the last remaining significant tract of what had once been a vast forest defining the entire mid-Atlantic region. It was a thing of great public value; it was, as Representative Bob Torricelli had pointed out, an "irreplaceable regional asset" to the tens of millions of people living in one of the most densely populated areas in the country. News stories and editorials reinforced this message that preservation of the intact forest was the right thing to do. And politically this growing public will accounted for the emergence of strong bipartisan political support, as reflected in the dramatic about-face of Representative Ben Gilman.

Wrote James Ahearn of the *Bergen Record*, "Benjamin Gilman got the message. He got the message in phone calls and letters from constituents, in public hearings, in newspaper editorials, and in comments citizens made in drop-in visits to his mobile district office. Gilman went from favoring development to co-sponsoring federal legislation for preservation."[3] And the dramatic finale, the success in getting federal funding, was powerfully enhanced by the need for both Republicans and Democrats to reaffirm their environmental credentials in the 1996 election year.[4]

To those who reckon wilderness by the vast tracts of intact open space and wilderness in the western United States, the 20,000 acres of Sterling Forest may seem too few to have warranted such a tidal wave of public outcry and substantial commitment of public dollars. But those 20,000 acres are a vast wild treasure to the millions of inhabitants of the nation's most crowded metropolitan area. To many of these people, it is a matter of relief and rejoicing that after a quarter century of effort, this wilderness tract was preserved, one that might have been expensively engineered to support an entire small city but now remains, intact, a rock-strewn forest that is still sanctuary for bears, timber rattlers, and people.

THE FIGHT FOR OPEN SPACE CONTINUES

The birth of the region's great public parks coincided with the period in American history when interest in conservation of nature and scenery converged with concern for the public good, and when dramatic gestures of philanthropy were initiated by prominent citizens with broad social vision.[5] The early decades of the twentieth century were characterized by community leaders with a clear vision for the future, with natural landscapes integral to that vision and with considerable expenditures of both public and private money to ensure the survival of natural landscapes into the future. Historian Frances Dunwell asserts, "The importance of the Highlands is that they remind us there is an alternative—one that involves conscious choices and the willingness to tackle the laws and politics which lead us down a path we may not want to go."[6] In working to save Sterling Forest, and to preserve the Highlands beyond, environmentalists are attempting to return to the early twentieth-century vision that believed in strong action on behalf of the public good.

But ours is a much different time, with many fewer social visionaries spending money on the public good and much more public and private money going to support poor patterns of development. Now, despite the Sterling Forest victory, publicly funded new sewage capacity and new sewer plants are encouraging new developments in the open spaces in and around Sterling Forest, creating the continuing fear that the forest, rather than being an undisturbed link in a vast greenway, will become gradually more like a city park, an island greensward surrounded by a dense tangle of roads, roofs, and driveways.[7]

Although private development has no automatic right to publicly-funded subsidies and although development brings staggering school, services, and infrastructure bills to municipalities, it is public money, largely in the form of water, sewer, and road subsidies, that is moving development along at a considerable pace in southeastern Orange County. The impacts on the Wanaque watershed and the Ramapo water supply will surely be a public health concern for future generations.

Beyond Sterling Forest is the surrounding larger area still facing development, the roughly 75,000-acre Sterling Forest-Wanaque Watershed-Wyanokie Highlands area. And from an even broader perspective, the 2 million-acre Highlands, stretching from Reading, Pennsylvania, to Litchfield, Connecticut, with its ancient twisted bedrock, its rocky outcrops, its crowded ridges and deep forests, has an increasingly uncertain future as an intact bioregion. Whereas much of the southern Appalachians and the Green and White Mountain National Forests in New England have been protected, in the area closest to the New York megalopolitan corridor, some 80 percent of the Highlands, including hundreds of thousands of acres of high-value biodiversity and watershed lands, remains unprotected. Today, with much of the easy land in the metropolitan New York City region already developed, the rockbound Highlands are becoming fodder for subdividers in the bewildering and largely uncoordinated jurisdiction of about 130 counties, towns, cities, and villages in four states. Some Highlands municipalities have seen their populations grow by more than 20 percent in the decade 1990–2000. More than 5,000 acres a year are being lost, endangering the purity of the many reservoir systems located in the Highlands and the volume and quality of the water available from its aquifers—threatening, in short, the drinking water supply of more than 11 million people in four states.[8]

At the February 1998 Bear Mountain press conference, Wilma Frey, of the New Jersey Conservation Foundation, said, "The Highlands are threatened. . . . Our work to preserve it is far from complete. Unless we take strong action very soon the Highlands region from Pennsylvania to Connecticut will not survive."[9] The Highlands Coalition, formed in 1988 to protect this critically important region, has compiled a list of "critical treasures" of New York and New Jersey Highlands that identifies the tracts in most urgent need of protection (a total of some 50,000 acres) and estimates the cost of acquiring or otherwise protecting those lands: ($258 million) (see Table 2).

While citizens advocate for a future that preserves the Highlands regional resource, day by day tracts of woodland become suburban housing. The hands-off political climate, the home-rule tradition, and the lack of regional coordination encourage creation of more of the same kind of suburb that has devoured so much of the land in the New York City metropolitan area. In New York State, for example, as the Land-Use Law Center at Pace University has noted, the zoning laws simply do not meet the needs of rural areas, where the need now is to protect agriculture, forestry, and other economically and socially essential land uses requiring open space. The Law Center observes, "Our fragmented maze of land-use laws provides many opportunities for battle but few opportunities for sound advance planning."[10]

In recent years, activists have had increasing success in raising public and government awareness about the regional nature of the Highlands watershed and its ecosystems and the ancient landform that all but defines the eastern seaboard and supplies much of the water its enormous populations depend on. With increased emphasis on the importance of a regional approach to preservation, many environmentalists hope a government body will be formed to make regionwide land-use decisions about the Highlands. But as of the summer of 2004 the idea of yet another layer of government lacks sufficient public understanding or support.[11]

And the Highlands, of course, is but one slender corridor in a much broader and more diverse landscape, so much of which has been swallowed up by fifty years of cheap gasoline and government subsidies for housing and industrial development in rural areas, for water and sewer systems, and for private auto transport and the building and maintenance of roads. These federal subsidies that spur the ongoing destruction of farmland, wildlife habitat, forest and watershed, increase air and water pollution, and endanger public water supplies. These policies are now so permanently entrenched, so deeply embedded in the fabric of our governed lives, and thereby so invisible, that for decades they have been for all intents and purposes beyond scrutiny and thus nearly out of public control.

And over the last decades these policies have shaped an entirely new America, one of boundaryless suburbs dominated by land-guzzling shopping malls, business parks, and housing subdivisions, all dependent on highway interchanges in areas where developers' land and building costs are low and profit margins are high. The Regional Plan Association's prescient 1969 scenario for Orange County, New York, has been repeated over and over, not just in Orange County but around the nation:

> Housing will be spread out, scattered and expensive. Jobs and facilities will encircle the expressway interchanges and then scatter farther and farther out. Travel will continue to be by auto only and traffic will mount with local tie-ups, which will be very difficult to solve. There will be few amenities of urban life, such as special entertainment,

Table 2. Wish List of Highlands Areas for Acquisition, 2000

Parcel	Size, Acres	Estimated Cost	Description
			New Jersey
Ramapo Mtns, Bergen & Passaic counties	2,500	$10 million	At eastern edge of NJ Highlands. Strategic privately owned inholdings adjacent to Ramapo Mtn. State Forest and Ringwood State Park vulnerable to intensive development.
Wyanokie Highlands, Passaic County	3,000	$12 million	Headwaters flow into Wanaque Reservoir. Completion of a critical greenway in the Wyanokies linking Long Pond Ironworks State Park with Norvin Green State Forest is threatened by development.
Pequannock Watershed, Passaic, Sussex, and Morris counties	33,000	$100 million	Wilderness core of NJ Highlands and largest unprotected forest tract. Enormous biological value. Much held by City of Newark to safeguard water supply but threatened by development proposals.
Farny Highlands, Morris County	3,600	$22 million	Headwaters of five rivers, important in water supply. Some areas preserved; others still in jeopardy.
Sparta Mtn Greenway, Sussex & Morris counties	4,000	$13 million	Western edge of NJ Highlands. Vulnerable to development, connects two major wildlife management areas.
Wallkill River Area, Sussex County		$8 million	Habitat sites threatened with development, immediate preservation needed.
Upper North Branch Raritan River, Morris & Hunterdon counties			Headwater areas and trout production streams need protection; already enjoy extensive preserve along Black River Greenway.
South Branch Raritan River Watershed, Morris & Hunterdon counties			May be most endangered watershed in NJ. Headwaters owned by major developers; farmland conversion could destroy the river's outstanding rural character; watershed development could degrade water quality in Spruce Run Reservoir.

Parcel	Size, Acres	Estimated Cost	Description
Pequest River Valley, Warren County	13,000	$78 million	Valley groundwater and surface water highly sensitive to nonpoint source pollution from sod and truck farms and residential subdivisions.
Musconetcong Mtn., Hunterdon County	20,000	$80 million	High wildlife, water, and recreational values. Upland in great demand for housing sites with a view and for proximity to businesses south.
Pohatcong Mtn. and Grasslands, Warren County	5,000	$26 million	Grasslands are home to threatened and endangered bird species. Two-thirds of the region is completely unprotected and under extreme development pressure.
Scotts Mtn., Warren County	30,000	$120 million	Provides critical habitat for interior forest bird species. Watershed areas in need of protection.
Totals	129,400	$500 million	

Parcel	Size, Acres	Estimated Cost	Description
			New York
Torne Valley, Rockland County	1,700	$9 million	A gateway into NY State. Federal sole-source aquifer for Ramapo River basin, important habitat, and Native American and colonial historic sites. Threatened with development proposals.
Greater Sterling Forest, Orange County	2,750	$20 million	Over 20,000 acres have been protected, acquisition of additional inholdings and adjacent lands will protect ecosystem, watershed, Appalachian Trail.
Schunemunk Mtn., Moodna Creek/ Woodcock Mtn, Orange County	1,600	$4 million	Much of Schunemunk ridge is protected but lands at both ends of ridge are vulnerable to development. Woodcock provides important habitat and local watershed. Public acquisition would enable Long Path trail to be suitably routed.
Fort Montgomery Gateway, Orange County	4	$1 million	Revolutionary War site. Battle Site is protected but several adjacent parcels need to be protected to preserve historic context.

Table 2. Wish List of Highlands Areas for Acquisition, 2000 (continued)

New York (continued)

Parcel	Size, Acres	Estimated Cost	Description
Hudson Highlands/ Fahnestock Link, Putnam County	150	$2.5 million	Woodlands linking Hudson Highlands State Park and Fahnestock State Park need to be acquired.
NYC Croton Watershed lands, Westchester & Putnam counties	30,000	$200 million	Vital NYC watershed for Croton Reservoir System. Many areas highly vulnerable to development.
Fishkill/Beacon Range, Putnam & Dutchess counties	1,200	$3.5 million	Wildlife habitat for diverse range of animals and plants, and extensive trail network for outstanding recreation. Protection of land would enhance integrity of this landscape.
Northern Putnam Greenway, Putnam & Dutchess counties			Protection will provide important linkages and corridors between Hudson Highlands and Great Swamp and help protect Croton watersheds.
Great Swamp, Putnam & Dutchess counties	6,700	$10 million	Largest freshwater wetland of its type in southeastern NY. Drainage flows into Croton Reservoir system.
Taconic Ridge, Dutchess County	6,000	$8 million	Conservation will protect sensitive ridgeline ecosystems and agricultural land in Harlem Valley and provide increased recreational opportunities.
Totals	50,100	$258 million	

specialty stores and the arts. Public services, such as water supply and waste disposal, will be inefficient, uncertain and costly. Tax burdens will increase rapidly but not necessarily fairly. More countryside than necessary will be bulldozed into backyards. Finally, what man builds will be uninspiring, frequently ugly.[12]

In addition, of course, these public policies have fostered an economic pattern in which land-rich townships have come to compete with cities and in which cities, which are land poor, generally are the losers: The evolving suburbs have essentially siphoned off the assets of cities. By sending the middle class outward, these policies have contributed to the decline of cities as cultural, educational, and commercial centers. As cities' troubles have grown, they have become a catalyst for additional waves of out-migration by middle-class, primarily white, residents, thus destabilizing once-solid urban neighborhoods. In such hollowed-out, job-poor urban communities, an inner-city underclass, largely nonwhite, becomes concentrated, but in many cities it is unable to find jobs and lacks the transportation needed to get to where the jobs are—in the suburbs.

Even in rural areas, sprawl contributes to the loss of a sense of community, as strip development replaces traditional commercial and social centers. Far from established jobs or the urban services they need, the new suburbanites now spend more and more time in their cars, spend more money on transportation than they might ever have imagined, and add mightily to the traffic congestion. These immigrants' sheer numbers eventually force their suburban towns to build water lines, sewer capacity, schools, and other infrastructure, thus raising taxes. This scenario explains the paradox of an ever-increasing suburban tax base that is nevertheless outstripped by rising property taxes and a middle class whose living costs spiral ever upward.

As *New York Times* columnist Russell Baker wrote in a much-quoted 1988 column,

> We head inexorably toward the 44-lane highway, cheered on by the incantation of real-estate developers and asphalt tycoons: no use crying, folks, because growth and development cannot be stopped, and anyhow it's good for you. . . . In my experience, growth and development raise your taxes, make a shameful mess on the countryside and disperse people from the civilizing influence of city living to barren new communities, which bind their victims to lifetimes of driving.[13]

Sprawl is thus a pattern that ultimately erodes the economic base and quality of life of both cities and suburbs. It is an affliction that cripples and decays cities and older suburbs, lifts all living costs, gobbles up natural resources, and divides our nation by income and race. It cries out for reform.

SPRAWL IS NOT INEVITABLE

People arguing for protection of open space inevitably encounter the property rights counterargument—"this land is mine and you can't tell me what to do with it; land-use regulation interferes with constitutional rights to private property." This position is widely held in the United States and, as John Humbach notes, when it is intertwined with the "philosophical garb of free-market theory and skepticism of government" it may sound highly compelling.

Nonetheless, "property rights" is not necessarily an all-or-nothing proposition—in many areas of life the personal freedoms associated with a free market must be, and are, to a great extent counterbalanced by our acceptance of the personal sacrifices associated with living within a social contract. For land-use policy the free market scenario doesn't make sense over the long term because it will ultimately and unavoidably result in our "spreading our population seamless across the countryside, like a blot on a paper towel, consuming land until it's almost all gone."

Fortunately, we can still retain many private property rights even as we institute restrictions that return us to the traditional land pattern, of human settlements separated by undeveloped farms, forests, and waters. As Robert Binnewies asserts, "We can do what most of the rest of the industrial capitalist, property-based first world does about land use planning and designate some areas for near-term growth and development, designate other areas as a reserve for later growth and development, and designate the bulk of our national land base for no foreseeable development whatsoever. We can, in other words, zone for permanent privately owned open space."[14]

As Kenneth Jackson has observed, in Europe land tends to be regarded as a scarce and valuable public resource, preservation of farms and open space is seen as desirable and suburban sprawl is not; and development for private profit is largely controlled.[15] Even in the United States, committed as it is to the primacy of private property rights, a number of states have refined their zoning codes to protect such open-land uses as agriculture and forestry, which are economically important and also constitute crucial elements in land-use planning. Protections are now in place for commercial forests in northern California; both Maine and Oregon require municipalities to discourage new development that is incompatible with farming or forestry by requiring localities to create and enforce urban growth boundaries, thus channeling growth into particular acceptable areas.

Perhaps the issue is not so much about property rights as it is about our failure to develop a coherent social policy. As James Kunstler says, we Americans have been living car-centered lives for so long that we have nearly lost the understanding of what it takes to make a place good for people to live in.[16] While the media often frame the debate as a struggle between activists and developers or as squabbles over implementation of the Clean Air Act, or report on epidemics of asthma in inner cities, they have not been entirely successful in making the connections between these seemingly random problems of postmodern life and the patterns of living we have encouraged.

If the public wants to slow or reverse sprawl, to revitalize downtown communities, to save farms, watersheds, and wilderness, to clean its air and water, it will have to recapture the formulation of public policy. Reversing sprawl will be a long-term, many-faceted effort, but it surely will include new policies that emphasize viable core cities and the explicit preservation of open space. In its details it must include new approaches to zoning and a commitment to regional planning. Above all, it will need a reaffirmation of mass transportation and a nononsense reexamination and reform of our massive subsidies—roads, bridges, and tunnels, parking lots, and gas selling for below-replacement value—of auto use.

And it will need a thoroughgoing reexamination of the traditional economic assumptions that land is merely a different form of capital—a free gift of nature; that anything that encourages economic growth is good; and that since sprawl development encourages economic growth (at least it appears to) it is also a good thing. These are assumptions that must be more carefully scrutinized by the people who make policy. Some of it has already come under scrutiny—for example, the assumption that exurban residential housing is productive from a "tax positive" point of view has been pretty well demolished by the numerous studies that show that housing demands far more in services than it provides in taxes.

By treating land as a commodity, mainstream economists have ignored its vital role in areas that are often not given weight in conventional economic accounting: ecosystem health, watershed protection, the social and community values of a working landscape, and, of course, aesthetic pleasure and spiritual sustenance. In decades to come, it is these externalities, ignored in some accounting schemes, barely acknowledged in others, that could well make the difference between living conditions that are unpleasant or even hazardous and those that support and enhance human health and well-being.

While we struggle mightily to change policy, we must meanwhile look at approaches to saving the land. Continuing public acquisition of land is one of the best and most immediate strategies available—even at the inflated prices paid for the Sterling Forest tracts, the purchases were worth it: They took the land off the development market and safeguarded a vital metropolitan watershed. Land acquisition will almost always turn out to be cheaper in the long run than providing infrastructure and services to new developments on private parcels and extending the range of auto use even farther into the countryside. And if public policy stops pouring money into activities that subsidize development, land prices can stay reasonable—developers would lose much of the incentive to build in still-undeveloped places.

We don't have too much time to save land in our most densely populated regions. As the U.S. population heads toward the 300-million mark, as we continue to pave the way for developers to make money from the rocks, sprawl will continue to eat away at the countryside. In the coming more crowded, paler green America, forested places like Sterling Forest will be even more desperately needed and more fiercely defended. Perhaps the best outcome of the Sterling Forest effort—a struggle that has lasted for more than a quarter century, where open space protection ultimately prevailed—was the realization that large-scale, long-term battles, fought against substantial odds, can be won and must be fought. In years to come, the struggle over the fate of our open spaces can only be propelled by this increasing urgency.

Epilogue

THE STERLING FOREST CORPORATION actively continued to market its remaining enterprises in the new millennium. It sold its South County Water Company, which provided water and sewage services to the various developments scattered throughout the forest, to United Water Company, which also included the rights to the water resources of the state park. The SFC's remaining 1,120 acres included a 545-acre parcel containing the long-established ski center and gardens that had been leased to the annual New York Renaissance Faire. This property was sold during 2004 to the fair operators.

The SFC, now reorganized as the Sterling Forest LLC, had previously submitted an application in 2000 to the Tuxedo Town Board for a golf course and 103 homes on its last 575-acre property. A Draft Environmental Impact Statement (DEIS) was completed during 2003 that focused on the impacts of the golf course, whose construction would have leveled mountains and filled in valleys—a gigantic remodeling of the forest to allow for a perfect tee shot. Water from the former iron mine shafts used for irrigation would percolate through fractured bedrock and contaminate the region's public water supply. The Sterling Forest Partnership contracted planning consultant Steve Gross and hydrologist Paul Rubin, who conducted their own environmental studies. Before the final EIS was approved, they documented a major rattlesnake population for which the golf course construction would be lethal. The NYS DEC stepped in and required further studies. On March 26, 2004, the Department of Environmental Conservation (DEC) confirmed the significance of the rattlesnake presence and the development plans were halted. After the Sterling Forest LLC consultants also verified the rattlesnake habitat studies, the corporation withdrew the golf course proposal.

In 1971, the Sterling Forest Corporation proposed 27,500 houses for its 22,000 acres straddling the NY–NJ border. More than thirty-five years and hundreds of public hearings later, the last remnant of the SFC is attempting to force development on its last remnant property. The corporation recently demanded a zoning change by the Town of Tuxedo to build 107 houses on 575 acres in the heart of Sterling Forest State Park. But the same environmental constraints and public policy issues that would prohibit construction and preserve the natural water and habitat resources are as present today as have been in each of the previous grand development incarnations.

To date, grassroots citizen activism and an incredible partnership of business, government, foundation, environmental group, and individual efforts have preserved 21,000 of those original acres. No building permit on the contested land has been issued during that entire time.

Throughout the spring of 2006 public hearings on the last 575 acres continued. Happily, as this book goes to press, these remaining acres are in final good-faith negotiations.

JÜRGEN WEKERLE
Chair of the Sterling Forest-Highlands Committee
Atlantic Chapter, Sierra Club
September 2006

Notes

CHAPTER ONE

1. This long corridor is known geologically as the Reading Prong and in rocks and its geological history it is a close match to the much longer Blue Ridge, which extends from Georgia into western Pennsylvania; only about 70 miles of generally flat Piedmont separates the two upland belts.

2. The statistical and natural history information relating to the Highlands is from *Draft New York—New Jersey Highlands Regional Study* (Washington, DC: USDA, 2002) and *New York–New Jersey Highlands Regional Study* (Washington, DC: USDA, 1992).

3. Andrew Jacobs, "At the last frontier, a crucial tug of war," *New York Times* 21 January 2001.

CHAPTER TWO

1. James M. Ransom, *Vanishing Ironworks of the Ramapos* (New Brunswick, NJ: Rutgers University Press, 1966), 3.

2. Susanna Lawrence and Barbara Grossman, *The Audubon Society Field Guide to the Natural Places of the Mid-Atlantic States* (New York: Pantheon Books, 1984), 152–154.

3. Adriaen Van Der Donck, *A Description of the New Netherlands*, ed. Thomas F. O'Donnell (Syracuse, NY: Syracuse University Press, 1968), 17, 36–37, 121.

4. Ransom, 6.

5. *Crevecoeur's Eighteenth-Century Travels in Pennsylvania & New York*, trans. and ed. Percy G. Adams (University of Kentucky Press, 196), 29–30.

6. The connection between this ironworks and the name Sterling is linked partly to Cornelius Board: historical evidence suggests that Board was an agent for the Earl of Stirling of Scotland. Also, at some time in the 1740s James Alexander, heir presumptive to the title Earl of Stirling (although he never assumed the title), bought a

portion of Cheesecock land; surveyor Charles Clinton specifically mentioned this as the "Sterling Iron Works" in 1745. See for example Ransom, 177–179.

7. Lincoln Diamant, *Chaining the Hudson: The Fight for the River in the American Revolution* (New York: Lyle Stuart, 1989), 155.

8. Thomas Taber, *Morristown & Erie Railroad: People, Paper, and Profits* (Morristown, NJ: Railroadians of America, 1967), 98.

9. Taber, 131.

10. James G. Sweeney, "Sterling Forest Myths," *OCHS Journal*, Publication of the Orange County Historical Society, 26 (1997), 8.

11. Christian R. Sonne, Historian, Town of Tuxedo, Email to author, 16 July 2003.

12. Frances F. Dunwell, *The Hudson River Highlands* (New York: Columbia University Press, 1991), 158.

13. Sweeney, 8.

14. Ransom, 205–206.

15. Rudy Abramson, *Spanning the Century: The Life of W. Averell Harriman, 1891–1986* (New York: William Morrow, 1992), 111.

16. "Memorial to E.H. Harriman," *Newburgh Daily Journal*, 25 February 1911.

17. Dunwell, 154.

18. Dunwell, 155.

19. Robert Moses address commemorating the gift of Mary Williamson Harriman establishing the Bear Mountain-Harriman State Park, 1940.

20. Phillip Shabecoff, *A Fierce Green Fire: The American Environmental Movement* (New York: Hill and Wang, 1993), 30.

21. Shabecoff, 34–35.

22. As discussed in Shabecoff, 56–58.

23. Dunwell, 141.

24. Dunwell, 160–161.

25. Raymond H. Torrey as quoted in JoAnn Dolan, "The New York–New Jersey Trail Conference—A Long History as Trailblazer and Partner," unpublished article.

26. Perhaps in the 1930s, according to JoAnn Dolan's history of the NY–NJ Trail Conference.

27. Letter from Louis A. Sigaud, Chairman, Special Committee on Sterling Park, New York-New Jersey Trail Conference, to R.W. Hart, Superintendent, Arden Estate, 23 January 1951.

28. Letter, R.W. Hart to Louis A. Sigaud, 29 January 1951.

29. Letter, R.W. Hart to Louis A. Sigaud, 29 January 1951.

30. Letter, A. K. Morgan, General Manager, Palisades Interstate Park Commission, to Hon. George W. Perkins, Assistant Secretary in Charge of European Affairs, Department of State, Washington, DC, 6 February 1951.

31. Sweeny, 8, and "Developers purchase more Sterling Property," *Newburgh Daily News*, 9 December, 1954.

CHAPTER THREE

1. U.S. Department of Transportation, "Development of the interstate program," *America's Highways: 1776–1976* (Washington, DC, Federal Highway Administration, 1976).

2. *Population of States and Counties of the United States: 1790–1990,* Twenty One Decennial Census Compiled and edited by Richard L. Forstall, March 1996. Dept. of Commerce, U.S. Bureau of the Census. Profile based on Regional Plan Association model.

3. "Sterling Forest: An interstate planning challenge," The Regional Plan Association, 1988.

4. Regional Plan Association, 1988, ii.

5. Regional Plan Association, Second Regional Plan, 1968.

6. Regional Plan Association report based on its 1969 Conference on the Future of Orange County.

7. John Humbach, interview by author, 22 June 1999.

8. "Developer opens 17,280-acre Tract," *New York Times*, 31 October 1954.

9. Harrison E. Salisbury, "Science town to adjoin Tuxedo," *New York Times*, 2 February 1957.

10. Anthony DePalma, "For sale: Sterling Forest's 19,990 acres," *New York Times*, 26 October 1986; Sterling Forest brochure circa 1957.

11. Jürgen Wekerle, interview by author, 13 February 1999.

12. Mark A. Uhlig, "Thruway unit suspends plans for interchange," *New York Times*, 11 February 1987.

13. "City Investing discloses plans," *Sterling Forest News*, 2, no. 12 (1967), 1.

14. Letter of transmittal from William L. Pereira, Chairman of the Board of City Investing Company to Mr. William Nicoson, Director, Office of New Communities Development, 29 April 1971; as appended to Regional Plan Association Report: "Sterling Forest: An Interstate Planning Challenge," 1988.

15. National Urban Policy and New Community Development Act of 1970. U.S. Code: Title 42. The Public Health and Welfare. Sec. 4501. Congressional statement of purpose.

16. Sterling One document quoted in *State of the Region*, Regional Plan Association, 1975, 15.

17. Sterling One Q & A sheets, 1975.

18. Josh Barbanel, "Bitter dispute over new homes divides Tuxedo," *New York Times*, 15 January 1978.

19. Barbanel.

20. Barbanel.

21. Tuxedo Conservation and Taxpayers Association, flyer, 23 March 1977.

22. Tuxedo Conservation and Taxpayers Association, brochure, June 1977.

23. Al Ewert, interview by author, 26 March 2000.

24. Ruth Bonapace, "State blasts Tuxedo on Sterling I statement," *Middletown Times Herald-Record*, 9 January 1978.

25. John W. Sweeny J.S.C., New York Supreme Court Appellate Division, Goshen NY, 28 July 1978.

26. Letter from Peter C. Arrighetti, Chairman, Tuxedo Planning Board, to Theodore A. Hoffman, Chairman, Tuxedo Town Board, 8 June 1976.

27. Ron Nowak, "Sad story of Sterling 1," *Greenwood Lake and West Milford News*, 5 March 1986.

28. In 1970 Senator Henry M. Jackson attempted to reform the nation's existing land-use system, introducing his National Land Use Policy Act, which would have created a comprehensive national program sufficiently funded to motivate state and local governments to work together for development and conservation and would have offered incentives to the states to develop strategic land-use plans. This landmark bill, which passed the Senate, failed to pass in the House. See, for example, Sidney Plotkin, *Keep Out: The Struggle for Land Use Control* (Berkeley: University of California Press, 1987), 168–173.

29. Donna Sylvester, "Conservation efforts focus on unique Sterling Forest swamp," *Advertiser Photo News*, 30 October 1985.

CHAPTER FOUR

1. JoAnn Dolan, interview by author, 8 March 2000.

2. Jeff Storey and Ruth Boice, "Sterling Forest land deal appears near," *Middletown Times Herald-Record*, 17 September 1986.

3. John Humbach, Chairman, Sterling Forest Coalition, at a Hearing of the Subcommittee on General Oversight and Investigations of the Committee on Interior and Insular Affairs, United States House of Representatives regarding Open Space in Urban Corridors on 2 October 1989, Tuxedo Town Hall, Tuxedo, NY. This development was never built.

4. JoAnn L. Dolan and Paul R. Dolan, letter, "Would protect a portion of Sterling Forest," *Advertiser Photo News*, 5 February 1986.

5. JoAnn L. Dolan and Paul R. Dolan, letter, "A plan to preserve Sterling Forest," *Warwick Valley Dispatch*, 12 February 1986.

6. Paul Dolan, interview by author, 10 July 1999.

7. Peter Grafton and Ruth Boice, "Monroe-West Milford 'green belt' proposed," *Middletown Times-Herald Record*, 10 March 1986.

8. Annual report, Palisades Interstate Park Commission, 1986.

9. Claire Luhrs, "They're mapping the Greenway," *West Milford Argus*, 7 September 1986.

10. Robert Hanley, "Disputes over forest turn fierce," *New York Times*, 22 November 1988.

11. JoAnn Dolan, interview.

12. Paul Dolan, interview.

13. Principles developed by the working group were as follows: A combination of techniques should be used to preserve open land, including outright purchase,

acquisition of development rights, government regulation, and clustering of buildings. Development should be confined to accessible and environmentally sound sites. A Greenwood Lake beach should be operated as a local recreation site. Consideration should be given to transfer of development rights from one part of Sterling Forest to another. The quality of drinking water in Lake Mombasha in the Town of Monroe and in New Jersey's Wanaque Reservoir system should be protected. DEC should keep local officials informed about any plans to use environmental bond issue funds to buy Sterling Forest land. The forest should not be developed in a piecemeal fashion but as part of an overall plan.

14. JoAnn Dolan, interview.

15. As Nina Easton reported in *American Banker*, state and federal regulators found numerous bad loans in the bank's portfolio. Nina Easton, "LA law firm linked to string of troubled banks closes up shop," *American Banker*, 25 January 1988.

16. In 1990, GDC pleaded guilty to federal indictments resulting from overpricing its houses and fraudulent housing appraisals. Investigators discovered that GDC had bilked 130,000 senior citizen retirees and immigrants in Florida of $2.25 billion. GDC agreed to pay a fine of $500,000 and restitution of $80 to $100 million to cheated homeowners, but, owing $10 million in Florida property taxes, eventually filed for bankruptcy. By the late 1980s, Home Group no longer held a financial interest in General Development Corporation, but by then many of the people managing Home Group were the same people who were managing GDC. Among the interlocking directorate of GDC and Home Group were David Brown, VP and general counsel of CI and chairman of GDC. George Scharffenberger, Marshall Manley, Hatch, and Pyne, the officers-directors of Home Group, were also the directors of GDC. Brown, Scharffenberger, and Manley resigned from GDC in 1990.

17. Robert Rieman and Jeff Storey, "Sterling Forest off seller's block," *Middletown Times Herald-Record*, 26 March 1987.

18. Two factors that might have been attractions to potential buyers were (1) the pending Article 78 lawsuit against Warwick by Lynmark Development Associates of Suffern, and (2) a decision by New York State officials to attempt to fund a full-trumpet interchange 15A. But the corporation said the major factor is that "prices have escalated very quickly [and] we became convinced we were under no pressure to sell. We're very close to the world's largest city." Lem Chaimowitz, "Sterling Forest yanks 'for sale' sign." *Greenwood Lake and West Milford News*, 1 April 1987.

19. "Thruway unit suspends plans for interchange," *New York Times*, 11 December 1987.

20. "Regan opposes thruway exit at Sterling Forest," *New York Times*, 28 December 1988.

21. Robert O. Binnewies, letter to author, 6 August 2000.

22. New York State Thruway Authority Proposed Sterling Forest Interchange, Report 88-S-83 Office of the State Comptroller, Edward V. Regan.

23. Binnewies, letter.

24. Adam Bryant, "Exit 15A plan gets new support," *Middletown Times Herald Record*, 11 July 1989.

25. John P. Keith, President, foreword, "Sterling Forest: An interstate planning challenge," Regional Plan Association, 1988, i.

26. Regional Plan Association, 1988, 28.

27. Len Chaimowitz, "Sterling Forest preservation has Torricelli support," *Greenwood Lake and West Milford News*, 15 May 1988.

28. Humbach, interview by author, 22 June 1999.

29. Humbach, interview.

30. Robert W. Biddle, Legislative Liaison, Conservation Committee, New York–North Jersey Chapter, Appalachian Mountain Club, letter to John Gebhards, 23 November, 1988.

31. Robert W. Biddle, letter to John Gebhards.

32. John Humbach, "Preservation of Sterling Forest," prepared for AMC Conservation Committee, 1988.

33. Humbach, "Preservation of Sterling Forest."

34. Ivan P. Vamos, Deputy Commissioner for Planning and Operations, NYS Office of Parks, Recreation and Historic Preservation, letter to James Goldwater, 2 February 1989.

35. Jeff Storey, "Sterling Forest chief to stress public relations," *Middletown Times Herald-Record*, 6 February 1989.

36. Robert Hanley, "Disputes Over Forest Turn Fierce," *New York Times*, 22 November 1988.

37. Robert E. Thomson, telephone interview by author, 5 September 2003.

38. "Sterling Forest to air planners' findings Dec. 19," *Middletown Times Herald-Record*, 29 November 1989.

39. Herbert Fliegner, "1,500 Orange citizens try to control growth," *Middletown Times Herald-Record*, 23 December 1989.

40. Carlos Ygartua, "Watchdog or lapdog?," *Middletown Times Herald-Record*, 8 October 1989.

41. Len Chaimowitz, letter, *Orange County Business Journal*. Chaimowitz was editor and publisher of the *Greenwood Lake News*. His source was Robert Thomson.

42. Ygartua.

43. Fliegner.

44. Ygartua.

45. Adam Bryant, "Heimbach named Sterling president," *Middletown Times Herald-Record*, 11 October 1989.

46. Binnewies, letter.

47. Adam Bryant, "Time short for state to buy Sterling land," *Middletown Times Herald-Record*, 25 September 1989.

48. Marita J. Licardi, "N.J. group seeks halt to Sterling development," *Middletown Times Herald-Record*, 14 November 1989.

49. The narrative summarizing the perspectives of both developers and environmentalists derives from "A Hearing of the Subcommittee on Oversight and Investigations of the Committee on Interior and Insular Affairs, United States House of

Representatives, "'Regarding open space in urban corridors,'" on Monday, October 2, 1989, Tuxedo Town Hall, Tuxedo, New York." The speakers cited here are: Roger Metzger, Citizens for Environmentally Responsible Development; Michael J. DiTullo, President and CEO, Orange County Partnership; William J. D. Boyd, President, Mid-Hudson Pattern for Progress, Inc.; George Boynton, general partner, Tuxedo Park Associates, a limited partnership owning 2,400 acres in Tuxedo; Robert E. Thomson, Chairman and CEO, Sterling Forest Corporation; Christopher J. Dunleavy, Executive Director, Orange County Chamber of Commerce; Jürgen Wekerle, Sierra Club activist; John Humbach, Professor of Law, Pace University School of Law and Chairman, Sterling Forest Coalition; Orin Lehman, Commissioner, Office of New York State Parks, Recreation, and Historic Preservation; Marge Roukema, U.S. Representative, New Jersey 5th Dist.; Hooper Brooks, Director, Regional Plan Association, Michael Vickerman, Conservation Director, Sierra Club Atlantic Chapter.

50. Jeff Storey, "Sterling Forest future interests House," *Middletown Times Herald Record*, 6 June 1989.

51. Kostmayer's legislation was actually submitted as two separate but nearly identical bills: one authorizing the National Park Service to conduct the study, to be referred to the House Interior Committee, on which Kostmayer served, and the other authorizing the U.S. Forest Service to conduct the study, to be referred to the House Agriculture Committee.

52. "Saving Sterling Forest," *Bergen Record*, 11 December 1991.

53. Adam Bryant, "Fed study of Sterling called waste of time," *Middletown Times Herald Record*, 11 November 1989.

54. Robert Torricelli ran for the U.S. Senate in 1996 and was elected. With a cloud of scandal hanging over his head—he was unable to clear himself from charges of taking bribes for favors—he was forced to withdraw from a second Senate run in 2002, only days before the election. His name was replaced on the ballot with that of previous Senator Frank Lautenberg, who was elected that November.

55. Len Chaimowitz, "Sterling Forest preservation has Torricelli support," *Greenwood Lake and West Milford News*, 18 May 1988.

56. Robert G. Torricelli, "Questions about Sterling Forest," *New York Times*, 22 May 1988.

57. JoAnn Dolan, interview.

CHAPTER FIVE

1. Alexandra Biesada, "Damn Yankee," *Financial World*, 17 April 1990.

2. Jürgen Wekerle, "Do sharks swim in Sterling Forest waters?" *Middletown Times Herald-Record*, 16 April 1990.

3. Besides Trygg-Hansa the consortium included Industrial Mutual Insurance Company, a major Finnish insurer; International Insurance Advisors, an offshore Caribbean

bank; Enskilda Securities, a Scandinavian investor; Vik Brothers International, the European investor group headquartered in the U.S.; and Donaldson Lufkin Jenrette, an investment house headquartered in Delaware.

4. Robert Hennelly, "Out on a limb," *Village Voice*, 9 April 1991.

5. Robert Frank, "Forest housing called costly," *Middletown Times Herald-Record*, 24 October 1990.

6. Adam Bryant, "Forest plan called 'mind-boggling,'" *Middletown Times Herald-Record*, 2 June 1990. Sedway Cooke also drafted development alternatives for the forest. Two alternatives presented at the public meetings held in June called for more conventional suburban development placed scattershot across the forest. A third alternative, known as the composite alternative, was developed from recommendations made by the Sterling Forest Coalition and the Orange County master plan; it put almost all the development in a corridor in the eastern portion of the property, thus preserving large expanses of the forest.

7. JoAnn Dolan, interview by author, 8 March 2000.

8. Thomas Jorling, Commissioner NYS DEC, letter to Robert Thomson, 15 August 1990.

9. "Sterling Forest needs an objective second pair of eyes," editorial, *Middletown Times Herald-Record*, 17 October 1990.

10. "Bond Act pipeline primed for Sterling deal," *Middletown Times Herald-Record*, 15 October 1990.

11. Judy Mathewson, "Gilman's maneuver kills Sterling Forest study," *Middletown Times Herald-Record*, 16 October 1990.

12. "Sterling Forest needs an objective second pair of eyes."

13. Robert Frank, "Forest study alive, Gilman foe says," *Middletown Times Herald-Record*, 17 October 1990.

14. Ron Nowak, "US Forest Service begins NY/NJ study," *Greenwood Lake and West Milford News*, 9 January 1991.

15. Robert Frank, "Sterling Forest study group adds town, business officials," *Middletown Times Herald-Record*, 14 February 1991.

16. Jim Gordon, "The forest's future," *Orange*, June/July 1991, 24.

17. Robert Frank, "Selling Sterling Forest," *Middletown Times Herald-Record*, 30 March 1992.

18. Sterling Forest Corporation advertisement, *Middletown Times Herald-Record*, 1991.

19. Jürgen Wekerle, "Sterling Forest deal just a come-on," *Middletown Times Herald-Record*, 21 November 1992.

20. Robert Frank, "Politicians back Exit 15-A fight," *Middletown Times Herald-Record*, 16 May 1991.

21. Michael DiTullo, opinion, "Sterling Forest can be example for the future," *Middletown Times Herald-Record*, 19 September 1991.

22. Sam Howe Verhovek, "Environmentalists criticize plan for Sterling Forest development," *New York Times*, 31 March 1991.

23. Jim Gordon, 25.

24. John Humbach, Business Forum, "You can't see the forest for the buffers," *Middletown Times Herald-Record*, 28 May 1991.

25. Jürgen Wekerle, "Sterling Forest deal just a come-on."

26. William Berezansky, "Business leaders beat the drums for Tuxedo exit," *Middletown Times Herald-Record*, 17 May 1991.

27. Ron Nowak, "Forest's 28-year phasing plan unveiled," *Greenwood Lake and West Milford News*, 15 January 1992.

28. Joseph L. Fucci, opinion, "Environmentalists wish to direct, not halt, growth," *Middletown Times Herald-Record*, 19 November 1991.

29. Deborah Bright and James Northup, "Potential Fiscal Impact of the Sterling Forest Corporation Development Proposal," prepared for Appalachian Mountain Club, Sierra Club Atlantic Chapter and Sierra Club North East Conservation Committee, Salisbury, Vermont, September 1991.

30. Robert Frank, "Land group orders study of Sterling," *Middletown Times Herald-Record*, 7 April 1991.

31. "The Conservation of Sterling Forest, Analysis and Recommendations," distributed by the Sterling Forest Coalition, 30 January 1989, and John Humbach, "You can't see the forest for the buffers."

32. Stephen Garmhausen, "Nuclear reactor cleanup likely to end this year," *Middletown Times Herald-Record*, 19 April 1994; Paula McMahan, "Barely a tracer's left," *Middletown Times Herald-Record*, 27 February 1995.

33. This report of the Land Acquisition Advisory Committee was required under the 1990 bond act legislation even though the bond act itself did not pass. Responding to the intense development pressures in the Hudson Valley, the committee targeted Sterling Forest as the state's third-highest priority for the state to acquire if and when funding became available.

34. Robert Frank, "Planners ask help for forest," *Middletown Times Herald-Record*, 24 December 1991.

35. Elizabeth Llorente, "N.Y. bows out of fight to save Sterling Forest," *Bergen Record*, 16 December 1991.

36. Allen J. Schacht, associate deputy chief of state and private forestry, U.S. Forest Service, "Concerning Options for the conservation of the Sterling Forest," before the Subcommittee on Energy and the Environment, Committee on Interior and Insular Affairs, 23 June 1992.

37. Robert O. Binnewies, *Palisades: 100,000 acres in 100 years* (New York: Fordham University Press and Palisades Interstate Park Commission, 2001), 324.

38. Elizabeth Auster, "House panel OKs Sterling Forest funds," *Bergen Record*, 30 June 1992.

39. Judy Mathewson, "Lawmakers clash over Forest land," *Middletown Times Herald-Record*, 24 June 1992.

40. "Gilman expects $5 million to buy Sterling Forest will 'just sit there,'" *Hudson Valley Business News*, 24 August 1992.

41. Binnewies (2001), 325.

42. Binnewies (2001), 329.

43. S. Roy Graham, "Sterling Forest plan moves ahead," *Bergen Record*, 22 September 1992; Robert Frank, "Fund match for Sterling ruled out," *Middletown Times Herald-Record*, 7 May 1992.

44. Elizabeth Auster, "Sterling Forest federal funding reduced to $3 M," *Bergen Record*, 23 September 1992.

45. Rep. Kostmayer was defeated in his reelection bid in the November 1992 congressional election.

46. Robert O. Binnewies, unpublished ms., 2000.

47. William Neil, letter, *Newark Star Ledger*, 22 February 1994.

48. Robert Binnewies, memo to Jim Tripp et al., 22 February 1994.

49. JoAnn Dolan, interview.

50. JoAnn Dolan, interview.

51. Binnewies (2000).

52. Louis V. Mills, memo to Bob Binnewies and Larry Rockefeller, 25 January 1993.

53. Hal Kalwasser, confidential memo, 1 August 1993.

54. Stephen D. Moore, "Swedish banks try to assess effects of huge interest rates, volatile markets," *Wall Street Journal*, 22 September 1992.

55. Robert Frank, "Forest parent firm says it's healthy," *Middletown Times Herald-Record*, 1 December 1992; Robert Frank, "Citizens to guide forest, owner says," *Middletown Times Herald-Record*, 2 December 1992.

CHAPTER SIX

1. Joseph Berger, "Economy aids a compromise over developing forest land," *New York Times*, 27 April 1993.

2. Robert Frank, "Sterling's parent to go public," *Middletown Times Herald-Record*, 28 September 1993.

3. Robert O. Binnewies, *Palisades: 100,000 acres in 100 years* (New York: Fordham University Press and Palisades Interstate Park Commission, 2001), 329.

4. "Compromise is best hope for Sterling Forest," editorial, *Middletown Times Herald-Record*, 9 May 1993.

5. Jürgen Wekerle, memo, "Sterling Forest Update," 2 July 1993.

6. Ron Nowak, "Nowak's notebooks (north): Cozy confines," *Greenwood Lake and West Milford News*, 4 August 1993.

7. Edward Morley, "Preserve all of Sterling," *Middletown Times Herald-Record*, 10 April 1994.

8. Ron Nowak, "Forest price tag at $80 million minimum," *Greenwood Lake and West Milford News*, 29 September 1993.

9. Gordon Bishop, "Activists call for U.S. aid to preserve Highlands," *Newark Star Ledger*, 4 April 1993. New Jersey conservation groups led by the Audubon Society and the Highlands Coalition asked the congressional delegation to push for more than $25 million as a start for saving portions of the New Jersey Highlands. These activists

focused particularly on lands owned by the Resolution Trust Corporation, the federal agency created in 1989 to help dispose of the assets of banks that failed in the late 1980s. The Resolution Trust Corporation had many large tracts for sale in northern New Jersey and, despite the U.S. Forest Service report calling for open-space preservation in the Highlands, the RTC was unloading Highlands properties as fast as it could.

10. "Conservation groups urge NY land purchase," editorial, *Bergen Record*, 14 February 1993.

11. Binnewies, *Palisades*, 330.

12. "A Sterling Bid," editorial, *Middletown Times Herald-Record*, 24 July 1993.

13. Robert Frank, "U.S. near Sterling purchase," *Middletown Times Herald-Record*, 22 July 1993.

14. Frank, "U.S. near Sterling purchase."

15. Michael Markowitz, "$35M sought to save Sterling Forest," *Bergen Record*, 27 July, 1993.

16. Julia Campbell, "Step taken for U.S. to buy Sterling tract," *Middletown Times Herald-Record*, 27 July 1993.

17. Jan Barry, "Roukema seeks $25 M for forest," *Bergen Record*, 17 September 1993. Marge Roukema, a key player in the congressional effort to acquire Sterling Forest funding, was an eleven-term Republican "moderate" from Ridgewood, NJ. Frequently at odds with her increasingly right-wing party leadership on a wide range of issues, from abortion rights and campaign finance reform to environmental policy, she decided to retire from the House at the end of 2002.

18. Binnewies, *Palisades*, 333.

19. Binnewies, *Palisades*, 333.

20. Binnewies, *Palisades*, 336.

21. Edward Moltzen, "Babbitt calls Sterling land-buy a first step," *Middletown Times Herald-Record*, 29 September 1993.

22. Binnewies, *Palisades*, 331.

23. Moltzen.

24. J. Scott Orr, "Bradley acts on Sterling Forest funds," *Newark Star-Ledger*, 19 November 1993.

25. Sari Harrar, "Setback in plan to safeguard Sterling Forest," *Bergen Record*, 18 May 1994.

26. "Sterling Forest can be preserved," editorial, *Rockland Journal-News*, 26 May 1994.

27. Robert Binnewies, letter to author, 6 August 2000.

28. Judy Mathewson, "Park Service now backs Sterling preservation," *Middletown Times Herald-Record*, 24 May 1994.

29. Paul Dolan, interview by author, 10 July 1999.

30. Judy Mathewson, "Park Service willing to buy Sterling Forest," *Middletown Times Herald-Record*, 27 May 1994.

31. Binnewies, *Palisades*, 336.

32. Emily Laber, "Sterling Forest funding backed," *Bergen Record*, 4 August 1994.

33. Jennifer Buksbaum, "Sterling Forest funding moves ahead," *Bergen Record*, 22 August 1994. The House spending bill for the Department of the Interior failed to provide an actual appropriation for the acquisition of Sterling Forest. The bill did set aside $3 million for the Appalachian Trail, but also required Congress to pass a separate bill to authorize the acquisition of Sterling Forest before the $3 million could be used.

34. "The federal Sterling Forest bill, which was introduced by the Public Lands Sub-committee in the Senate, was part of a package of amendments to the Steamtown bill. The House passed the Steamtown bill . . . by a voice vote months ago. The House would only have had to vote on the amendments if the package had passed in the Senate. Late last week, Sen. Richard Shelby Democrat of Alabama, put a hold on all bills coming out of the Senate's Public Lands subcommittee, which included the Steamtown package. As of 6 p.m. Friday, the senator had not released his hold, so the bills could not go to a vote." Amy Beth Terdiman and Kristen Georgi, "Sterling bill dies with Congress," *Middletown Times Herald-Record*, 13 October 1994.

35. Emily Laber, "Senate delays preservation vote," *Bergen Record*, 13 October 1994.

36. Laber, "Senate delays preservation vote."

37. Emily Laber, "Whitman sets limits on watershed deal," *Bergen Record*, 10 November 1994.

38. Laber, "Whitman sets limits on watershed deal."

39. Devin Leonard, "Sterling Forest price tag may balloon to $9M," *Bergen Record*, 20 July 1993. In February 1992 Passaic County Superior Court Judge Joseph J. Salerno sided with Passaic County, but his death in mid-year stalled the long-simmering case. In March 1993, a new judge was assigned; the possibility of an upcoming trial kicked off another round of negotiations leading to the settlement.

40. Eric Durr, "Environmental trust fund approved at last," *Waterville Times* [NY], 9 July 1993.

41. Thomas J. Fitzgerald, "Pace slows on deal to preserve Sterling," *Bergen Record*, 9 July 1993.

42. Leslie Scism, "Home Holdings is seeking $250 million in capital as it posts 3rd-quarter loss," *Wall Street Journal*, 8 November 1994.

43. Judy Rife, "Sterling Forest parent sold," *Middletown Times Herald-Record*, 8 December 1994.

44. Michael Quint, "Zurich Insurance will control Home Holdings," *New York Times*, 28 December 1994.

45. "Home Holdings plan OK'd," *Middletown Times Herald-Record*, June 8, 1995, from the *Wall Street Journal*; "Home Holdings Inc. faces bond default deadline," *Business Insurance*, 23 June 1997.

46. "Home in Chapter 11," *Business Insurance*, 19 January 1998.

47. Robert Riemann, "Heimbach moves up," *Middletown Times Herald-Record*, 11 August 1994; Robert Thomson, telephone interview by author, 5 September 2003.

CHAPTER SEVEN

1. In September 1996, Sterling Forest Resources was incorporated as a 501(c)(3) not for profit organization known as Sterling Forest Partnership, a more structured grant-funded organization.

2. JoAnn Dolan, interview by author, 8 March 2000. The Palisades Interstate Parks Commission raised an additional $165,000, which also went toward funding experts who would critique the impacts of development.

3. JoAnn Dolan.

4. Julia Campbell, "Two towns let DEC have say over Sterling," *Middletown Times Herald-Record*, 12 February 1993. On July 5 1991, the Tuxedo Town Board declared itself "lead agency" for the project, not wanting the state DEC to dominate the review process. Tuxedo was concerned that the DEC would worry primarily about strictly environmental concerns, whereas the town needed to address its specific concerns about police, fire, traffic, and schools. Prodded by the Palisades Interstate Park Commission, on August 9, the DEC challenged the town's lead agency designation. The DEC wanted to look at the project from a three-town perspective and with a view toward keeping as much land in open space as possible. But in its challenge the DEC got a few things technically wrong: it mistakenly referred to the wrong project—and it missed the legal thirty-day deadline for a challenge. Within a month, the towns of Warwick and Monroe had joined Tuxedo in seeking lead agency status (Monroe later dropped out). In October, Ralph Manna, the DEC's regional director, asked DEC Commissioner Thomas Jorling for lead agency status and that November Jorling ruled that his agency was best suited to be lead agency. The towns challenged the DEC in state Supreme Court, claiming that the DEC had violated their home rule. In the summer of 1992, a state supreme court justice ruled in favor of the DEC as lead agency, and by February 1993 the towns agreed to drop their lawsuit over the "lead agency" designation, allow DEC to assume lead agency status, and have themselves listed as "involved agencies" if the state would pay for the project consultants.

5. JoAnn Dolan.

6. "Scoping document input for the proposed Sterling Forest project" 2 April 1993.

7. Jürgen Wekerle, letter to Lou Mills, 15 January 1995.

8. JoAnn Dolan, Executive Director, New York–New Jersey Trail Conference, testimony, 12 January 1993.

9. Julia Campbell, "Speakers urge caution in forest development," *Middletown Times Herald-Record,* 26 March 1993.

10. JoAnn Dolan, testimony.

11. S. Roy Graham, "The battle for Sterling Forest," *Bergen Record,* 27 January 1993.

12. "Speak up for Sterling Forest," *Bergen Record,* 13 June 1995.

13. JoAnn Dolan, interview.

14. Mary Yrizarry, letter, "Sterling Forest planning flawed," *Middletown Times Herald-Record,* 2 February 1997.

15. Ron Nowak, "Nowak's notebooks: Planned people," *Greenwood Lake and West Milford News,* 21 June 1995.

16. "Editor's corner: Reality check," *Greenwood Lake and West Milford News,* 21 June 1995.

CHAPTER EIGHT

1. "Crunch time in the fight to save Sterling Forest," editorial, *Bergen Record,* 10 March 1995.

2. Michael Mello, "Forest suffers a blow," *Middletown Times Herald-Record,* 29 July 1995.

3. Kristen Georgi, "Sterling purchase backed," *Middletown Times Herald-Record,* 25 April 1995.

4. "Senate passes $17.5 M bill to help buy Sterling Forest," *Bergen Record,* 1 July 1995.

5. Bonnie Brewer and Michael Mello, "Panel hears Sterling case; owner needs answer soon," *Middletown Times Herald-Record,* 26 September 1995.

6. Michael Markowitz, "Torricelli: Ax may hit Sterling," *Bergen Record,* 2 June 1995.

7. Michael Mello, "Forest friends plead case," *Middletown Times Herald-Record,* 29 September 1995.

8. "Hypocrisy on Sterling Forest," editorial, *Rockland Journal-News,* 3 October 1995.

9. Ian Fisher, "Western voices break into the debate over Sterling Forest," *New York Times,* 16 October 1995.

10. "Sterling Forest is at stake in preservation-funds poker," *Bergen Record,* 11 October 1995.

11. Rod Allee, "Supporters of forest buyout take a beating," *Bergen Record,* 29 September 1995.

12. David Kibbe, "Parks chief backs forest buy," *Middletown Times Herald-Record,* 5 May 1995.

13. "Save Sterling Forest," editorial, *New York Times,* 23 October 1995.

14. "A Sterling idea," editorial, *Bergen Record,* 26 October 1995.

15. J. Scott Orr, "Gingrich backs buying Sterling Forest as Dems doubt motives," *Newark Star Ledger,* 14 December 1995.

16. "Wrong way on Sterling Forest," editorial, *New York Times,* 18 December 1995.

17. Jan Barry, "Sterling Forest deal '99% there'" *Bergen Record,* 25 January 1996.

18. "Supporters of Sterling Forest plan turn up heat," *Rockland Journal-News,* 26 January 1996.

19. John H. Cushman, Jr., "G.O.P. backing off from tough stand over environment," *New York Times,* 26 January 1996.

20. Jan Barry, "Sterling Forest funding coup?" *Bergen Record,* 1 February 1996.

21. Adam Piore, "Clinton aide sees threat to Sterling Forest plan," *Bergen Record,* 27 February 1996.

22. "The Sterling Forest crunch," editorial, *Bergen Record,* 23 February 1996.

23. "Sterling's odd savior," *Bergen Record,* 6 March 1996.

24. The Coast Guard was abandoning its base on the 173-acre Governor's Island, located in New York Harbor, leaving the island's future uncertain.

25. Wayne A. Hall and Paula McMahon, "'Save Sterling Forest': Gingrich has plans to buy land," *Middletown Times Herald-Record*, 5 March 1996.

26. "The Orrin Hatch Land Grab," editorial, *New York Times*, 19 March 1996.

27. Adam Piore, "GOP lays out strategy on Sterling Forest," *Bergen Record*, 16 March 1996.

28. "Sterling Forest item sidelined: Utah land debate stops Senate bill," *Middletown Times Herald-Record*, 28 March 1996.

29. Adam Piore, "Sterling Forest funds blocked," *Bergen Record*, 28 March 1996.

30. Carl Weiser, "Forest fund bill dies in Senate," *Rockland Journal-News*, 28 March 1996.

31. Adam Piore, "Sterling Forest going wild?" *Bergen Record*, 19 April 1996.

32. "Snowbasin land swap wins OK," *Desert News*, 2 May 1996.

33. JoAnn Dolan, interview by author, 8 March 2000.

34. Robert O. Binnewies, *Palisades: 100,000 acres in 100 years* (New York: Fordham University Press and Palisades Interstate Park Commission, 2001), 346–347.

35. Robert O. Binnewies, letter to author, June 2000.

36. Paula McMahon and Kenneth Lovett, "Sterling deal goes through," *Middletown Times Herald-Record*, 16 May 1996.

37. Jan Barry, "Sterling buyout: 90% not enough, some say," *Bergen Record*, 28 May 1996.

38. Kate Boylan, Jay Gallagher, and Carl Weiser, "Preservation groups buy Sterling Forest," *Rockland Journal-News*, 16 May 1996.

39. "The rewards of patience . . . ," editorial, *Middletown Times Herald-Record*, 17 May 1996.

40. Sterling Forest Corporation, letter to Town of Tuxedo Town Board, 10 July 1996.

41. Ian Fisher, "2 States Agree: $55 Million for Sterling Forest," *New York Times*, 16 May 1996.

42. "Mr. Gingrich and Sterling Forest," editorial, *New York Times*, 6 June 1996.

43. Adam Piore, "House panel commits $9M to buy Sterling Forest," *Bergen Record*, 6 June 1996.

44. Michael Mello, "Babbitt doubts Sterling money," *Middletown Times Herald-Record*, 18 June 1996.

45. Piore, "House panel commits $9M to buy Sterling Forest."

46. Adam Piore, "Sterling Forest deal approved," *Bergen Record*, 27 July 1996.

47. Ian Fisher, "House G.O.P. strikes deal to save New York forest from development," *New York Times*, 27 July 1996.

48. Mark Wigfield, "Forest buy wins support: House OKs bill to help Sterling preservation," *Middletown Times Herald-Record*, 31 July 1996.

49. Carl Weiser, "House approves Sterling Forest funding," *Rockland Journal-News*, 31 July 1996.

50. Fisher, "House G.O.P. strikes deal to save New York forest from development."

51. Adam Piore, "Sterling Forest bill hits another hurdle," *Bergen Record*, 3 August 1996.

52. Piore, "Sterling Forest bill hits another hurdle."

53. Adam Piore, "House OKs Sterling Forest measure," *Bergen Record*, 31 July 1996.

54. Kathy DeCoster, TPL-DEC "Action plan for August."

55. "Sterling Forest showdown," editorial, *Bergen Record*, 13 September 1996.

56. Binnewies, *Palisades*, 352.

57. "Sterling Forest showdown."

58. "No add-ons for parks bill," editorial, *Rockland Journal-News*, 17 September 1996.

59. "House approves Sterling Forest buy," *Middletown Times Herald-Record*, 29 September 1996; John H. Cushman Jr., "House passes measure to preserve Sterling Forest," *New York Times*, 29 September 1996.

60. Adam Piore, "Senate defers Sterling Forest vote," *Bergen Record*, 1 October 1996.

61. Adam Piore, "Sterling Forest funds approved," *Bergen Record*, 4 October 1996; "Federal Money for Sterling Forest," *The Sterling Messenger*, November 1996; John H. Cushman Jr., "Senate Passes parks legislation, preserving big New York forest," *New York Times*, 4 October 1996.

62. Piore, "Sterling Forest funds approved."

63. Michael Mello, "Way paved for Sterling," *Middletown Times Herald-Record*, 4 October 1996.

64. Rod Allee, "Bradley would make a great champion for Highlands," editorial, *Bergen Record*, 4 October 1996.

65. Bruno Tedeschi, "Stumping for Sterling Forest," *Bergen Record*, 7 October 1996.

66. "Obtain all funds on Sterling Forest," editorial, *Rockland Journal-News*, 26 November 1996.

CHAPTER NINE

1. Jan Barry and Adam Piore, "2nd $8.5 M to save Sterling Forest in Clinton budget," *Bergen Record*, 29 January 1997.

2. "Sterling Forest funding request gets more congressional attention," *Rockland Journal-News*, 5 March 1997.

3. "Environmental priorities," *Middletown Times Herald-Record*, 12 March 1997.

4. "Parkland bill faces veto threat," *Bergen Record*, 29 October 1997.

5. Jan Barry, "Final $5 M given for Sterling Forest buyout," *Bergen Record*, 10 December 1997.

6. Judith Miller, "Sterling Forest among first Doris Duke fund grants," *New York Times*, 10 December 1997.

7. The reserved water rights might even have allowed the corporation to become a large water broker: Conceivably, the company could have eventually used the large new population at Sterling Forest to justify the need for new, publicly-funded, water and sewer that it then would broker throughout the region. The corporation sold its water and sewer utility to New Jersey's United Water, a utility giant, in 2002.

8.   Ron Pirani, interview by author, 23 March 1999.

9.   It did this by allowing the corporation to retain the "development rights" to 1,000 acres of the future park land. The 1,000 acres would not be immediately conveyed to the Palisades Interstate Park Commission but would remain in escrow. Only after it obtained building permits on its retained 2,220 acres or when it decided to sell its remaining 2,220 acres would the corporation convey the 1,000 acres to PIPC. In effect, this complicated deal would allow the corporation to "transfer development rights" and increase the density of building on its retained acreage—it could be allowed up to 3,220 housing units on the 2,220-acre tract it was holding.

10. Michael Edelstein, opinion, "Must we be the prey of developers?," *Middletown Times Herald-Record*, 18 September 1997.

11. It was an irony that some of New York's environmental bond act money in effect would be paying for new sewage capacity, which would dump nearly 3 million gallons a day of additional sewage effluent into the already-stressed Ramapo River. Furthermore, New York State and Orange County were pushing for yet another sewage treatment plant discharging into the Ramapo, one capable of releasing an additional 12 million gallons per day.

12. Robert Hennelly, "Merry developers of Sterling Forest chop away at Pataki's green image," *New York Observer*, 18 August 1997.

13. Glenn Blain, "State buys part of Sterling Forest for preservation," *Rockland Journal-News*, 15 August 1997.

14. Pauline Greenberg, "Sterling Forest land sold," *Middletown Times Herald-Record*, 14 August 1997.

15. Pauline Greenberg, "First 1,400 acres of Sterling sold," *Middletown Times Herald-Record*, 15 August 1997.

16. Hoping to look green, the corporation made much of its intention to transfer 1,525 acres to the Palisades Interstate Park Commission upon completion of the project. But it failed to mention that 1,000 of those acres was already going to PIPC as per the 1996 purchase contract. Moreover, the Town of Tuxedo would require the other 500 acres to be kept as open space as a condition of any development permit. In short, the corporation were taking credit for open space set-asides that for all intents and purposes had already been set aside.

17. Rich Newman, "Developer unveils big plans for Sterling Forest," *Middletown Times Herald-Record*, 18 April 1998.

18. Juliet Greer, "Another exit off Thruway: sterling idea," *Middletown Times Herald-Record*, 31 March 1998.

19. Chris McKenna, "Protection of Sterling Forest land omits parcels," *Middletown Times Herald-Record*, 13 December 2000.

CHAPTER TEN

1.   Robert E. Thomson, telephone interview by author, 5 September 2003.

2.   Paul Dolan, interview by author, 10 July 1999.

3.   James Ahearn, "A park grows despite odds," *Bergen Record*, 5 June 1994.

4.   Robert O. Binnewies, *Palisades: 100,000 acres in 100 years* (New York: Fordham University Press and Palisades Interstate Park Commission, 2001), 350.

5.   See, for example, Frances Dunwell, *The Hudson River Highlands* (New York: Columbia University Press, 1991), 161.

6.   Dunwell, 232.

7.   Juliet Greer, "Town's wealthy history faces modern times," *Middletown Times Herald-Record*, 8 September 1998; *Sterling Messenger*, January 1999. Other large developments were planned for the Town of Monroe. Meanwhile, the Town of Tuxedo was also grappling with another large development, Tuxedo Reserve (known in a much earlier proposal as Tuxedo Estates), which originally sought to build 2,450 housing units on 2,450 acres it owned surrounding the northern end of Tuxedo Park. Tuxedo Reserve first came before the board in 1989 and got preliminary approval in 1991. By the time it returned to the Town in the late 1990s, new regulations forced the developer, Tuxedo Park Associates, to reduce its proposal to 1,375 units.

8.   New York–New Jersey Highlands Regional Study, USDA Forest Service, 1992, 45; Draft New York-New Jersey Highlands Regional Study, 2002.

9.   In 2002, Representative Ben Gilman, the politician who once so adamantly and outspokenly opposed Sterling Forest protection, introduced the Highlands Stewardship Act of 2002, a bill that would have provided $25 million annually for Highlands land conservation and $7 million a year for "smart growth" projects, and also would have helped create a public awareness of the Highlands as an identifiable single region. Poised to retire after 15 terms in Congress, Gilman saw this as his personal legacy for the region. The 107th Congress failed to pass the act but a similar bill, co-sponsored by Senators Jon S. Corzine and Frank R. Lautenberg and Representative Rodney Frelinghuysen, all of New Jersey, was reintroduced in 2003. John Milgrim, "Bill would protect Highlands region," Middletown *Times Herald-Record*, 18 July 2002; "A Highlands Boost," editorial, *Bergen Record*, 9 July 2003.

10. John Humbach, "A land use law agenda for the 1990's," Center for Environmental Legal Studies at Pace University School of Law, prepared at the request of the Regional Plan Association, 14 January 1991.

11. The Highlands Coalition advocates creation of a Highlands National Forest Preserve, with acquisition and management of key Highlands tracts by the U.S. Forest Service. Acquisition of critical tracts would be pursued as the need and opportunity arose. The coalition also seeks creation of a multistate commission with representation from state agencies, local government, landowners, and the Forest Service, which would have some general planning authority with the goal of directing development away from critical areas and preserving the overall natural and rural character of the region.

12. The Future of Orange County, Regional Plan Association, April 1969.

13. Russell Baker, "On the road to nowhere," *New York Times*, reprinted in the *Middletown Times Herald-Record*, 15 May 1988.

14. This concept is eloquently developed by John Humbach in a speech given on November 9, 1991 at the National Growth Management Leadership Project Conference, Annapolis, Maryland.

15. Kenneth T. Jackson, *Crabgrass Frontier, the Suburbanization of the United States* (New York: Oxford University Press, 1985).

16. See his important book *The Geography of Nowhere: The Rise and Decline of America's Man-Made Landscape* (New York: Simon and Schuster, 1993).

Index